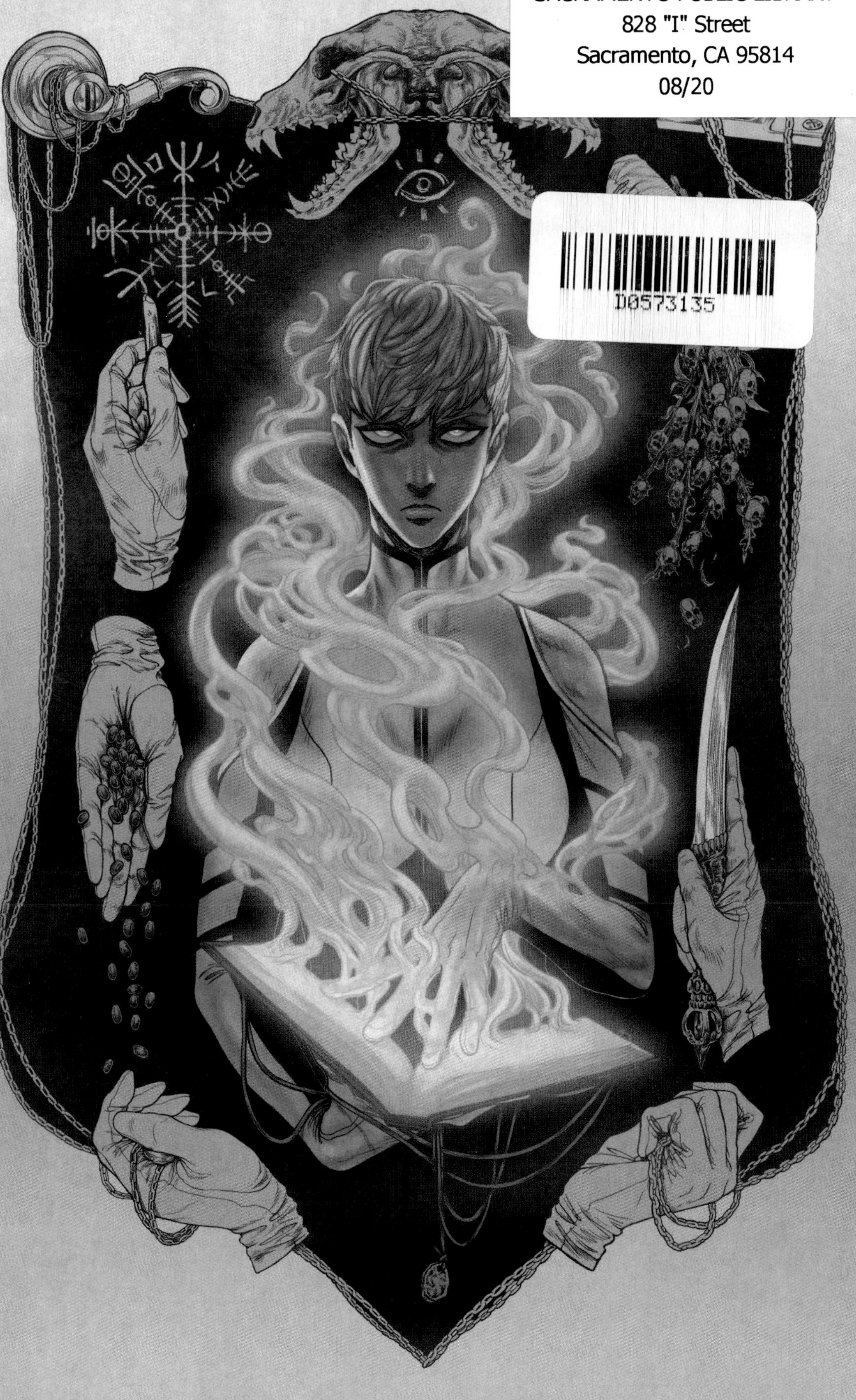

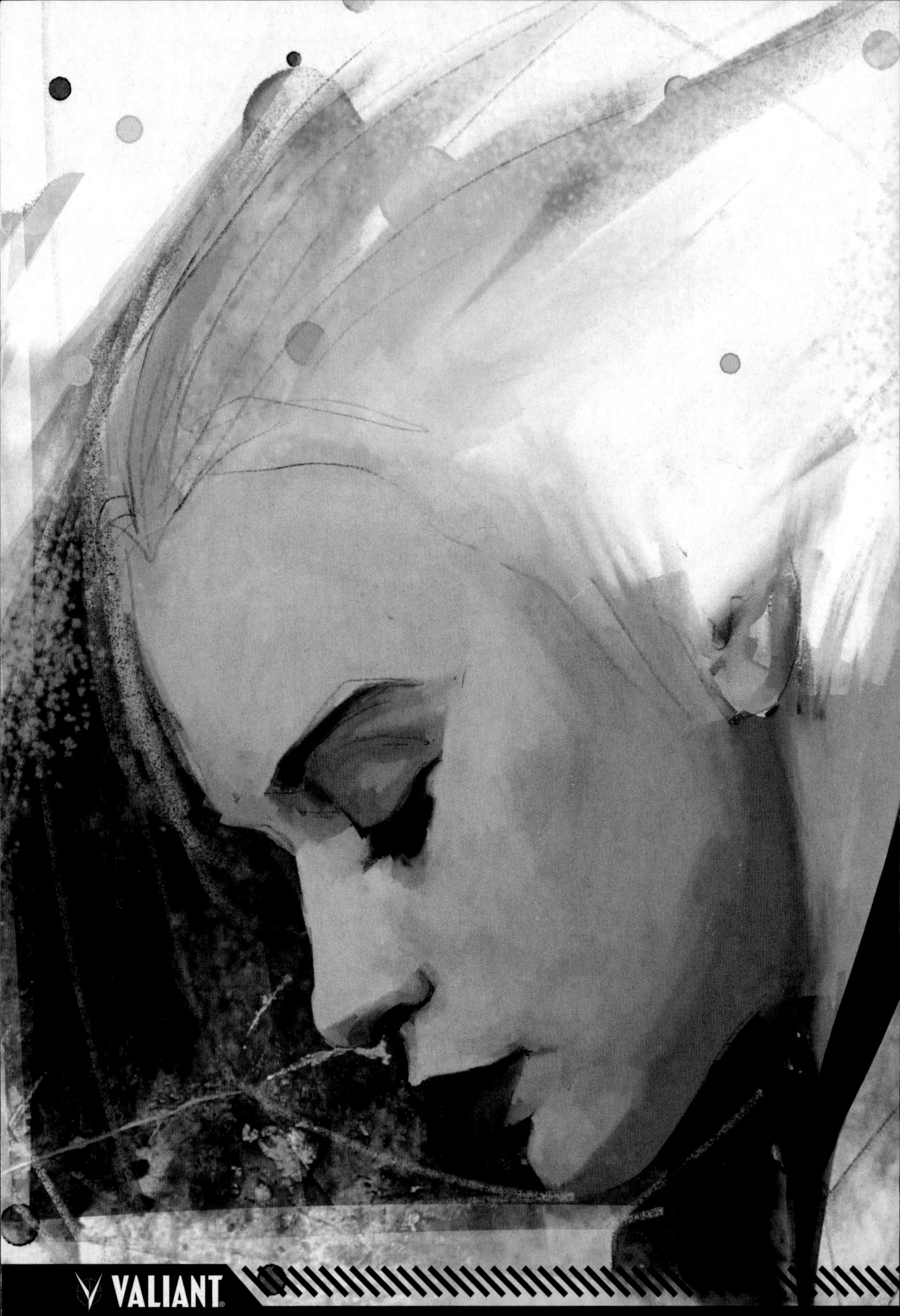

VALIANT®

DAN MINTZ Chairman **FRED PIERCE** Publisher **WALTER BLACK** VP Operations **MATTHEW KLEIN** VP Sales & Marketing **ROBERT MEYERS** Senior Editorial Director
TRAVIS ESCARFULLERY Director of Design & Production **PETER STERN** Director of International Publishing & Merchandising **LYSA HAWKINS, HEATHER ANTOS & GREG TUMBARELLO** Editors
DAVID MENCHEL Associate Editor **DREW BAUMGARTNER** Assistant Editor **JEFF WALKER** Production & Design Manager **GREGG KATZMAN** Marketing Manager **EMILY HECHT** Digital Marketing Manager
JOHN PETRIE Senior Sales Manager **KAT O'NEILL** Sales & Live Events Manager **CONNOR HILL** Sales Operations Coordinator **DANIELLE WARD** Sales Manager

ED CASEY Licensing **OLIVER TAYLOR** International Licensing Coordinator

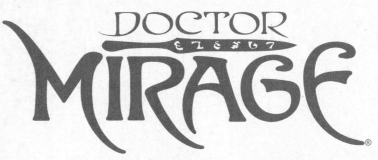

DOCTOR MIRAGE®

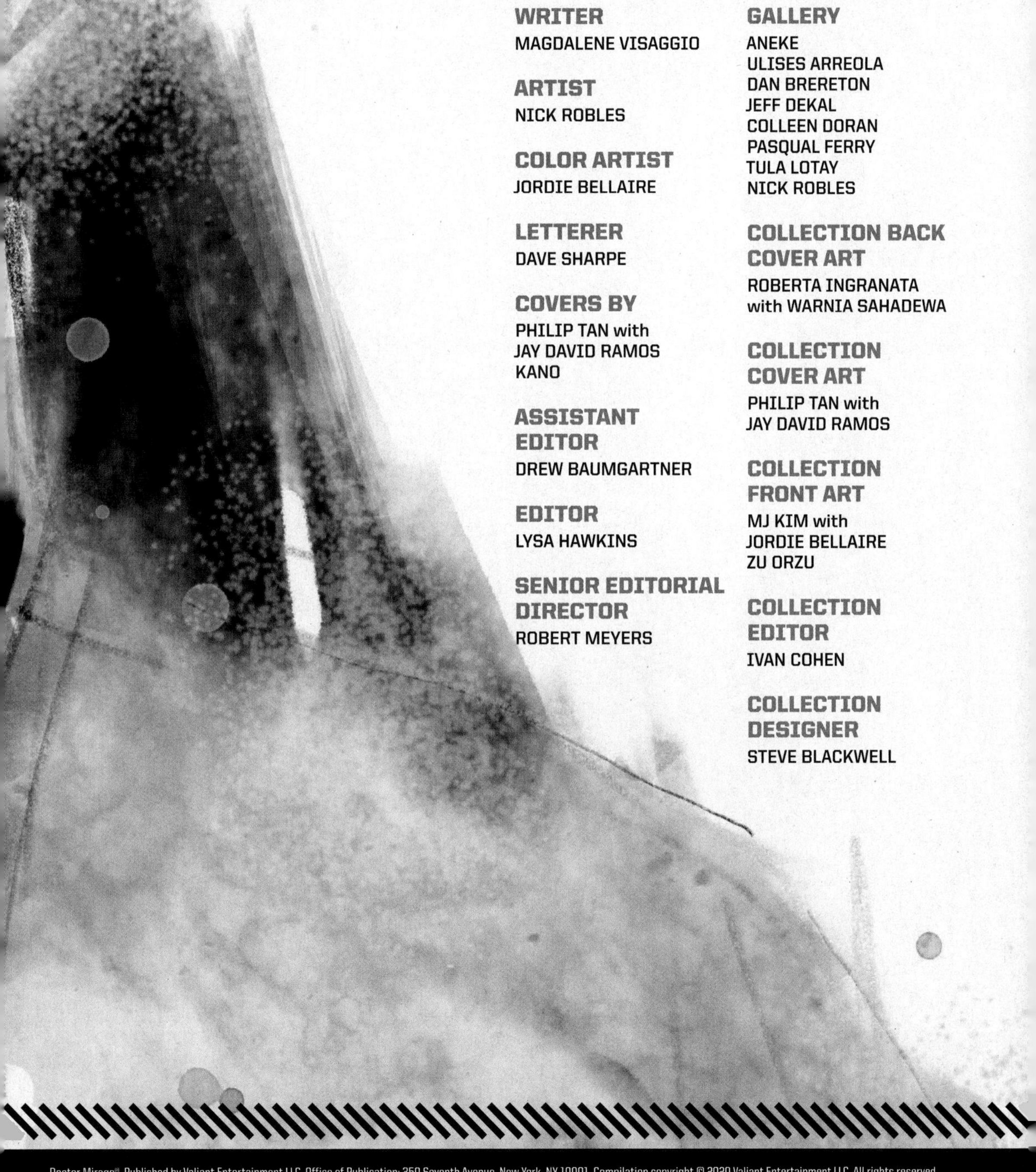

WRITER
MAGDALENE VISAGGIO

ARTIST
NICK ROBLES

COLOR ARTIST
JORDIE BELLAIRE

LETTERER
DAVE SHARPE

COVERS BY
PHILIP TAN with
JAY DAVID RAMOS
KANO

ASSISTANT EDITOR
DREW BAUMGARTNER

EDITOR
LYSA HAWKINS

SENIOR EDITORIAL DIRECTOR
ROBERT MEYERS

GALLERY
ANEKE
ULISES ARREOLA
DAN BRERETON
JEFF DEKAL
COLLEEN DORAN
PASQUAL FERRY
TULA LOTAY
NICK ROBLES

COLLECTION BACK COVER ART
ROBERTA INGRANATA
with WARNIA SAHADEWA

COLLECTION COVER ART
PHILIP TAN with
JAY DAVID RAMOS

COLLECTION FRONT ART
MJ KIM with
JORDIE BELLAIRE
ZU ORZU

COLLECTION EDITOR
IVAN COHEN

COLLECTION DESIGNER
STEVE BLACKWELL

Doctor Mirage®. Published by Valiant Entertainment LLC. Office of Publication: 350 Seventh Avenue, New York, NY 10001. Printed in the U.S.A. First Printing. ISBN: 9781682153468

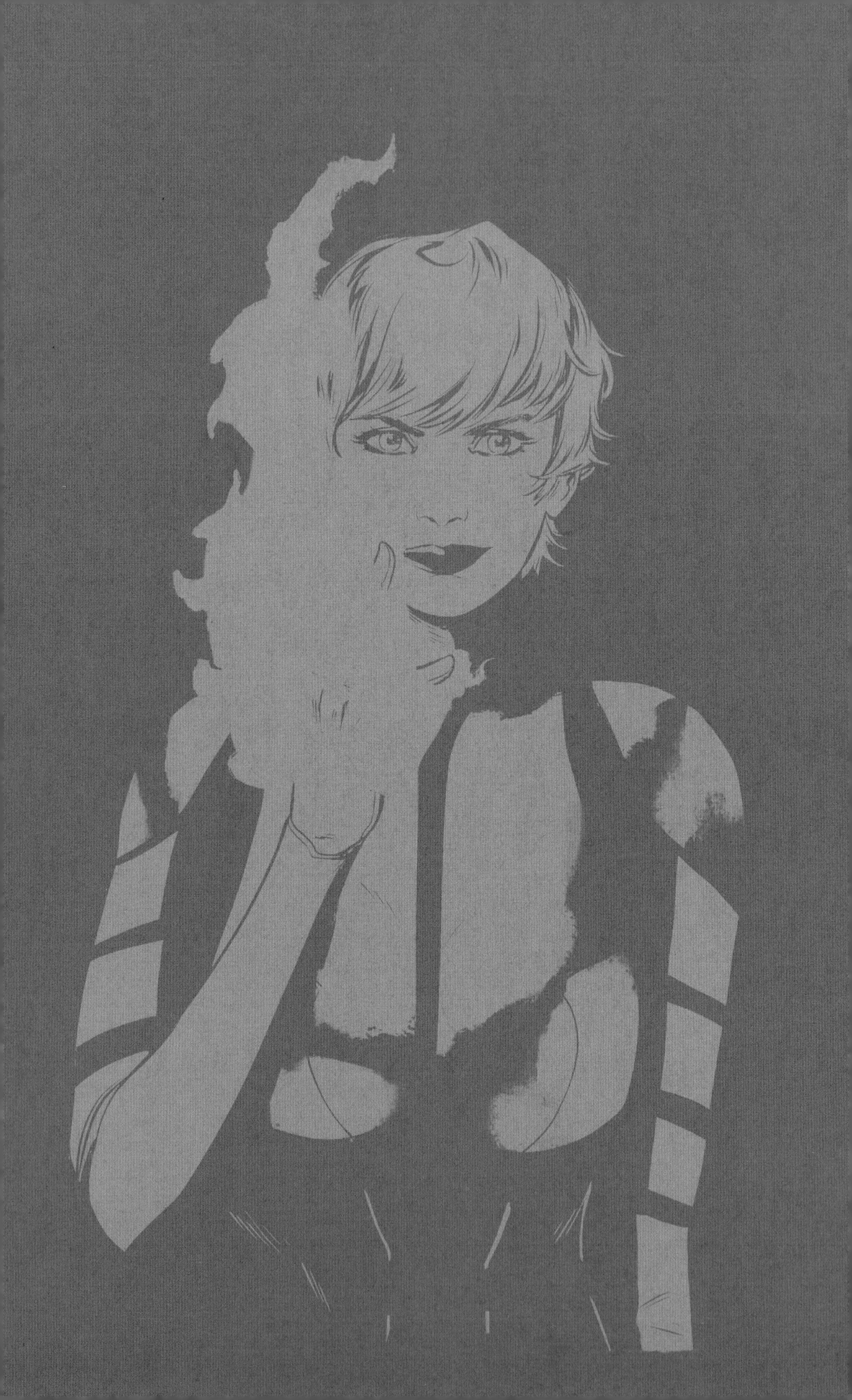

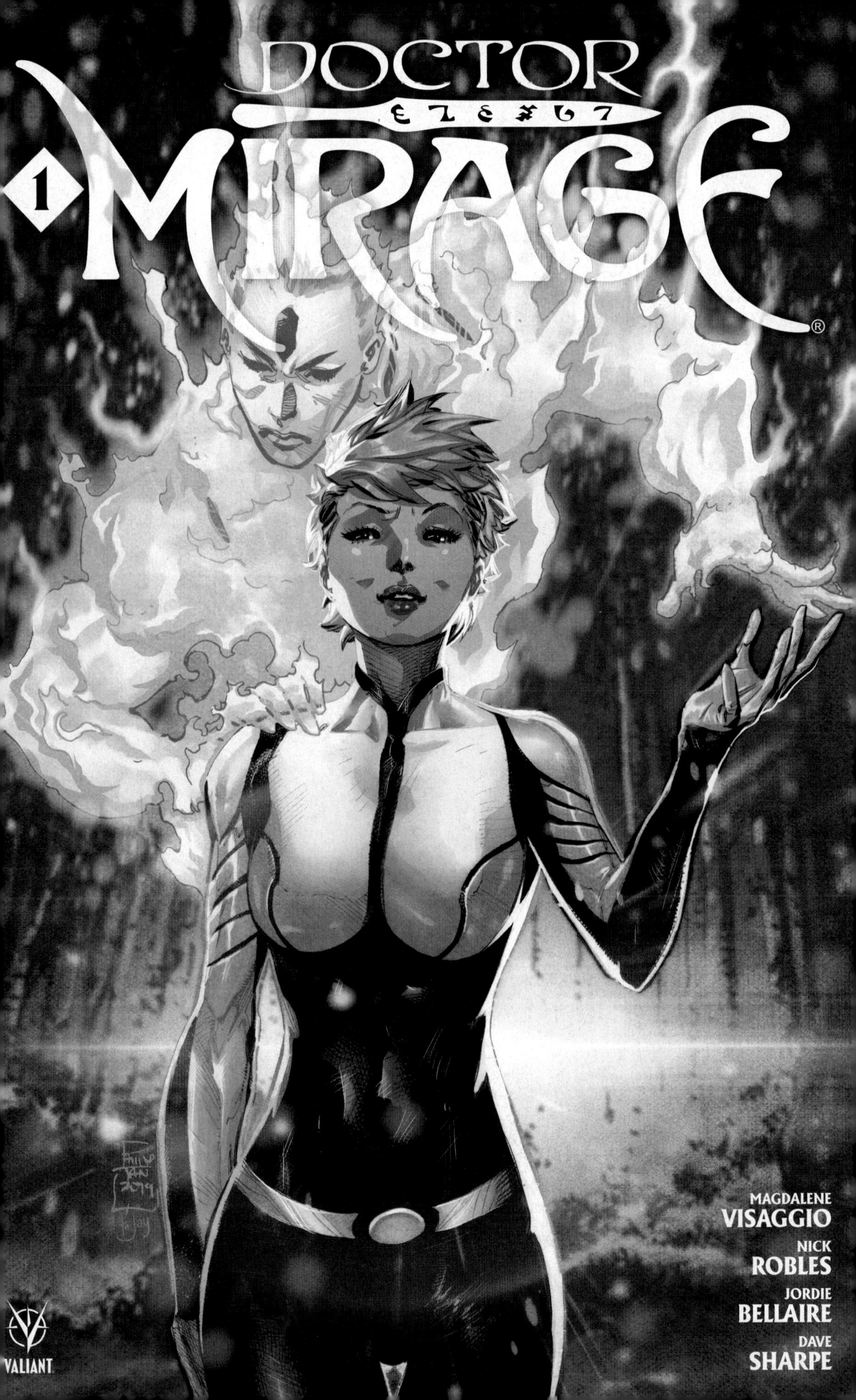
DOCTOR
MIRAGE
1
MAGDALENE
VISAGGIO
NICK
ROBLES
JORDIE
BELLAIRE
DAVE
SHARPE
VALIANT

DOCTOR MIRAGE #1

WRITER: Magdalene Visaggio
ART: Nick Robles
COLORS: Jordie Bellaire
LETTERS: Dave Sharpe
COVER ARTIST: Philip Tan with Jay David Ramos
ASSISTANT EDITOR: Drew Baumgartner
EDITOR: Lysa Hawkins

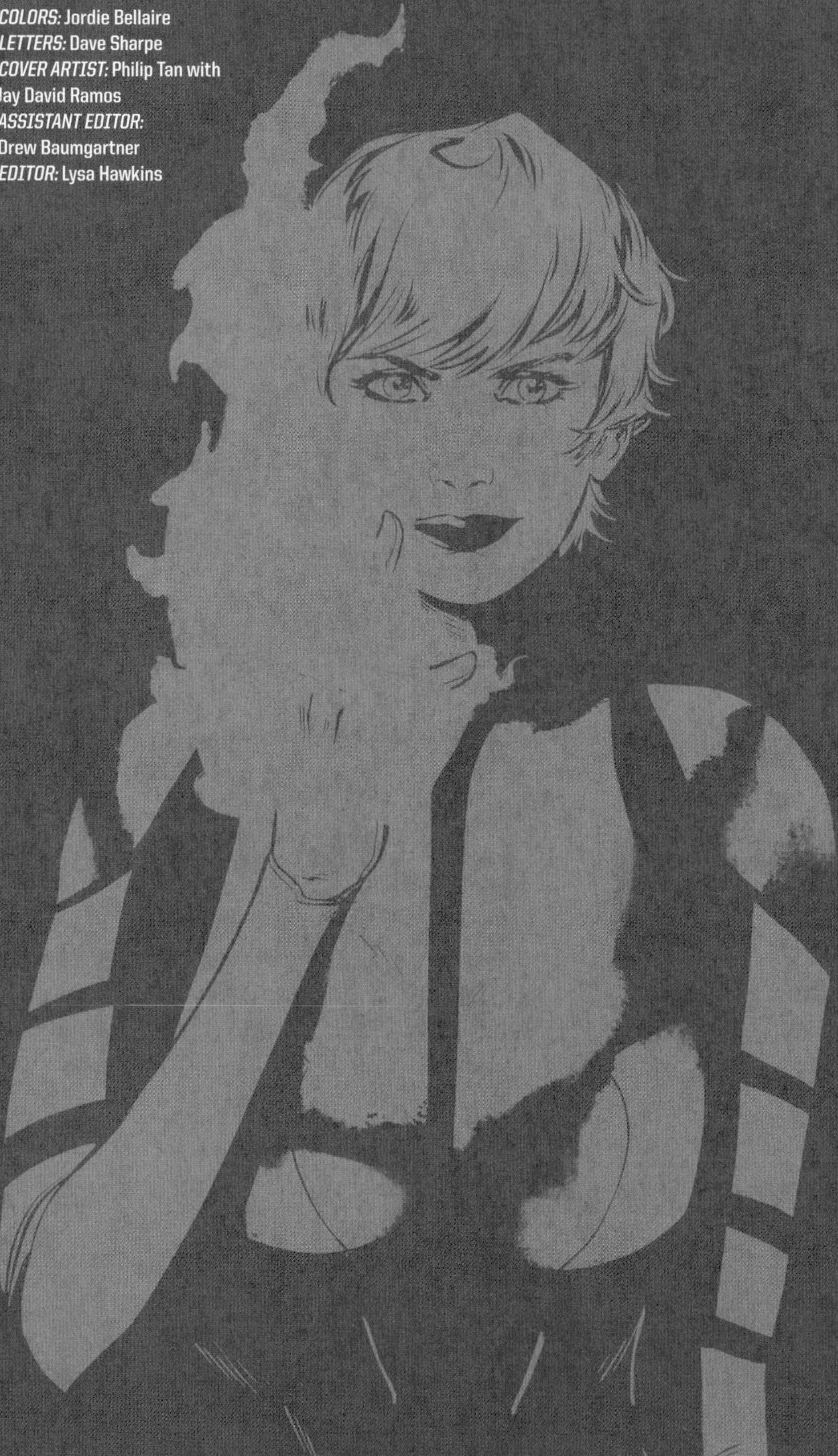

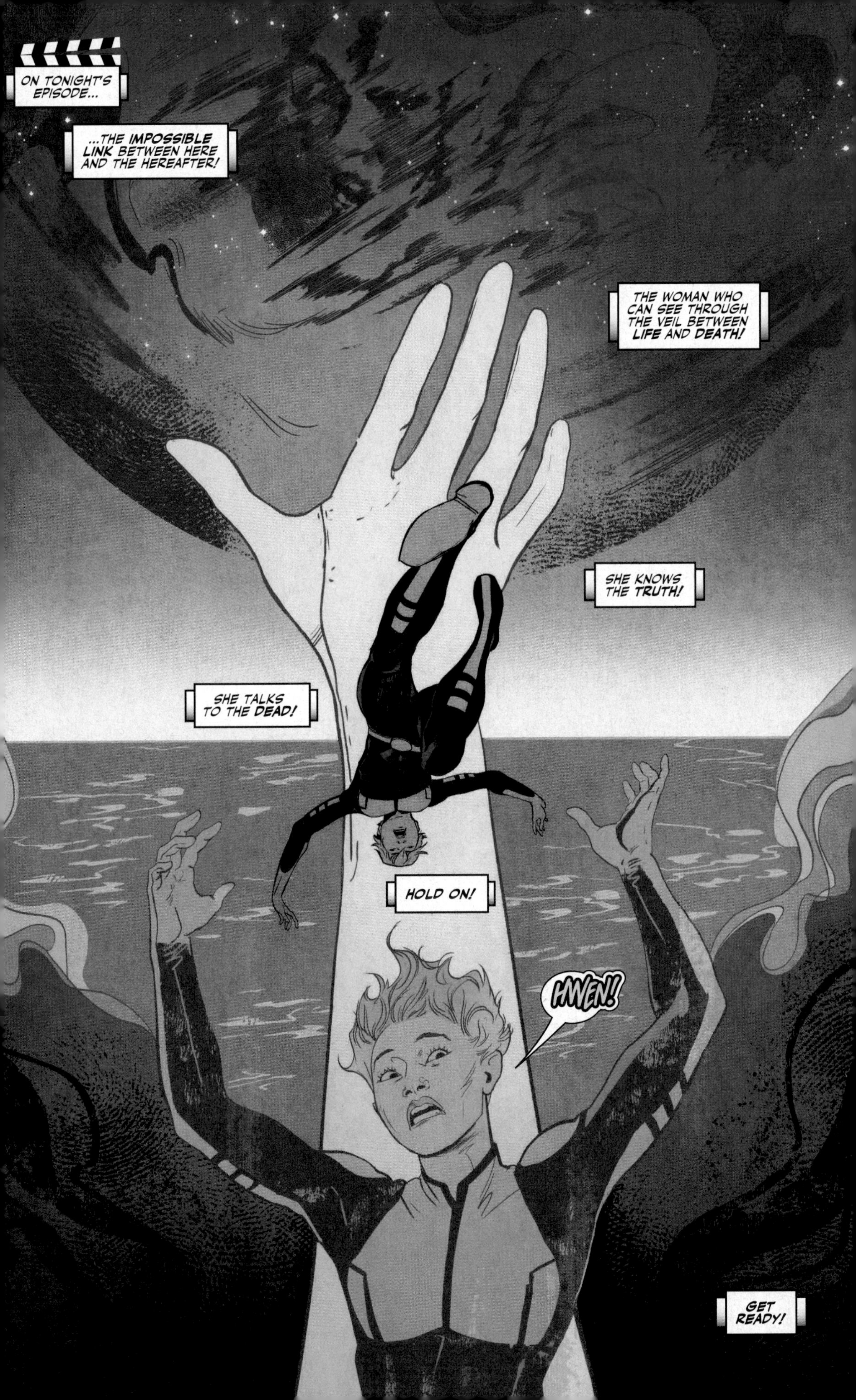
ON TONIGHT'S EPISODE...
...THE IMPOSSIBLE LINK BETWEEN HERE AND THE HEREAFTER!
THE WOMAN WHO CAN SEE THROUGH THE VEIL BETWEEN LIFE AND DEATH!
SHE KNOWS THE TRUTH!
SHE TALKS TO THE DEAD!
HOLD ON!
HAVEN!
GET READY!

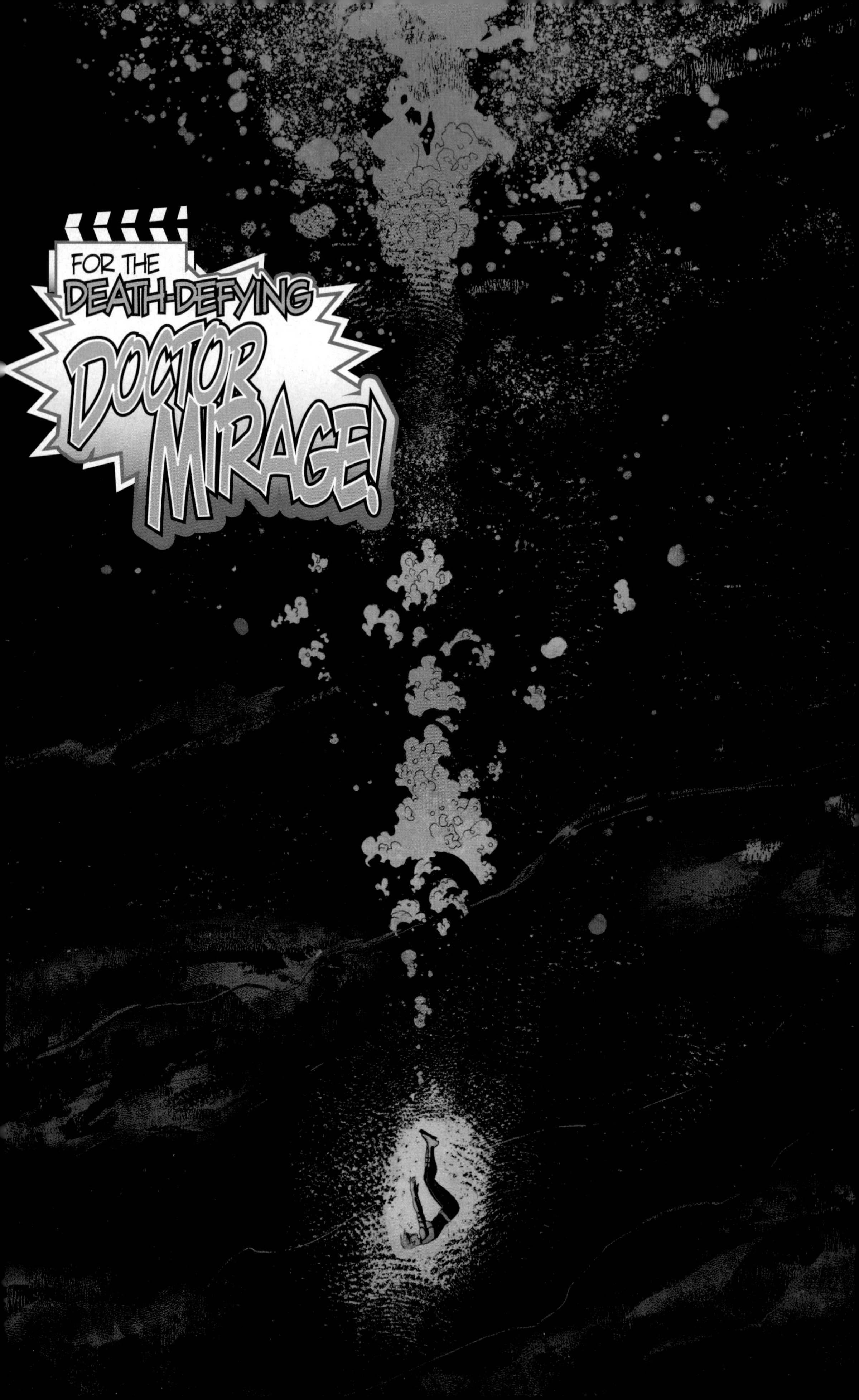
FOR THE
DEATH-DEFYING
DOCTOR
MIRAGE!

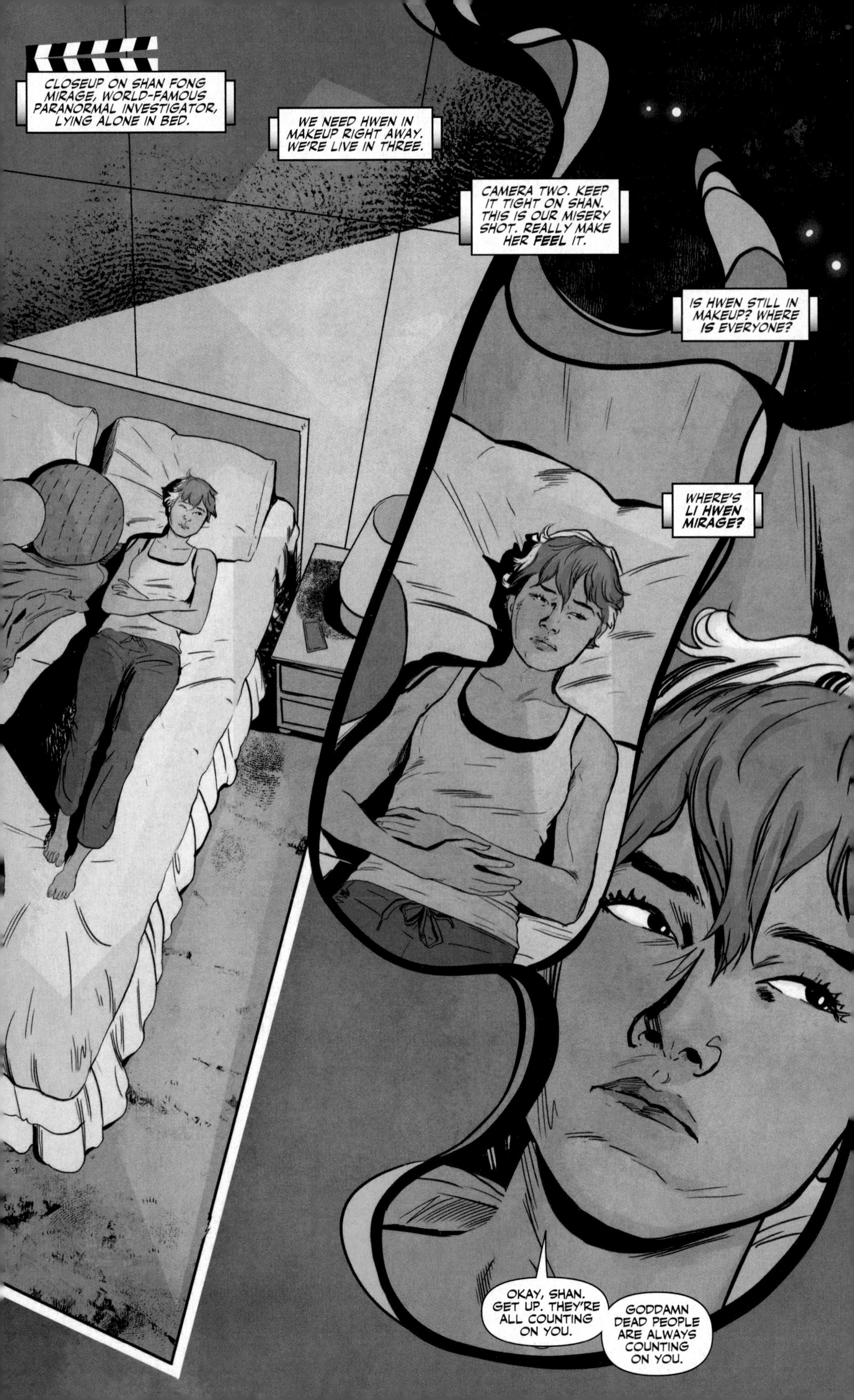
CLOSEUP ON SHAN FONG MIRAGE, WORLD-FAMOUS PARANORMAL INVESTIGATOR, LYING ALONE IN BED.
WE NEED HWEN IN MAKEUP RIGHT AWAY. WE'RE LIVE IN THREE.
CAMERA TWO. KEEP IT TIGHT ON SHAN. THIS IS OUR MISERY SHOT. REALLY MAKE HER FEEL IT.
IS HWEN STILL IN MAKEUP? WHERE IS EVERYONE?
WHERE'S LI HWEN MIRAGE?
OKAY, SHAN. GET UP. THEY'RE ALL COUNTING ON YOU.
GODDAMN DEAD PEOPLE ARE ALWAYS COUNTING ON YOU.

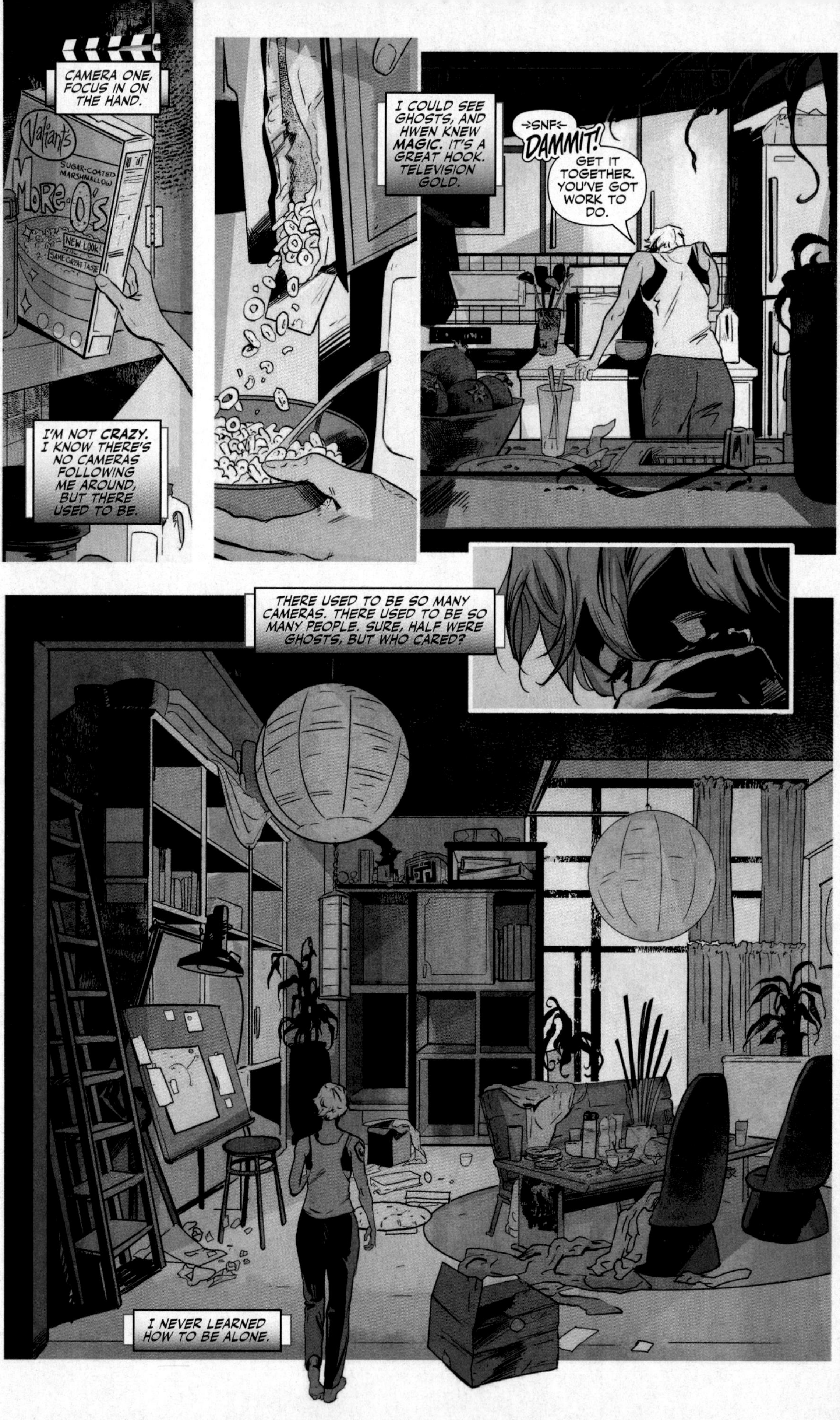
CAMERA ONE, FOCUS IN ON THE HAND.
Valiant's
SUGAR-COATED MARSHMALLOW
More-O's
NEW LOOK!
SAME GREAT TASTE
I'M NOT CRAZY. I KNOW THERE'S NO CAMERAS FOLLOWING ME AROUND, BUT THERE USED TO BE.
I COULD SEE GHOSTS, AND HWEN KNEW MAGIC. IT'S A GREAT HOOK. TELEVISION GOLD.
SNF
DAMMIT!
GET IT TOGETHER. YOU'VE GOT WORK TO DO.
THERE USED TO BE SO MANY CAMERAS. THERE USED TO BE SO MANY PEOPLE. SURE, HALF WERE GHOSTS, BUT WHO CARED?
I NEVER LEARNED HOW TO BE ALONE.

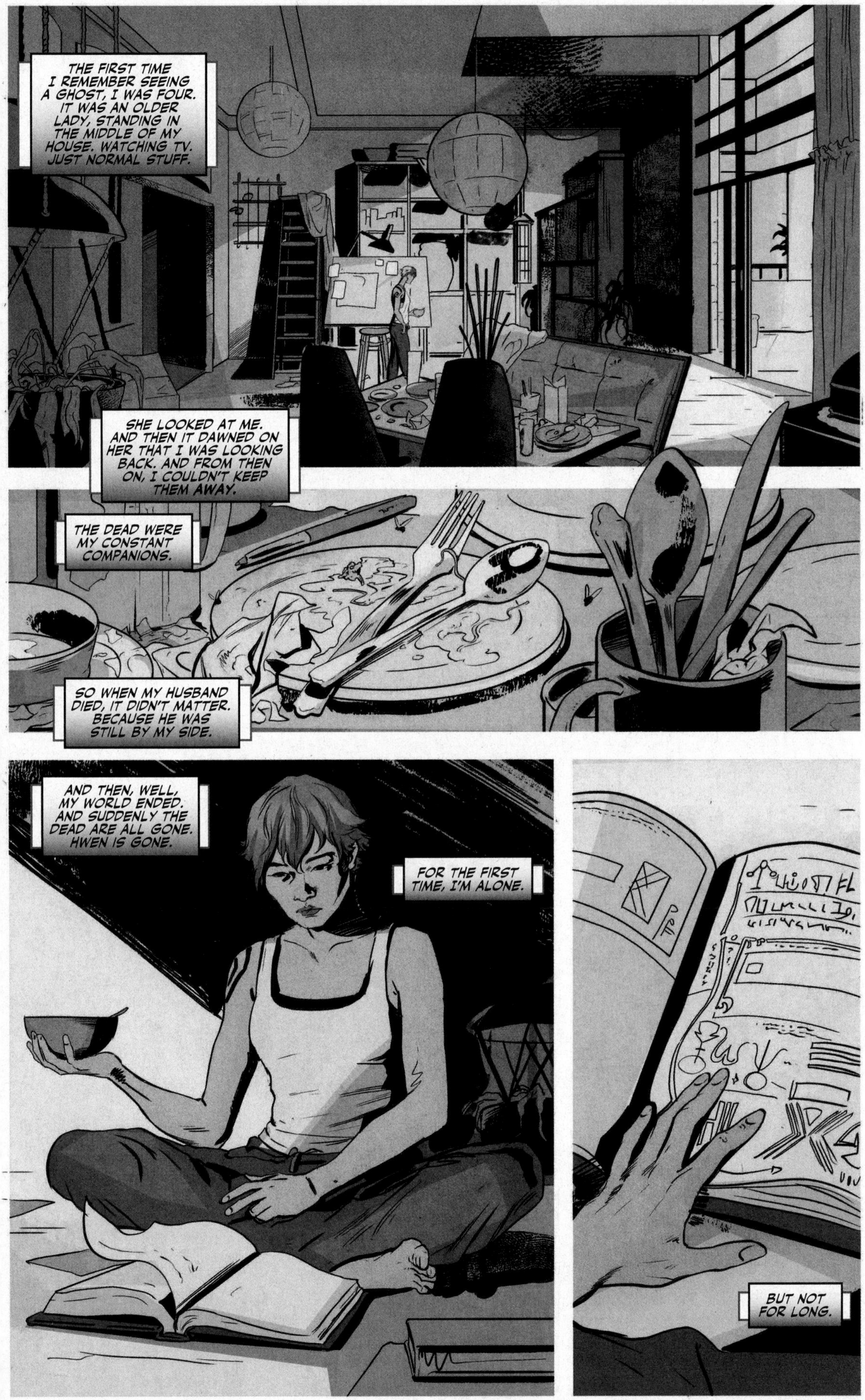
THE FIRST TIME I REMEMBER SEEING A GHOST, I WAS FOUR. IT WAS AN OLDER LADY, STANDING IN THE MIDDLE OF MY HOUSE. WATCHING TV. JUST NORMAL STUFF.
SHE LOOKED AT ME. AND THEN IT DAWNED ON HER THAT I WAS LOOKING BACK. AND FROM THEN ON, I COULDN'T KEEP THEM AWAY.
THE DEAD WERE MY CONSTANT COMPANIONS.
SO WHEN MY HUSBAND DIED, IT DIDN'T MATTER. BECAUSE HE WAS STILL BY MY SIDE.
AND THEN, WELL, MY WORLD ENDED. AND SUDDENLY THE DEAD ARE ALL GONE. HWEN IS GONE.
FOR THE FIRST TIME, I'M ALONE.
BUT NOT FOR LONG.

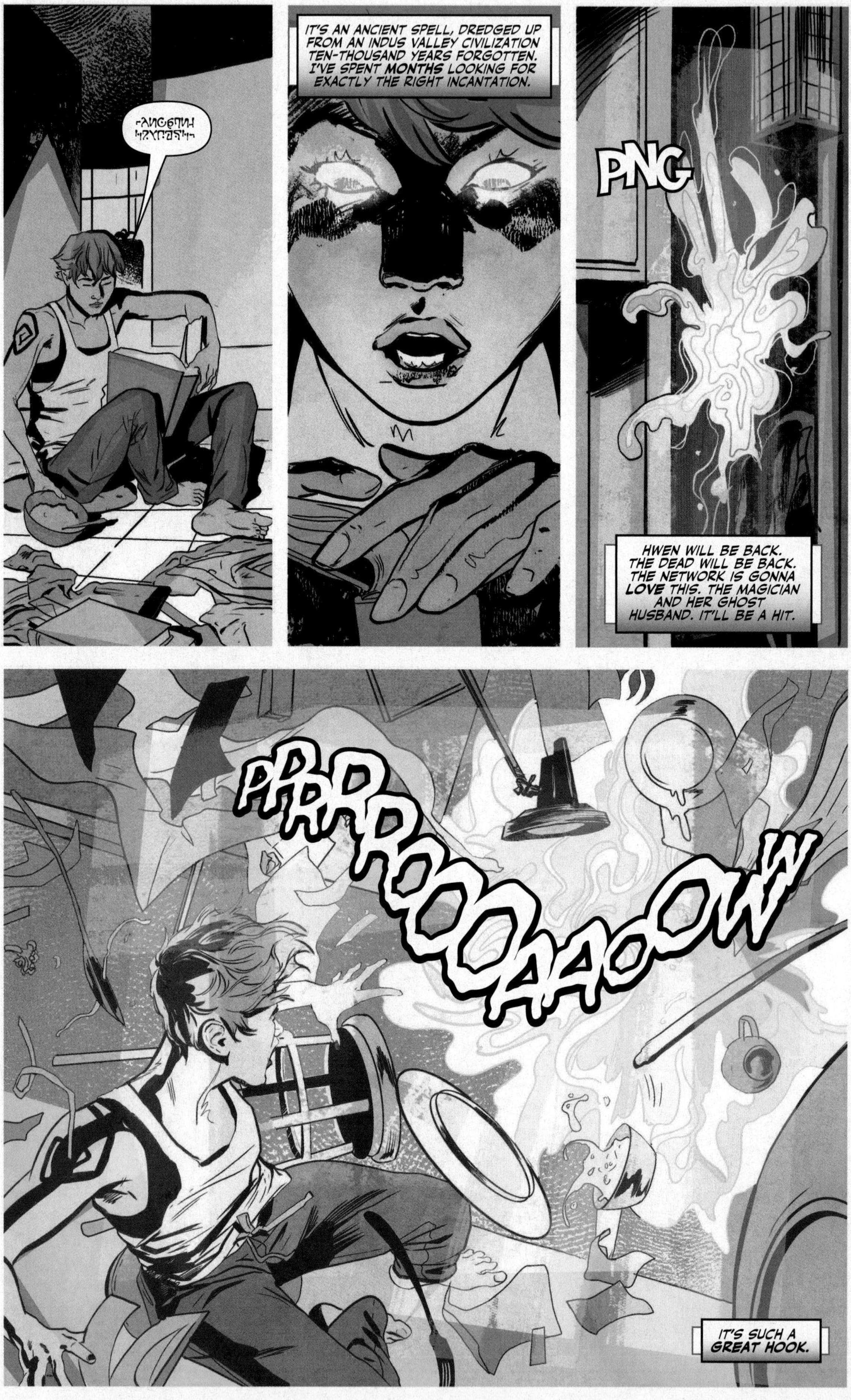
IT'S AN ANCIENT SPELL, DREDGED UP FROM AN INDUS VALLEY CIVILIZATION TEN-THOUSAND YEARS FORGOTTEN. I'VE SPENT MONTHS LOOKING FOR EXACTLY THE RIGHT INCANTATION.
PNG
HWEN WILL BE BACK. THE DEAD WILL BE BACK. THE NETWORK IS GONNA LOVE THIS. THE MAGICIAN AND HER GHOST HUSBAND. IT'LL BE A HIT.
PRRROOOAAOOW
IT'S SUCH A GREAT HOOK.

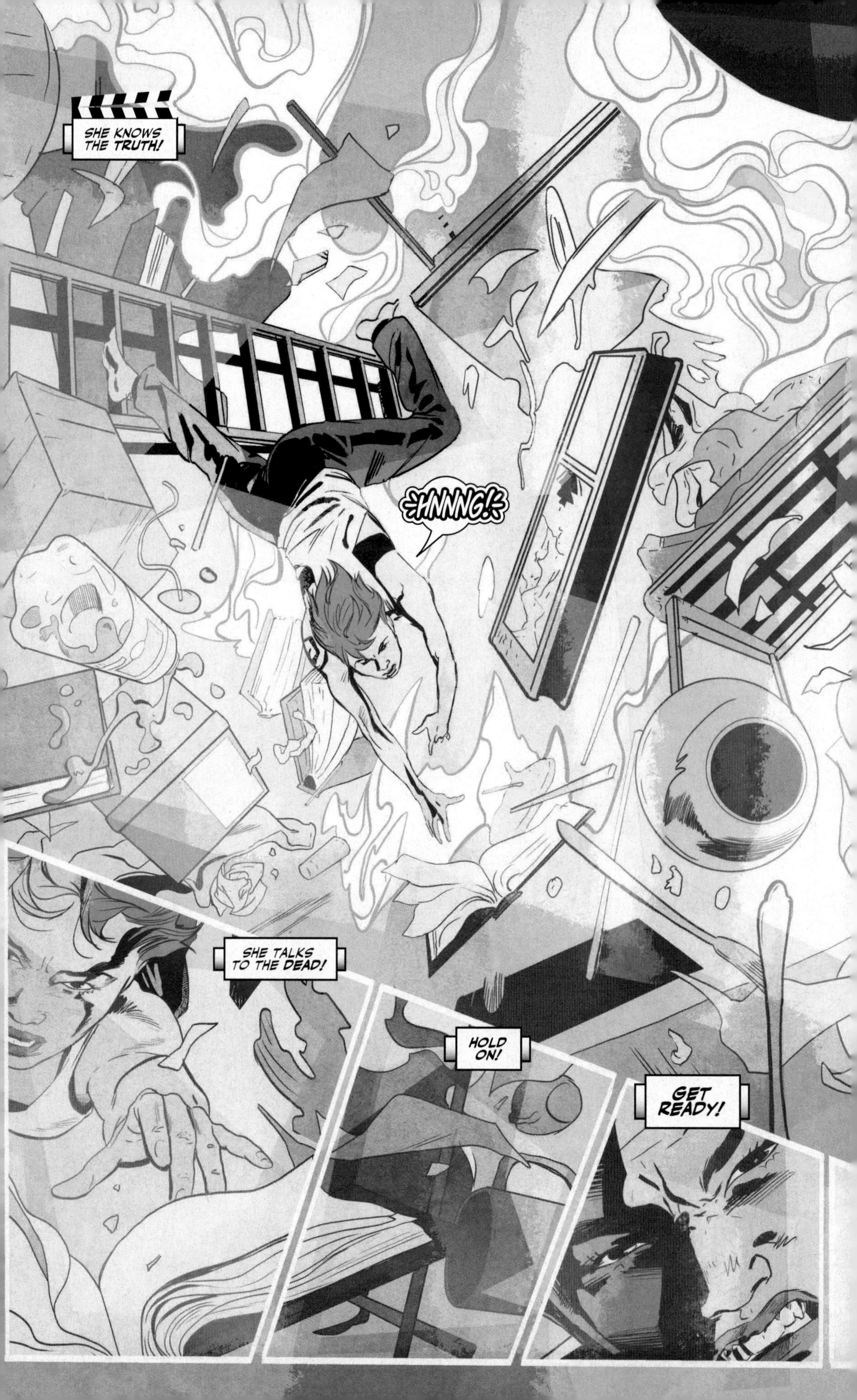
SHE KNOWS THE TRUTH!
HNNNG!
SHE TALKS TO THE DEAD!
HOLD ON!
GET READY!

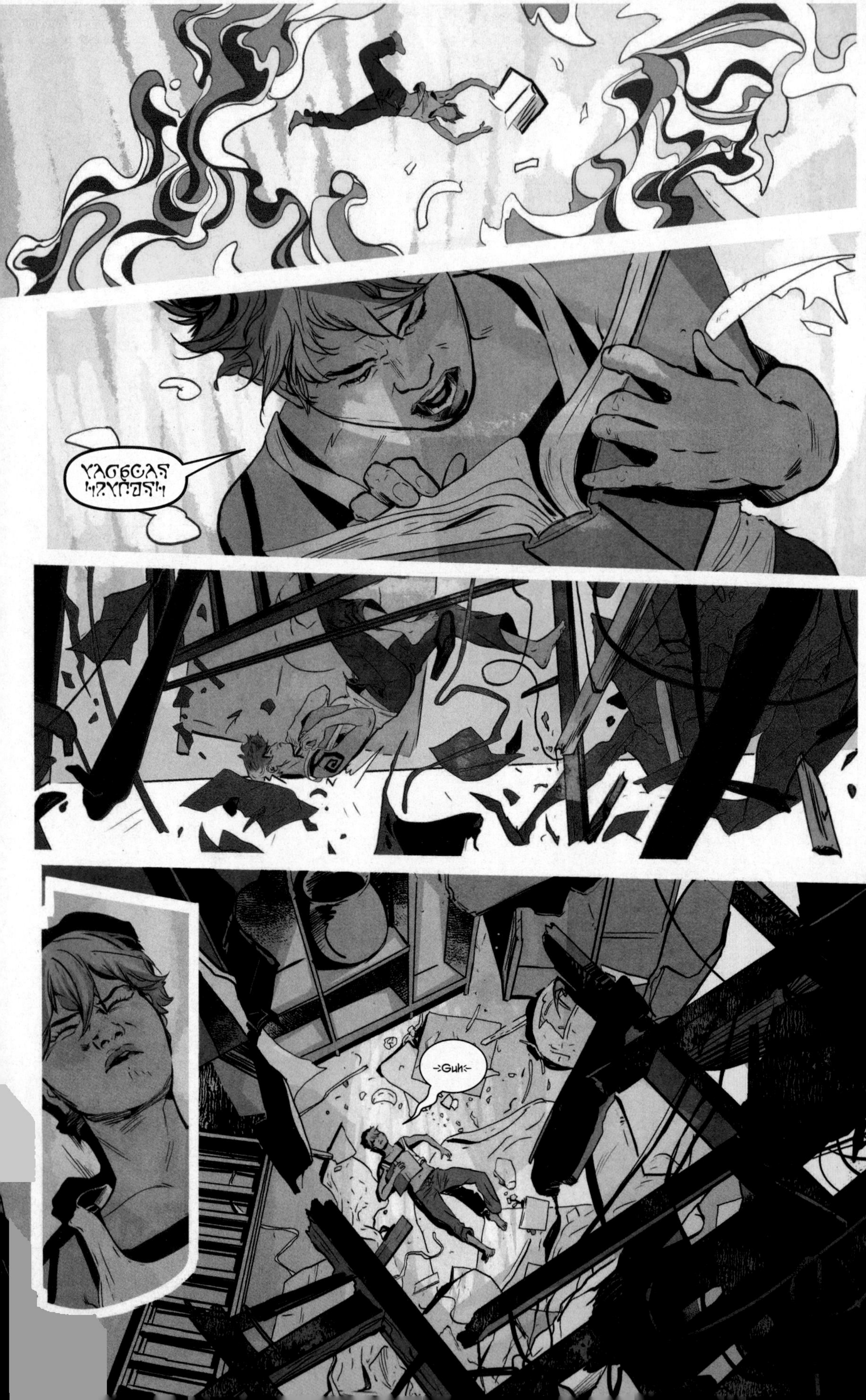
Guh

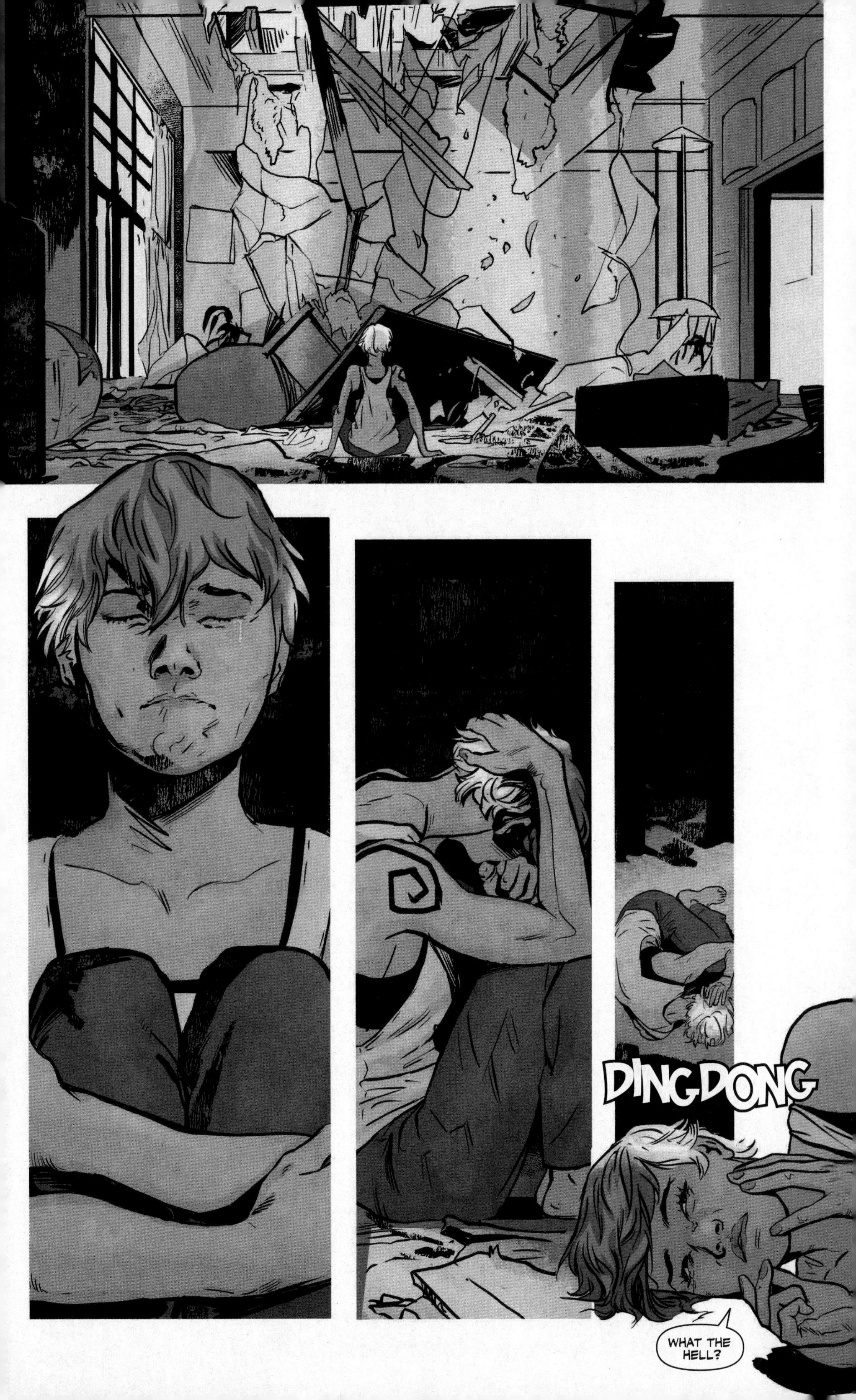
DING DONG
WHAT THE HELL?

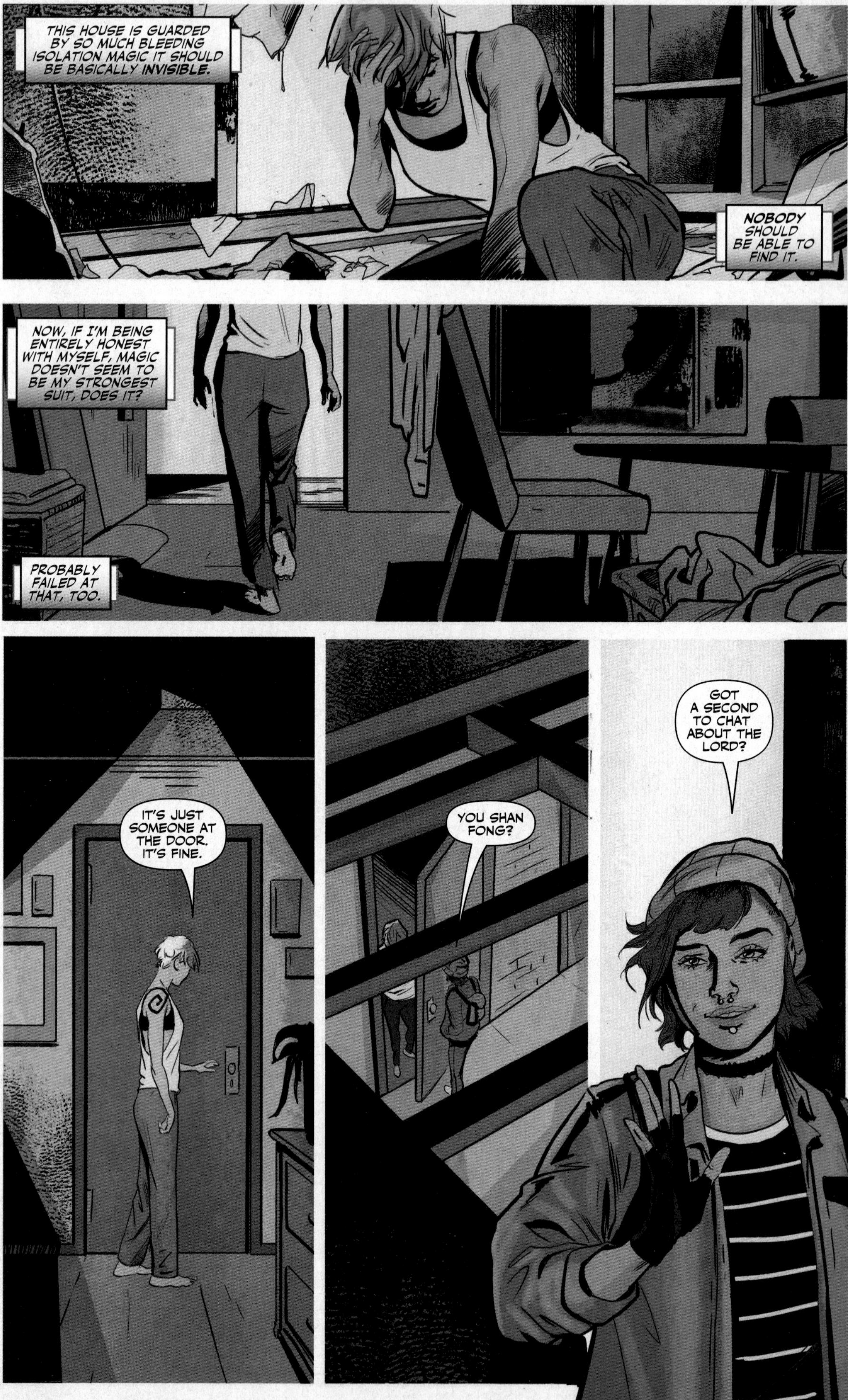
THIS HOUSE IS GUARDED BY SO MUCH BLEEDING ISOLATION MAGIC IT SHOULD BE BASICALLY INVISIBLE.
NOBODY SHOULD BE ABLE TO FIND IT.
NOW, IF I'M BEING ENTIRELY HONEST WITH MYSELF, MAGIC DOESN'T SEEM TO BE MY STRONGEST SUIT, DOES IT?
PROBABLY FAILED AT THAT, TOO.
IT'S JUST SOMEONE AT THE DOOR. IT'S FINE.
YOU SHAN FONG?
GOT A SECOND TO CHAT ABOUT THE LORD?

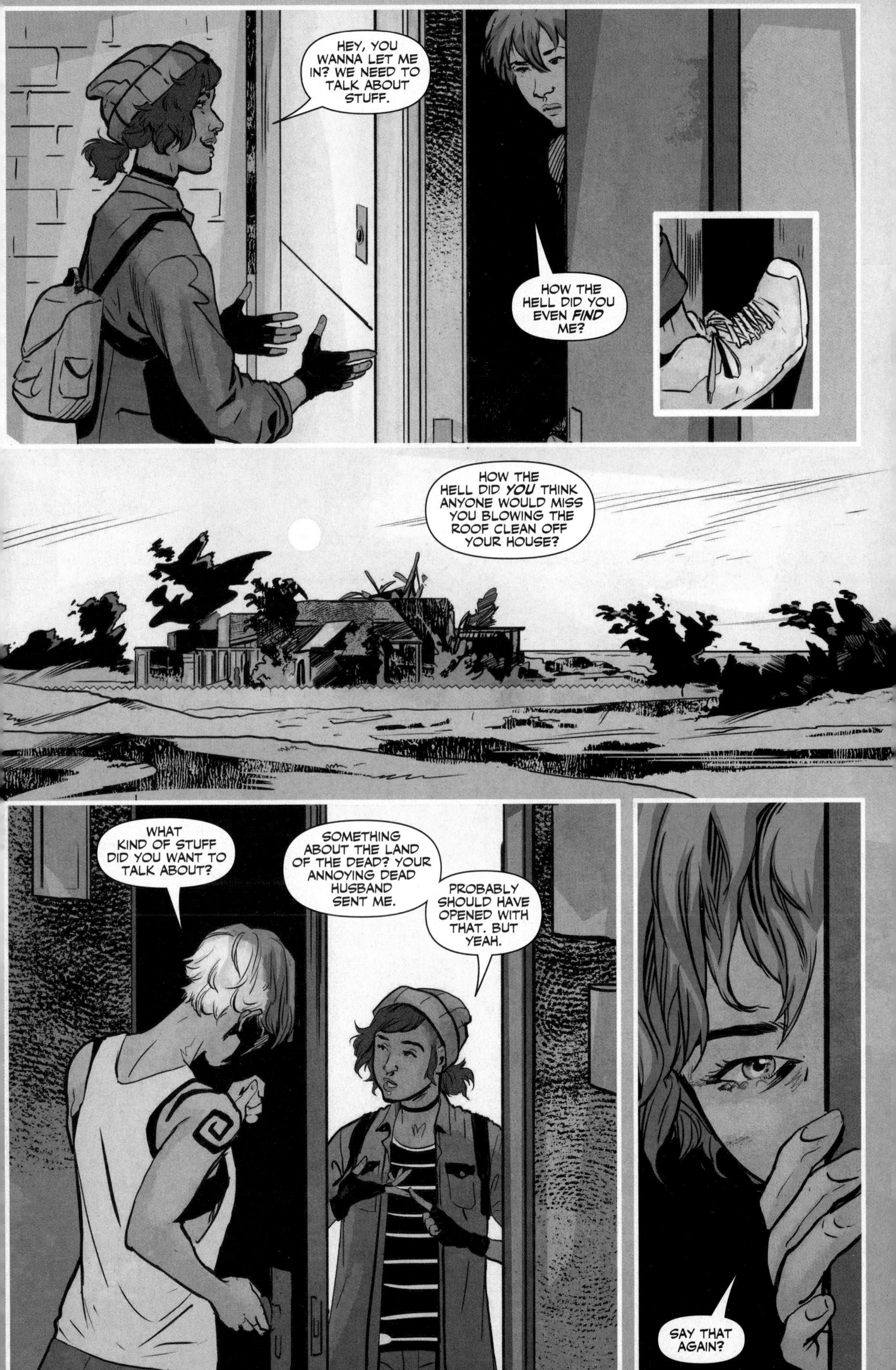
HEY, YOU WANNA LET ME IN? WE NEED TO TALK ABOUT STUFF.
HOW THE HELL DID YOU EVEN FIND ME?
HOW THE HELL DID YOU THINK ANYONE WOULD MISS YOU BLOWING THE ROOF CLEAN OFF YOUR HOUSE?
WHAT KIND OF STUFF DID YOU WANT TO TALK ABOUT?
SOMETHING ABOUT THE LAND OF THE DEAD? YOUR ANNOYING DEAD HUSBAND SENT ME.
PROBABLY SHOULD HAVE OPENED WITH THAT. BUT YEAH.
SAY THAT AGAIN?

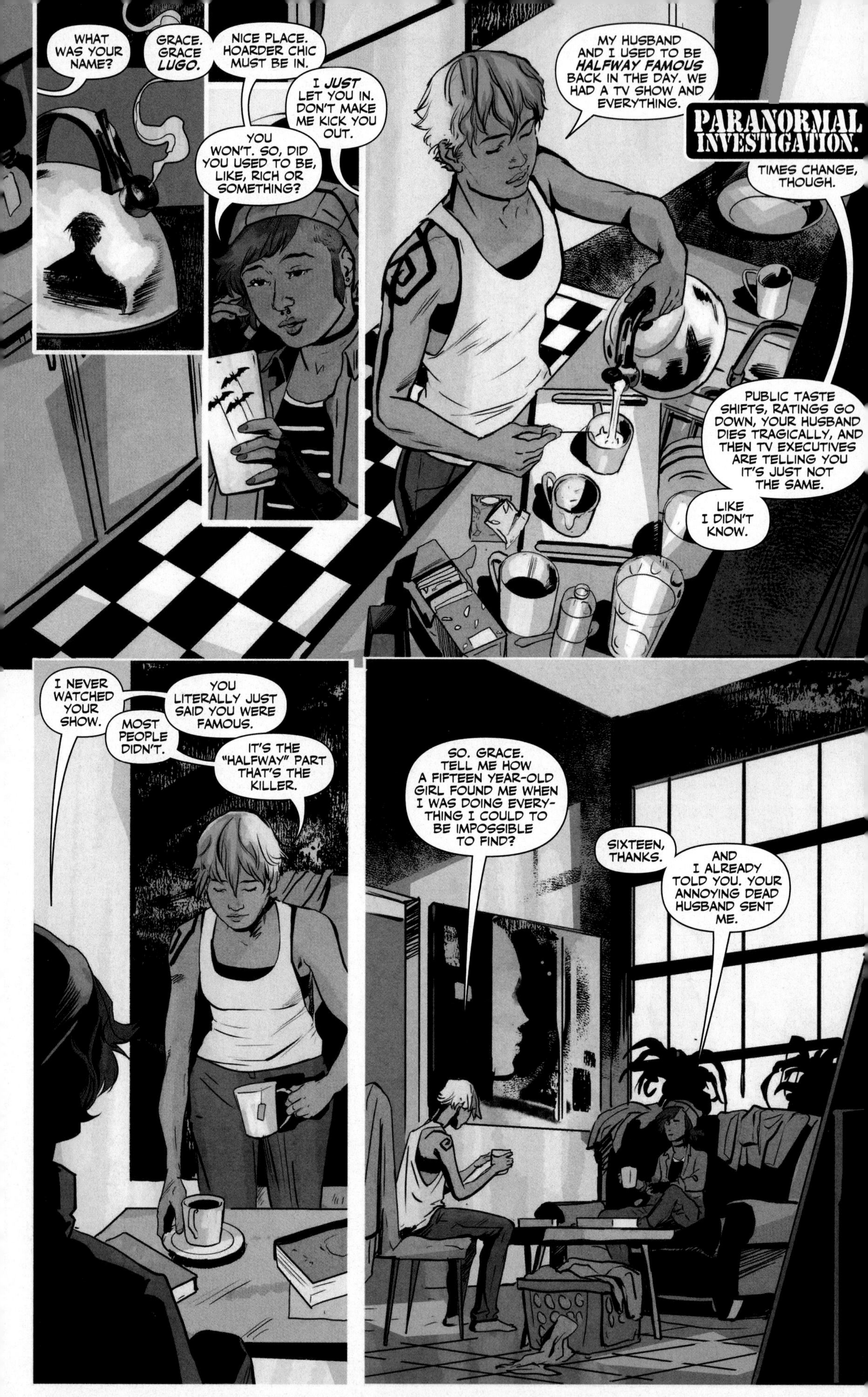
WHAT WAS YOUR NAME?
GRACE. GRACE LUGO.
NICE PLACE. HOARDER CHIC MUST BE IN.
I JUST LET YOU IN. DON'T MAKE ME KICK YOU OUT.
YOU WON'T. SO, DID YOU USED TO BE, LIKE, RICH OR SOMETHING?
MY HUSBAND AND I USED TO BE HALFWAY FAMOUS BACK IN THE DAY. WE HAD A TV SHOW AND EVERYTHING.
PARANORMAL INVESTIGATION.
TIMES CHANGE, THOUGH.
PUBLIC TASTE SHIFTS, RATINGS GO DOWN, YOUR HUSBAND DIES TRAGICALLY, AND THEN TV EXECUTIVES ARE TELLING YOU IT'S JUST NOT THE SAME.
LIKE I DIDN'T KNOW.
I NEVER WATCHED YOUR SHOW.
YOU LITERALLY JUST SAID YOU WERE FAMOUS.
MOST PEOPLE DIDN'T.
IT'S THE "HALFWAY" PART THAT'S THE KILLER.
SO. GRACE. TELL ME HOW A FIFTEEN YEAR-OLD GIRL FOUND ME WHEN I WAS DOING EVERY-THING I COULD TO BE IMPOSSIBLE TO FIND?
SIXTEEN, THANKS.
AND I ALREADY TOLD YOU. YOUR ANNOYING DEAD HUSBAND SENT ME.

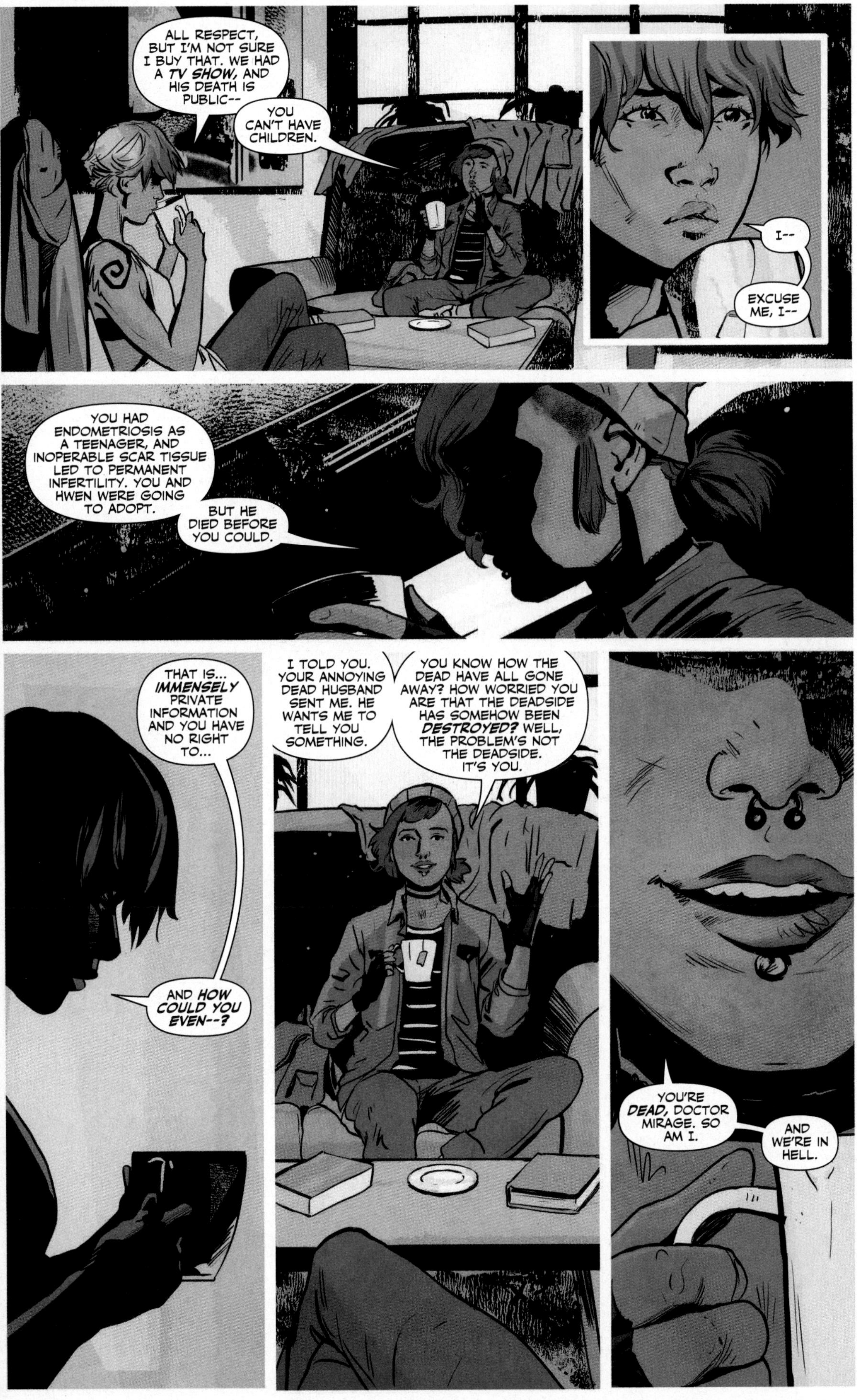
ALL RESPECT, BUT I'M NOT SURE I BUY THAT. WE HAD A TV SHOW, AND HIS DEATH IS PUBLIC--
YOU CAN'T HAVE CHILDREN.
I--
EXCUSE ME, I--
YOU HAD ENDOMETRIOSIS AS A TEENAGER, AND INOPERABLE SCAR TISSUE LED TO PERMANENT INFERTILITY. YOU AND HWEN WERE GOING TO ADOPT.
BUT HE DIED BEFORE YOU COULD.
THAT IS... IMMENSELY PRIVATE INFORMATION AND YOU HAVE NO RIGHT TO...
AND HOW COULD YOU EVEN--?
I TOLD YOU. YOUR ANNOYING DEAD HUSBAND SENT ME. HE WANTS ME TO TELL YOU SOMETHING.
YOU KNOW HOW THE DEAD HAVE ALL GONE AWAY? HOW WORRIED YOU ARE THAT THE DEADSIDE HAS SOMEHOW BEEN DESTROYED? WELL, THE PROBLEM'S NOT THE DEADSIDE. IT'S YOU.
YOU'RE DEAD, DOCTOR MIRAGE. SO AM I.
AND WE'RE IN HELL.

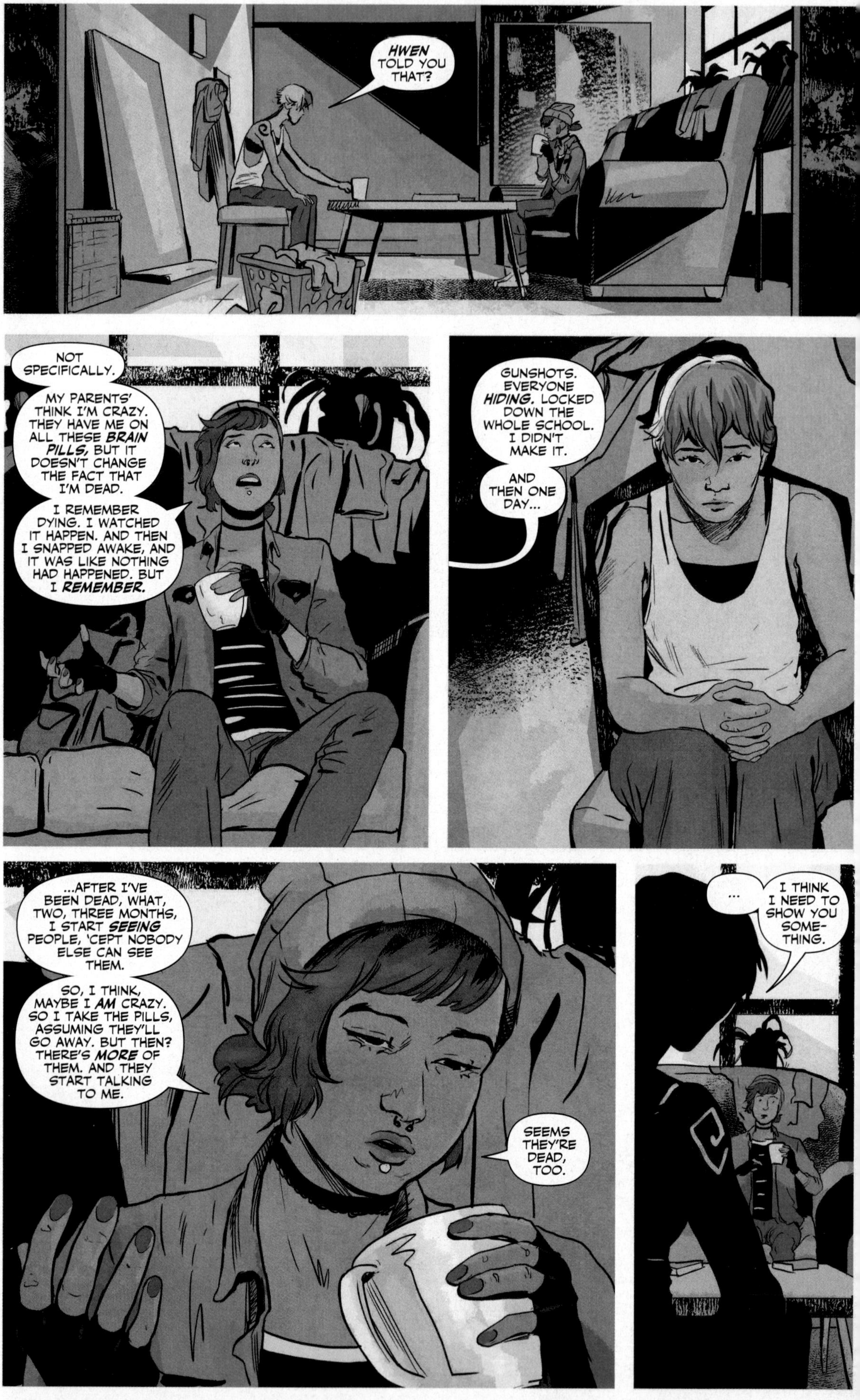
HWEN TOLD YOU THAT?
NOT SPECIFICALLY.
MY PARENTS' THINK I'M CRAZY. THEY HAVE ME ON ALL THESE BRAIN PILLS, BUT IT DOESN'T CHANGE THE FACT THAT I'M DEAD.
I REMEMBER DYING. I WATCHED IT HAPPEN. AND THEN I SNAPPED AWAKE, AND IT WAS LIKE NOTHING HAD HAPPENED. BUT I REMEMBER.
GUNSHOTS. EVERYONE HIDING. LOCKED DOWN THE WHOLE SCHOOL. I DIDN'T MAKE IT.
AND THEN ONE DAY...
...AFTER I'VE BEEN DEAD, WHAT, TWO, THREE MONTHS, I START SEEING PEOPLE, 'CEPT NOBODY ELSE CAN SEE THEM.
SO, I THINK, MAYBE I AM CRAZY. SO I TAKE THE PILLS, ASSUMING THEY'LL GO AWAY. BUT THEN? THERE'S MORE OF THEM. AND THEY START TALKING TO ME.
SEEMS THEY'RE DEAD, TOO.
...
I THINK I NEED TO SHOW YOU SOME-THING.

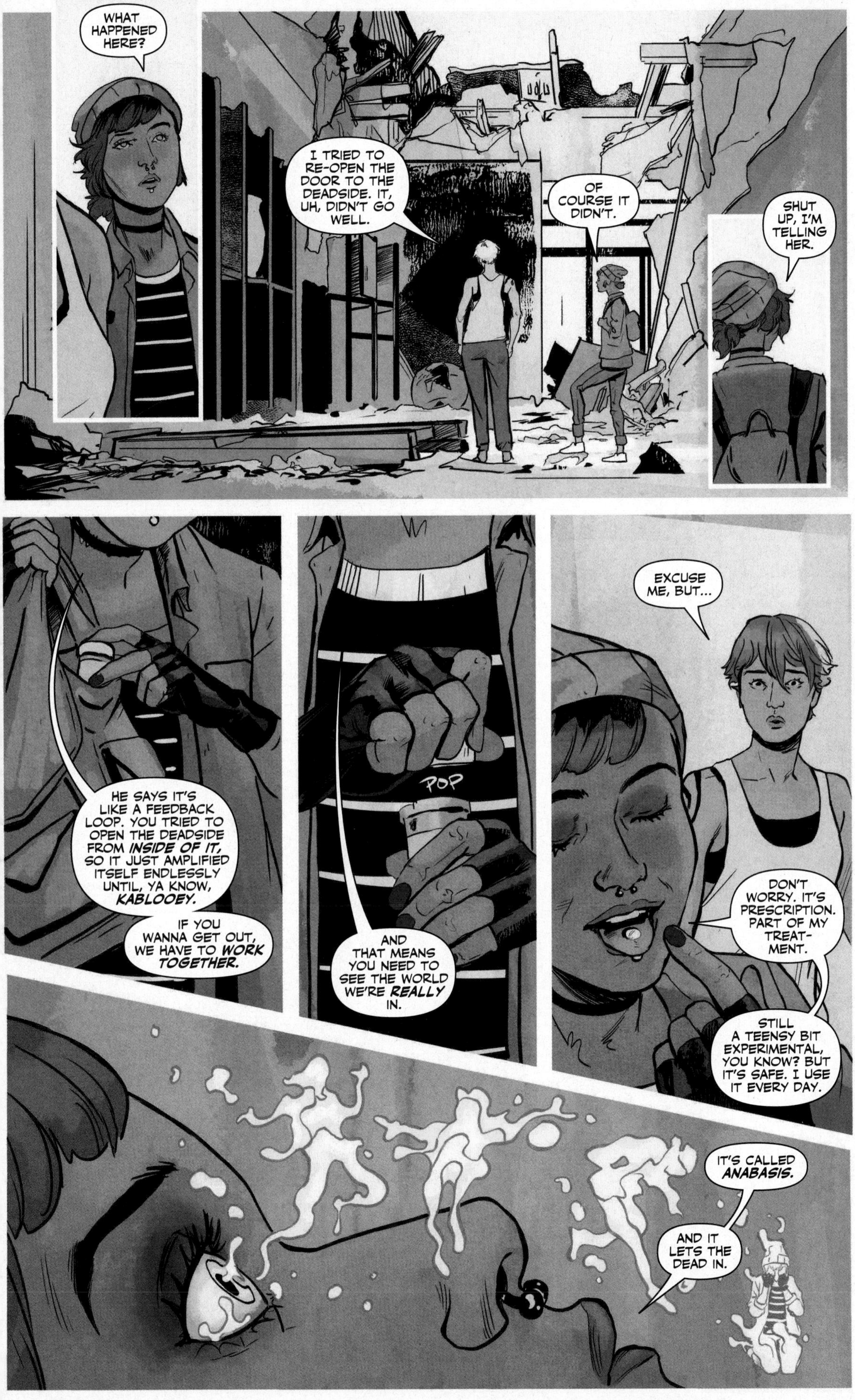
WHAT HAPPENED HERE?
I TRIED TO RE-OPEN THE DOOR TO THE DEADSIDE. IT, UH, DIDN'T GO WELL.
OF COURSE IT DIDN'T.
SHUT UP, I'M TELLING HER.
HE SAYS IT'S LIKE A FEEDBACK LOOP. YOU TRIED TO OPEN THE DEADSIDE FROM INSIDE OF IT, SO IT JUST AMPLIFIED ITSELF ENDLESSLY UNTIL, YA KNOW, KABLOOEY.
IF YOU WANNA GET OUT, WE HAVE TO WORK TOGETHER.
POP
AND THAT MEANS YOU NEED TO SEE THE WORLD WE'RE REALLY IN.
EXCUSE ME, BUT...
DON'T WORRY. IT'S PRESCRIPTION. PART OF MY TREAT-MENT.
STILL A TEENSY BIT EXPERIMENTAL, YOU KNOW? BUT IT'S SAFE. I USE IT EVERY DAY.
IT'S CALLED ANABASIS.
AND IT LETS THE DEAD IN.

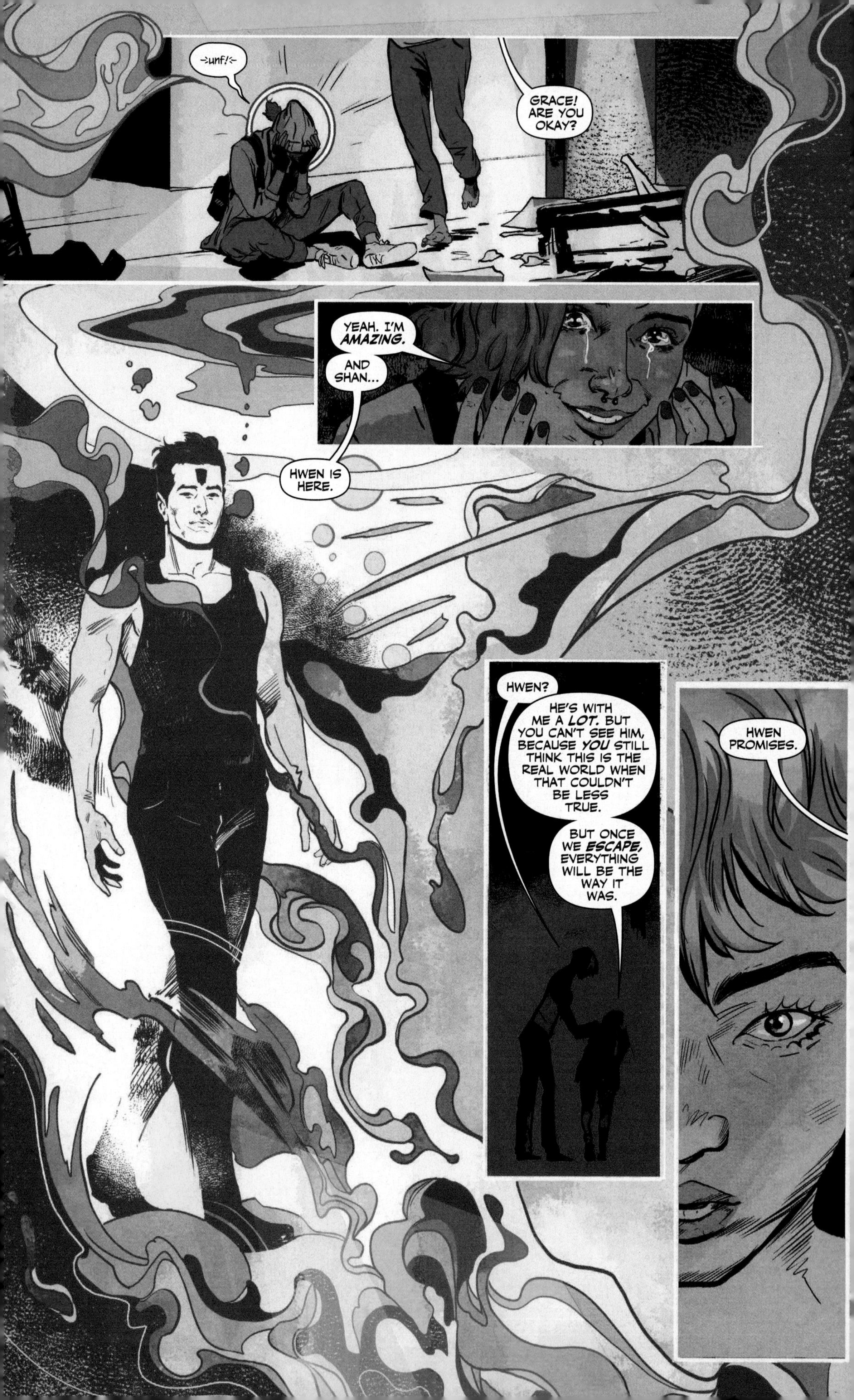

~unf!~
GRACE! ARE YOU OKAY?
YEAH. I'M AMAZING.
AND SHAN...
HWEN IS HERE.
HWEN?
HE'S WITH ME A LOT. BUT YOU CAN'T SEE HIM, BECAUSE YOU STILL THINK THIS IS THE REAL WORLD WHEN THAT COULDN'T BE LESS TRUE.
BUT ONCE WE ESCAPE, EVERYTHING WILL BE THE WAY IT WAS.
HWEN PROMISES.

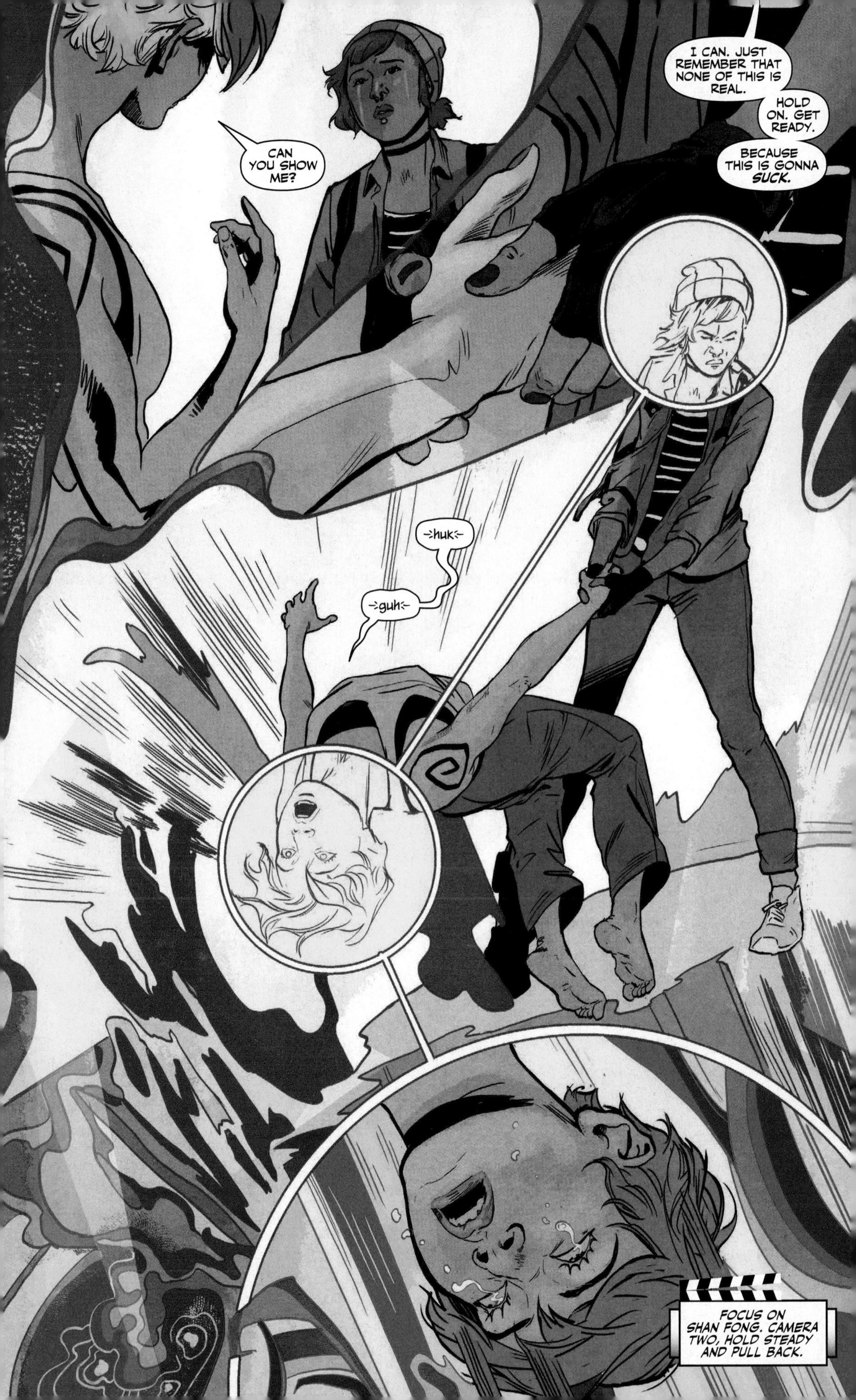
CAN YOU SHOW ME?
I CAN. JUST REMEMBER THAT NONE OF THIS IS REAL.
HOLD ON. GET READY.
BECAUSE THIS IS GONNA SUCK.
-huk-
-guh-
FOCUS ON SHAN FONG. CAMERA TWO, HOLD STEADY AND PULL BACK.

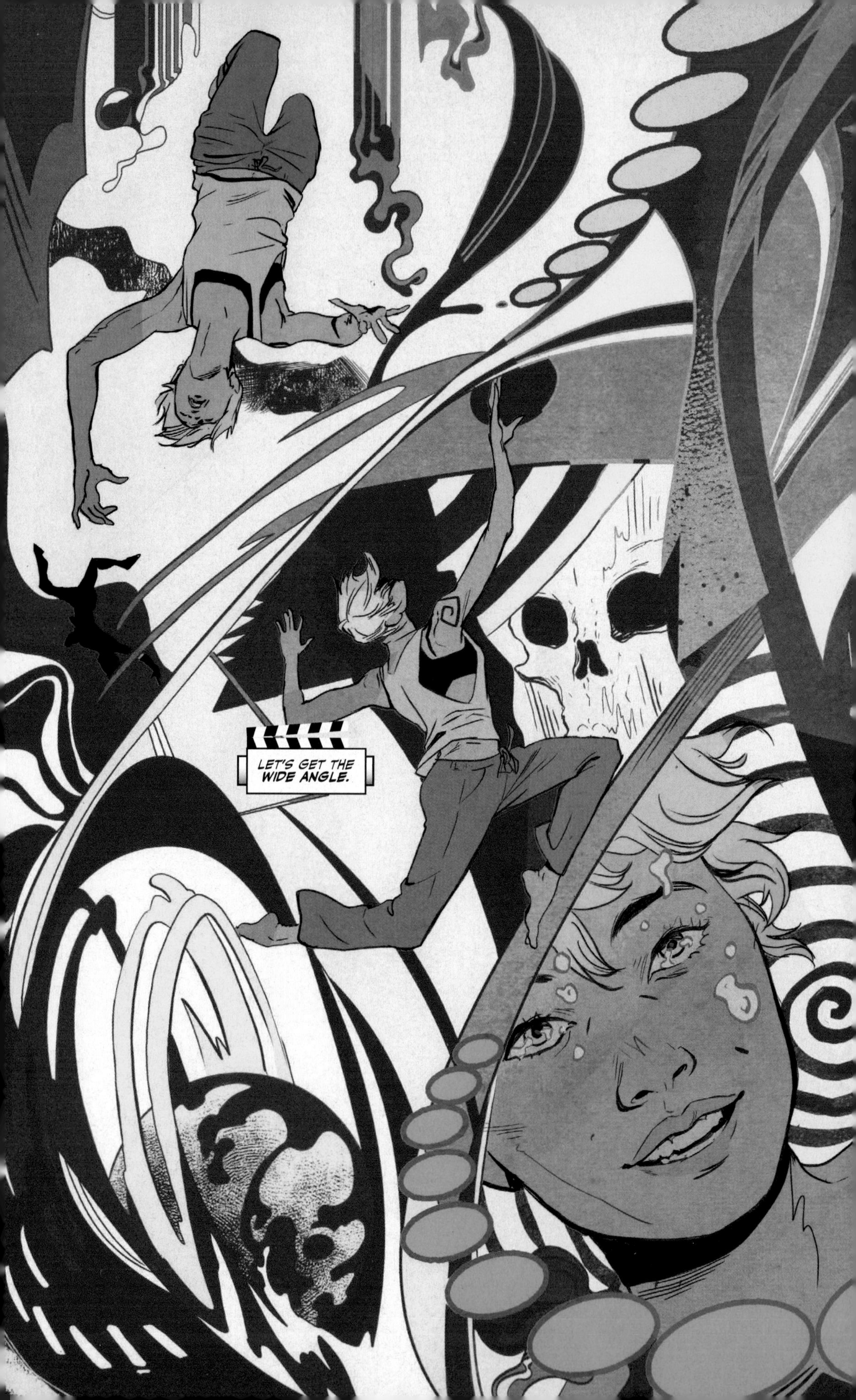
LET'S GET THE WIDE ANGLE.

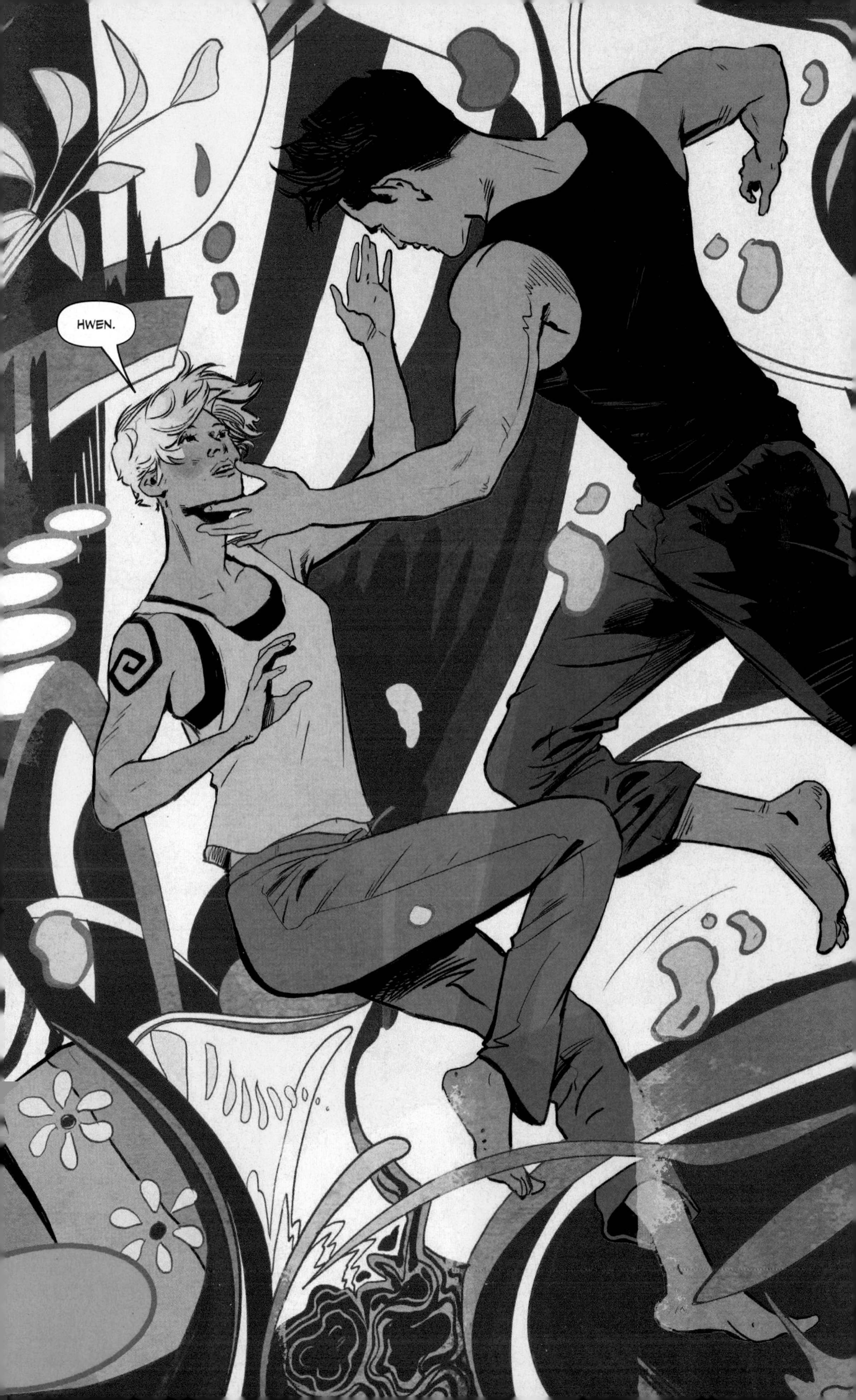
HWEN.

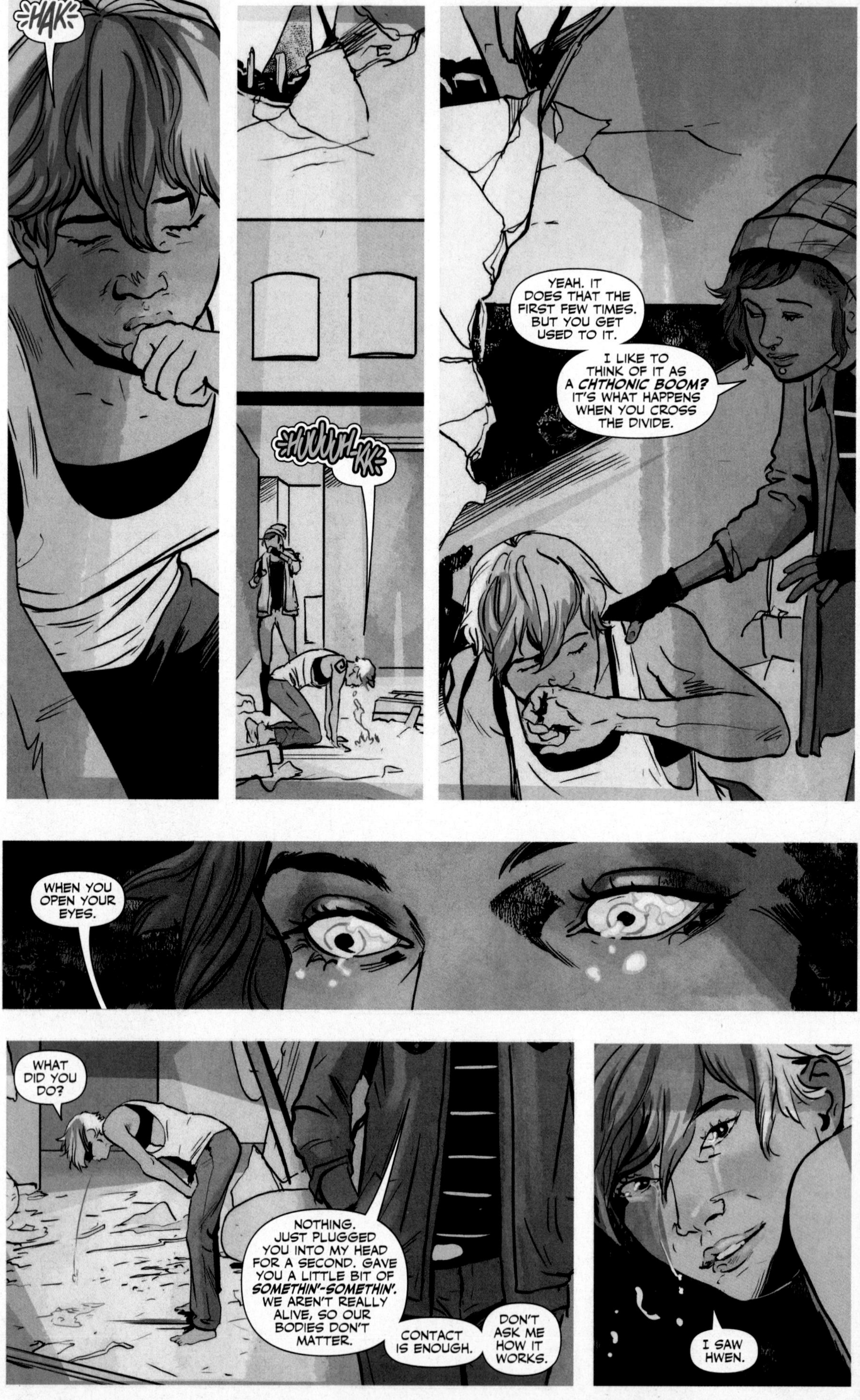
HAK
HUUUUHLKK
YEAH. IT DOES THAT THE FIRST FEW TIMES. BUT YOU GET USED TO IT.
I LIKE TO THINK OF IT AS A CHTHONIC BOOM? IT'S WHAT HAPPENS WHEN YOU CROSS THE DIVIDE.
WHEN YOU OPEN YOUR EYES.
WHAT DID YOU DO?
NOTHING. JUST PLUGGED YOU INTO MY HEAD FOR A SECOND. GAVE YOU A LITTLE BIT OF SOMETHIN'-SOMETHIN'. WE AREN'T REALLY ALIVE, SO OUR BODIES DON'T MATTER.
CONTACT IS ENOUGH.
DON'T ASK ME HOW IT WORKS.
I SAW HWEN.

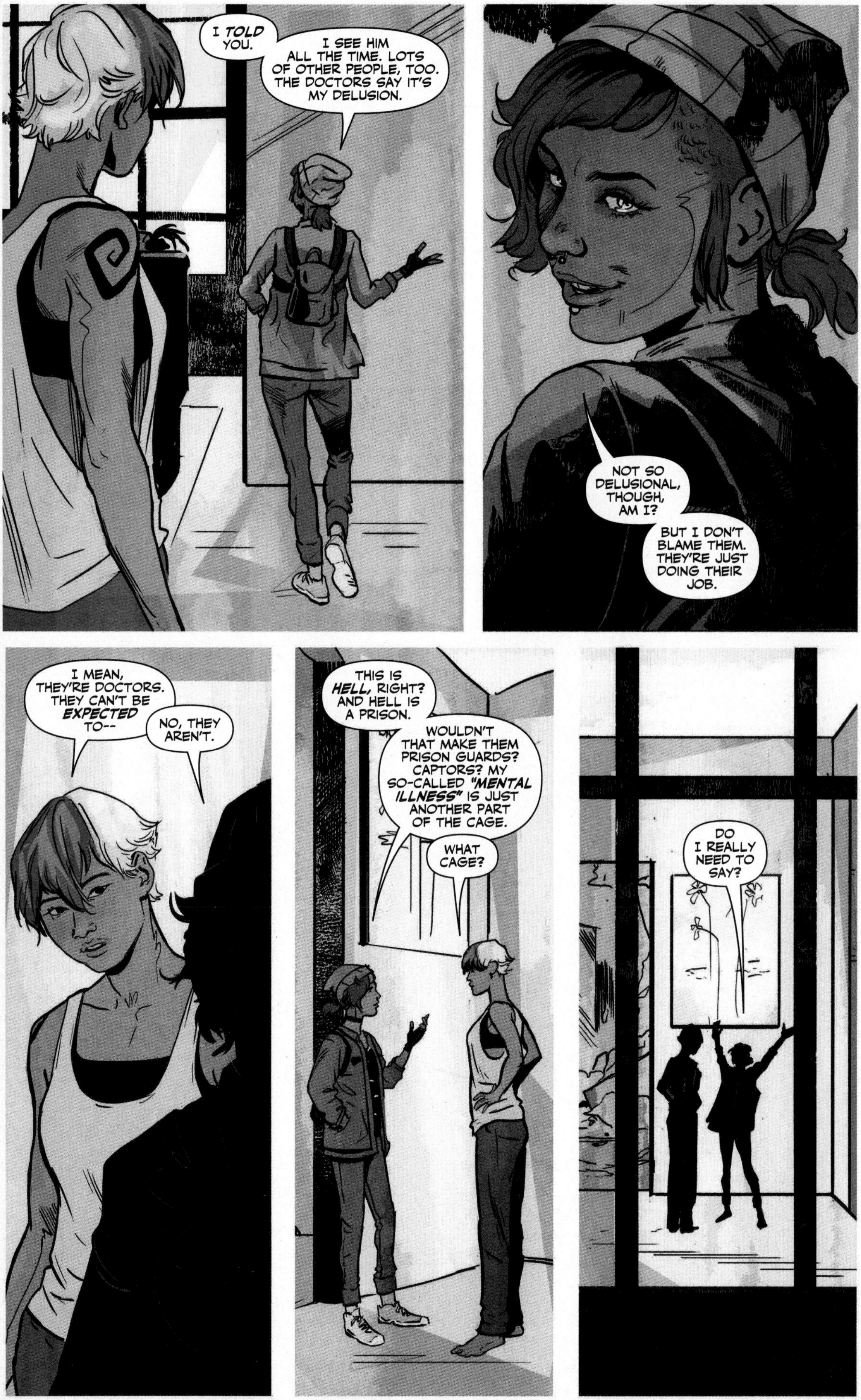
I *TOLD* YOU.
I SEE HIM ALL THE TIME. LOTS OF OTHER PEOPLE, TOO. THE DOCTORS SAY IT'S MY DELUSION.
NOT SO DELUSIONAL, THOUGH, AM I?
BUT I DON'T BLAME THEM. THEY'RE JUST DOING THEIR JOB.
I MEAN, THEY'RE DOCTORS. THEY CAN'T BE *EXPECTED* TO--
NO, THEY AREN'T.
THIS IS *HELL*, RIGHT? AND HELL IS A PRISON.
WOULDN'T THAT MAKE THEM PRISON GUARDS? CAPTORS? MY SO-CALLED *"MENTAL ILLNESS"* IS JUST ANOTHER PART OF THE CAGE.
WHAT CAGE?
DO I REALLY NEED TO SAY?

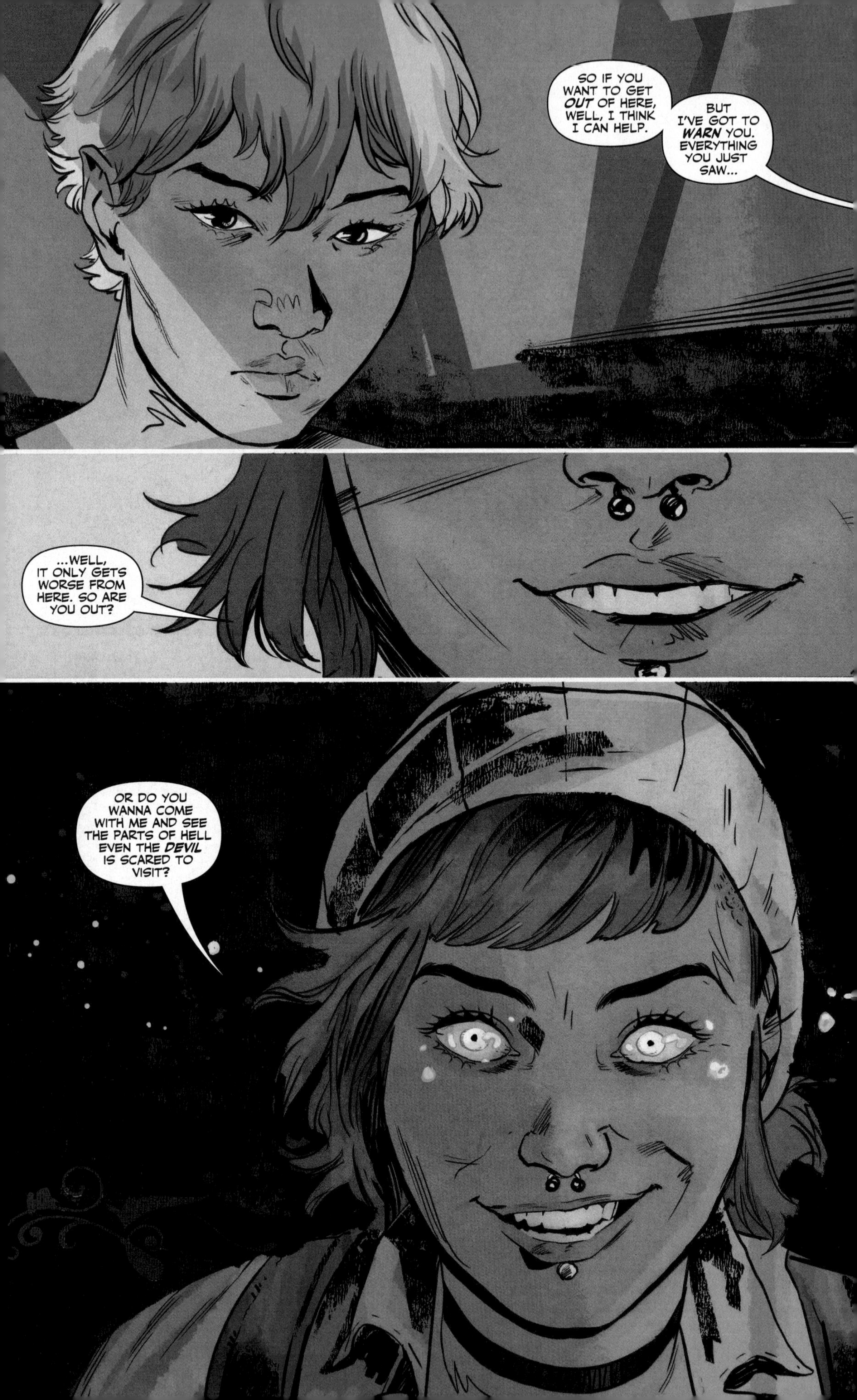
SO IF YOU WANT TO GET *OUT* OF HERE, WELL, I THINK I CAN HELP.
BUT I'VE GOT TO *WARN* YOU. EVERYTHING YOU JUST SAW...
...WELL, IT ONLY GETS WORSE FROM HERE. SO ARE YOU OUT?
OR DO YOU WANNA COME WITH ME AND SEE THE PARTS OF HELL EVEN THE *DEVIL* IS SCARED TO VISIT?

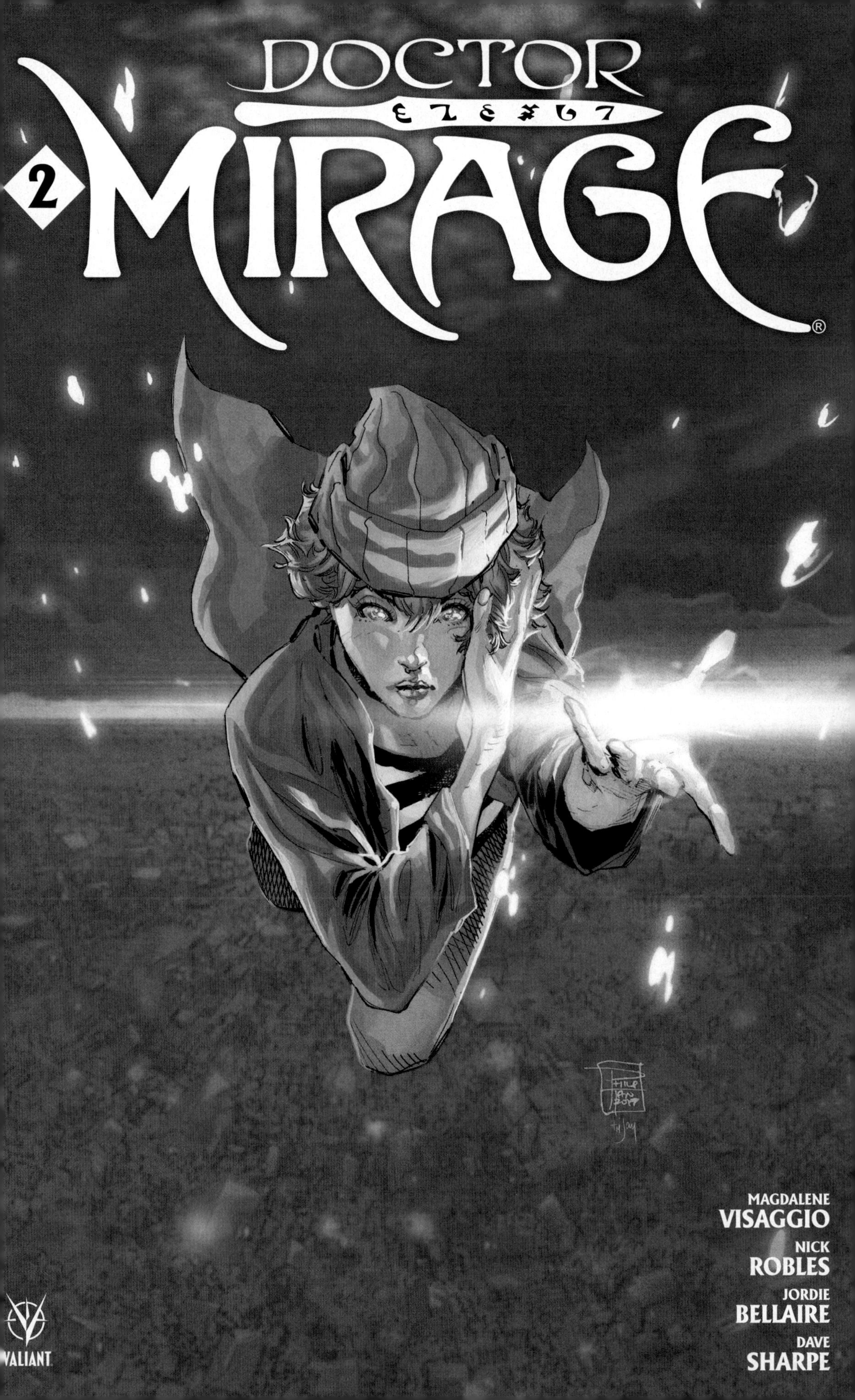

DOCTOR
MIRAGE
2
MAGDALENE
VISAGGIO
NICK
ROBLES
JORDIE
BELLAIRE
DAVE
SHARPE
VALIANT

DOCTOR MIRAGE #2

WRITER: Magdalene Visaggio
ART: Nick Robles
COLORS: Jordie Bellaire
LETTERS: Dave Sharpe
COVER ARTIST: Philip Tan with Jay David Ramos
ASSISTANT EDITOR: Drew Baumgartner
EDITOR: Lysa Hawkins

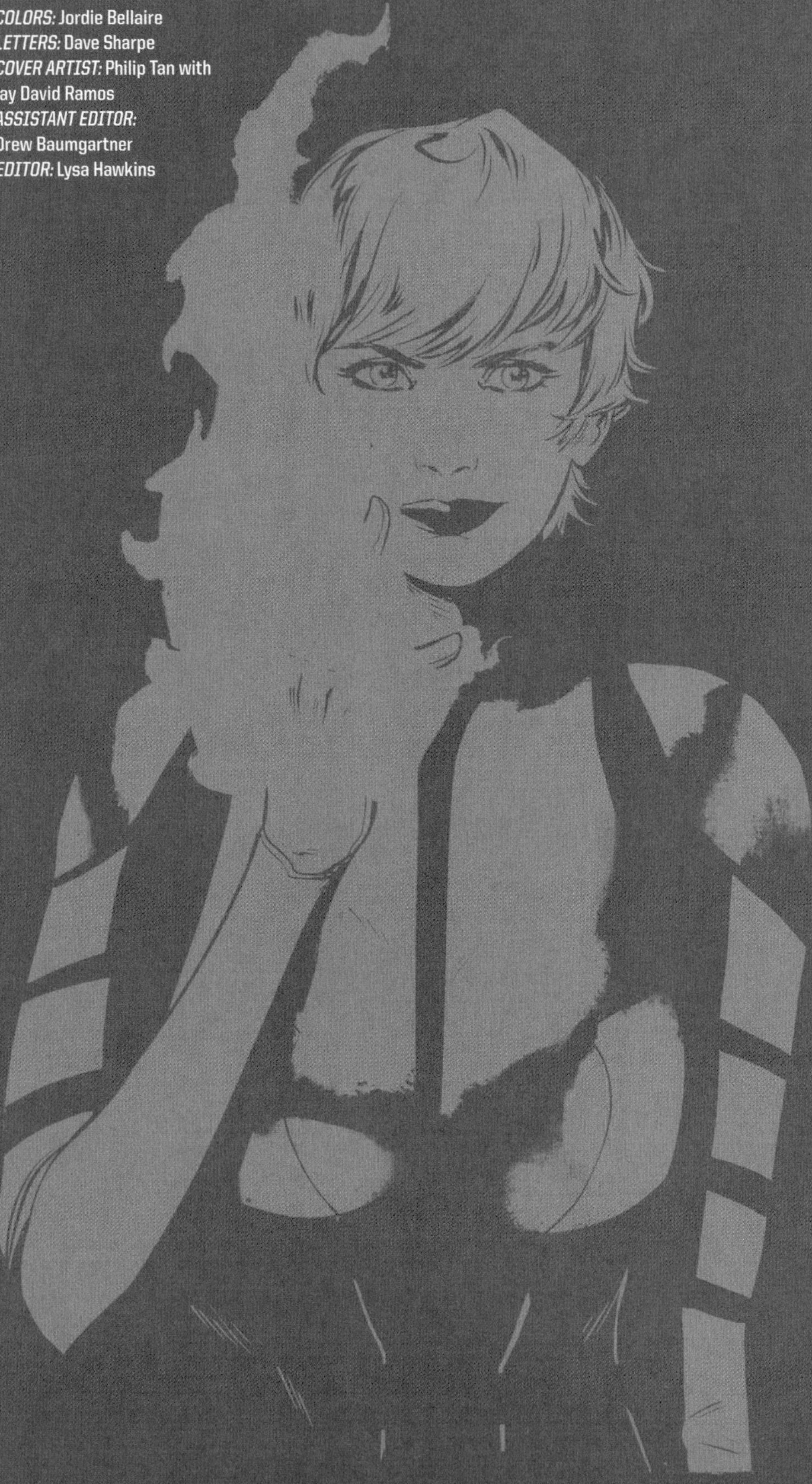

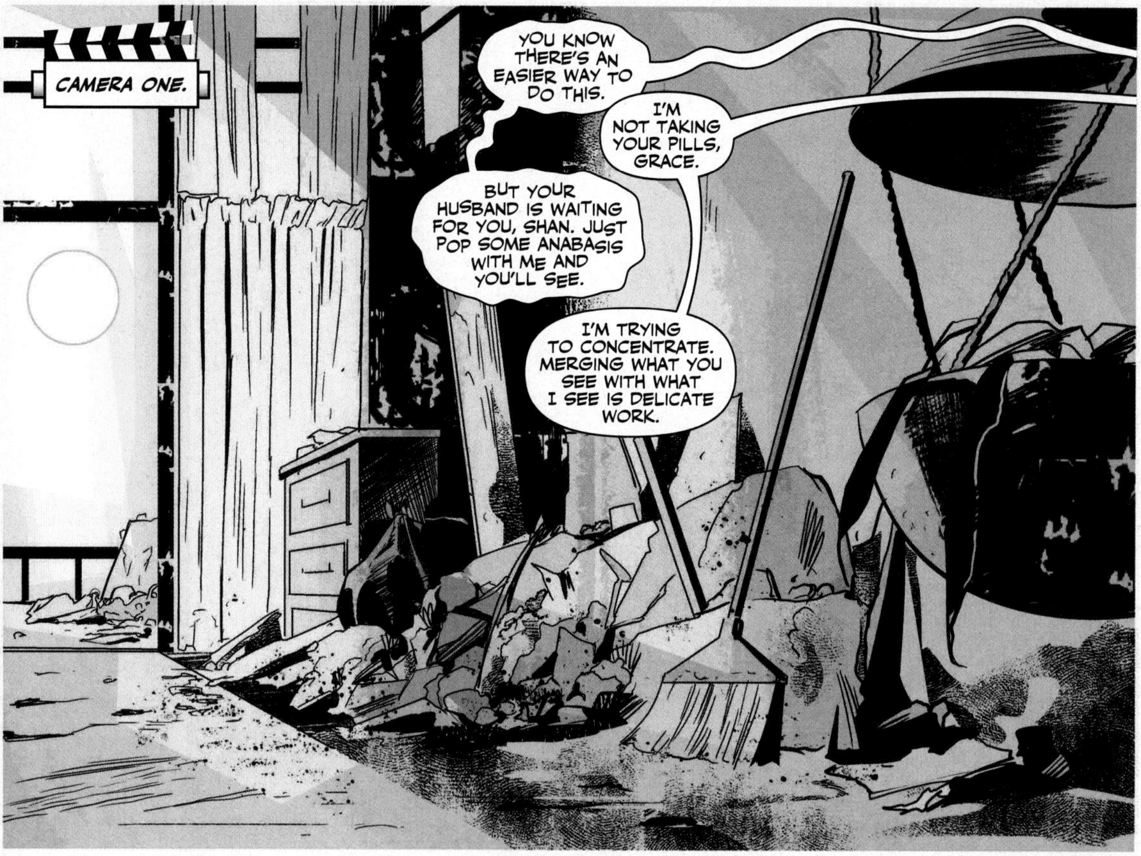
CAMERA ONE.
YOU KNOW THERE'S AN EASIER WAY TO DO THIS.
I'M NOT TAKING YOUR PILLS, GRACE.
BUT YOUR HUSBAND IS WAITING FOR YOU, SHAN. JUST POP SOME ANABASIS WITH ME AND YOU'LL SEE.
I'M TRYING TO CONCENTRATE. MERGING WHAT YOU SEE WITH WHAT I SEE IS DELICATE WORK.

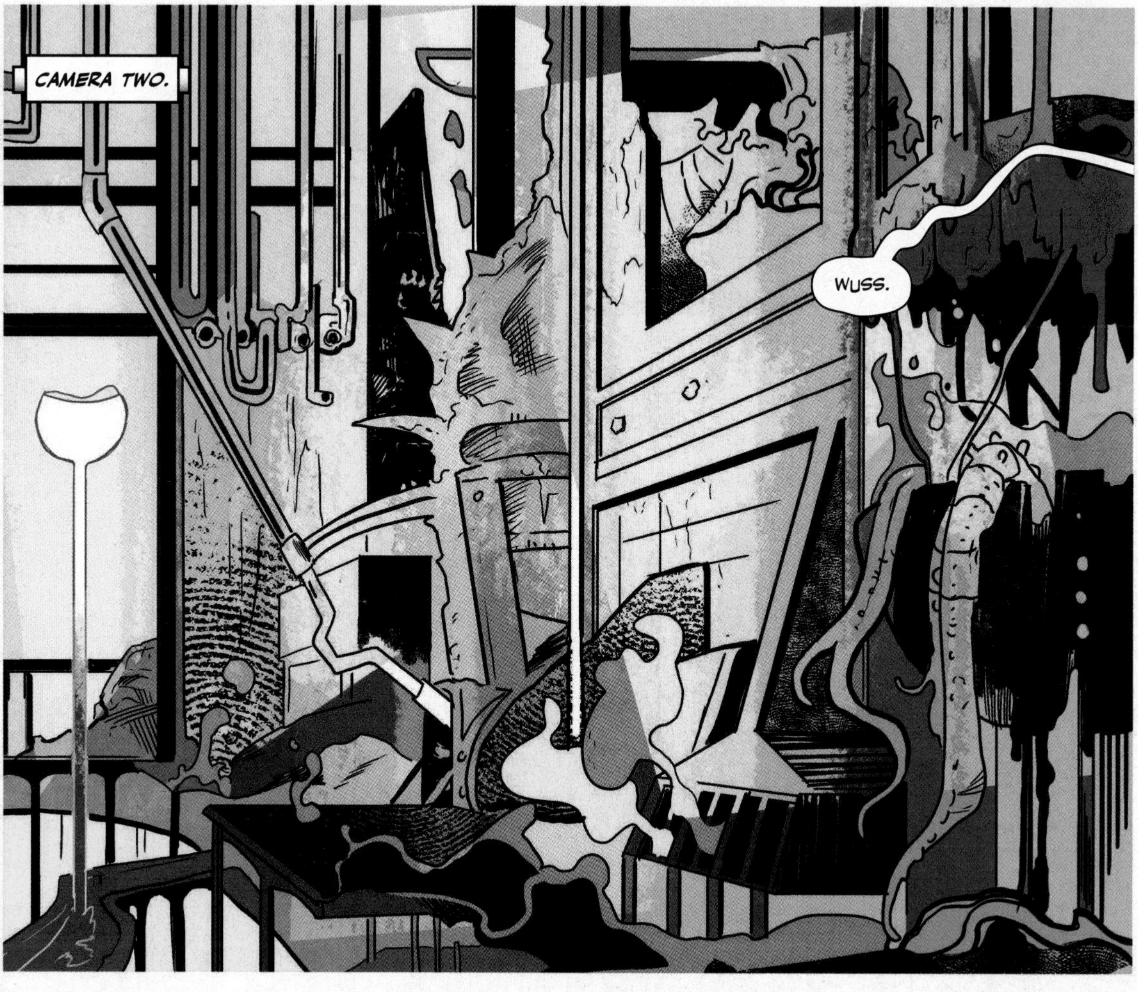
CAMERA TWO.
WUSS.

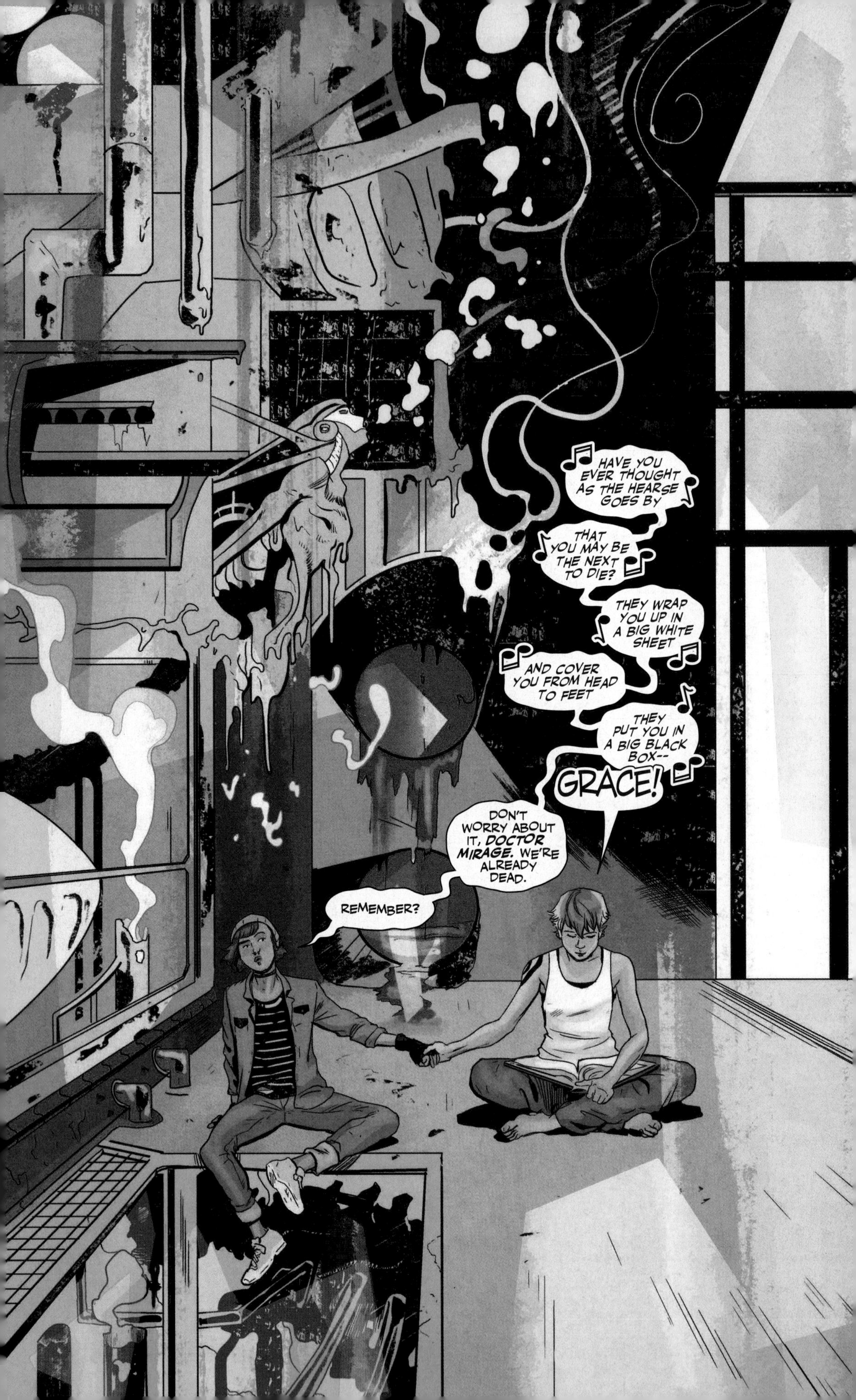
HAVE YOU EVER THOUGHT AS THE HEARSE GOES BY
THAT YOU MAY BE THE NEXT TO DIE?
THEY WRAP YOU UP IN A BIG WHITE SHEET
AND COVER YOU FROM HEAD TO FEET
THEY PUT YOU IN A BIG BLACK BOX--
GRACE!
DON'T WORRY ABOUT IT, DOCTOR MIRAGE. WE'RE ALREADY DEAD.
REMEMBER?

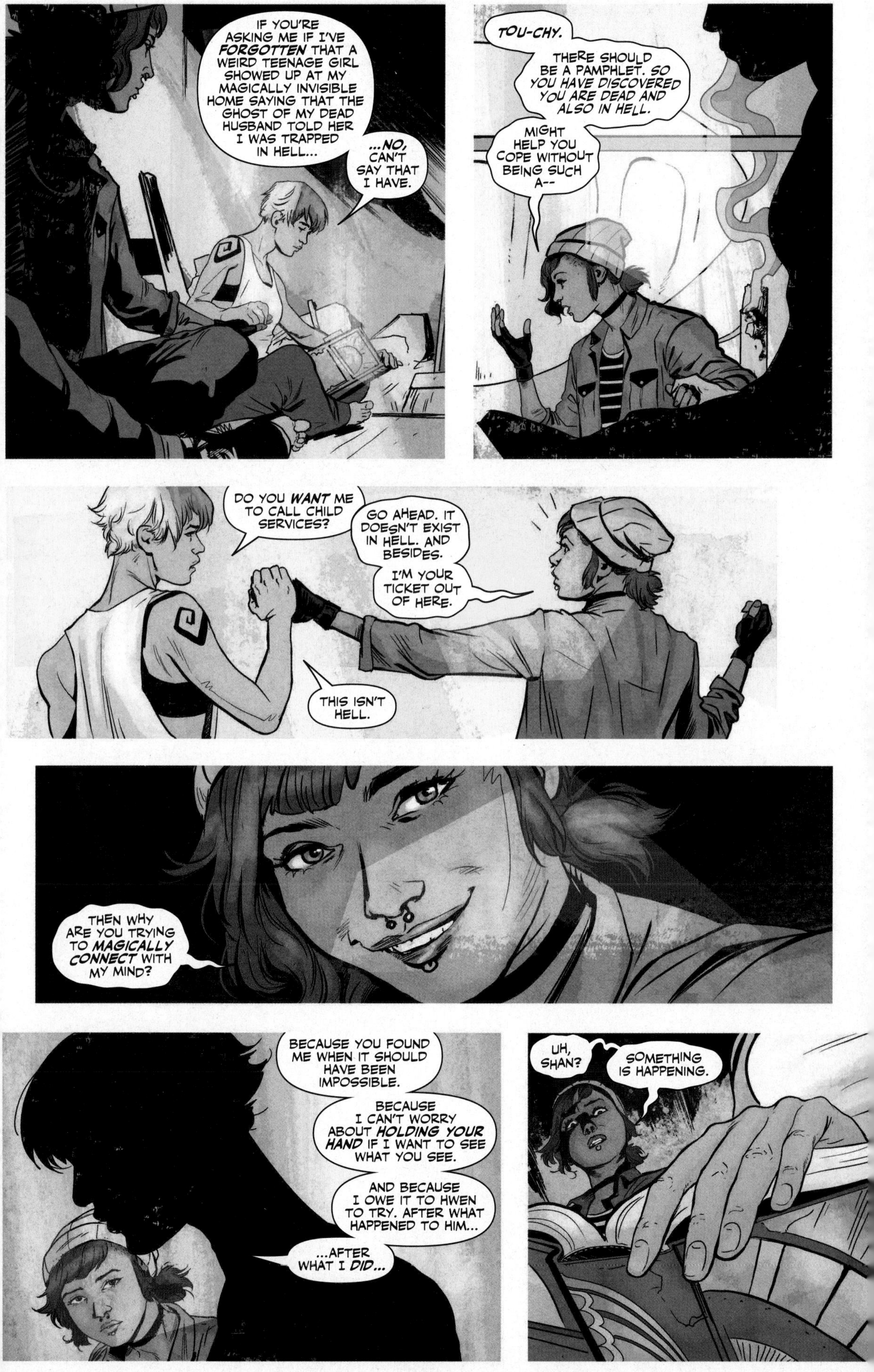
IF YOU'RE ASKING ME IF I'VE FORGOTTEN THAT A WEIRD TEENAGE GIRL SHOWED UP AT MY MAGICALLY INVISIBLE HOME SAYING THAT THE GHOST OF MY DEAD HUSBAND TOLD HER I WAS TRAPPED IN HELL...
...NO, CAN'T SAY THAT I HAVE.
TOU-CHY.
THERE SHOULD BE A PAMPHLET. SO YOU HAVE DISCOVERED YOU ARE DEAD AND ALSO IN HELL.
MIGHT HELP YOU COPE WITHOUT BEING SUCH A--
DO YOU WANT ME TO CALL CHILD SERVICES?
GO AHEAD. IT DOESN'T EXIST IN HELL. AND BESIDES.
I'M YOUR TICKET OUT OF HERE.
THIS ISN'T HELL.
THEN WHY ARE YOU TRYING TO MAGICALLY CONNECT WITH MY MIND?
BECAUSE YOU FOUND ME WHEN IT SHOULD HAVE BEEN IMPOSSIBLE.
BECAUSE I CAN'T WORRY ABOUT HOLDING YOUR HAND IF I WANT TO SEE WHAT YOU SEE.
AND BECAUSE I OWE IT TO HWEN TO TRY. AFTER WHAT HAPPENED TO HIM...
...AFTER WHAT I DID...
UH, SHAN?
SOMETHING IS HAPPENING.

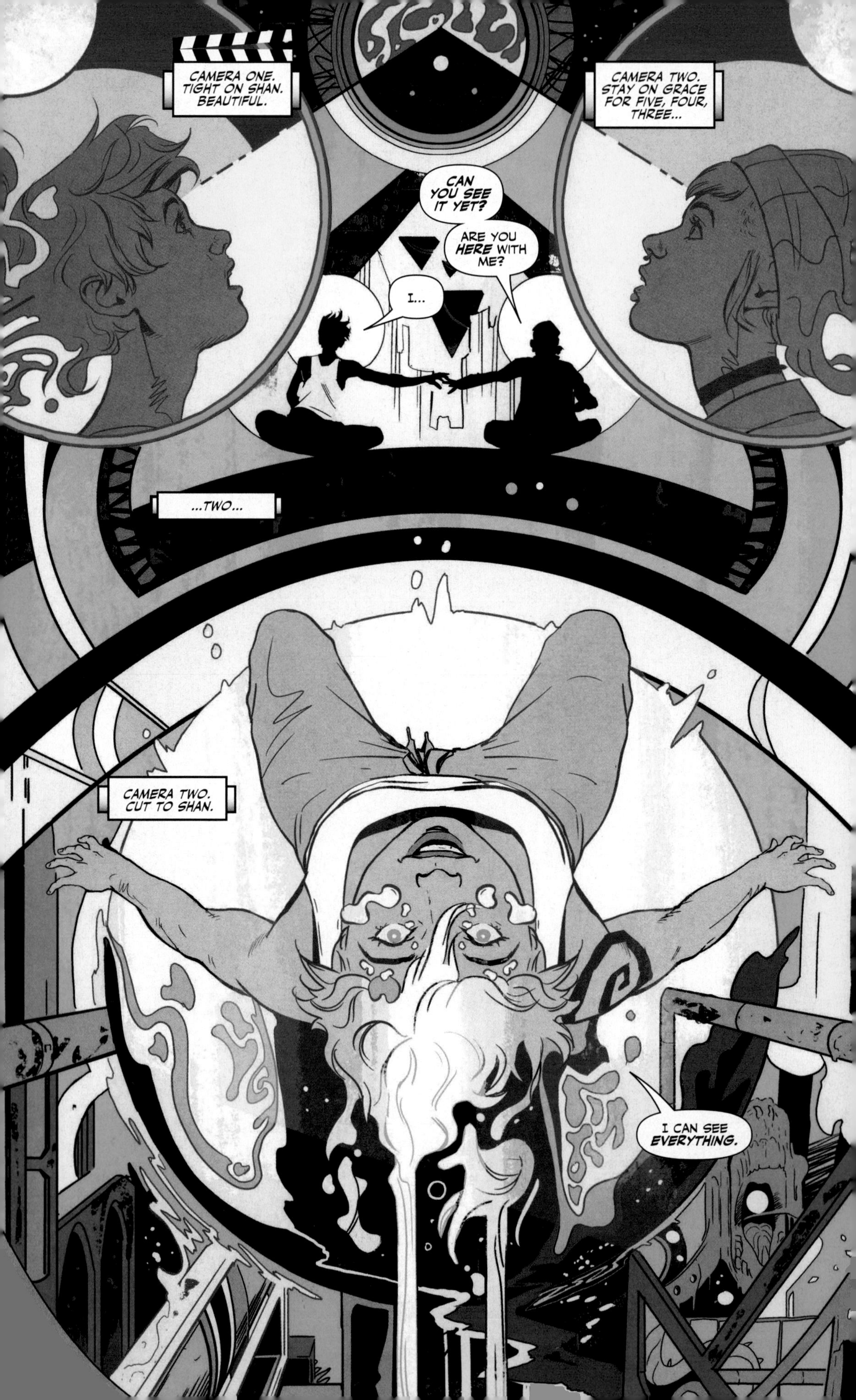
CAMERA ONE. TIGHT ON SHAN. BEAUTIFUL.
CAMERA TWO. STAY ON GRACE FOR FIVE, FOUR, THREE...
CAN YOU SEE IT YET?
ARE YOU HERE WITH ME?
I...
...TWO...
CAMERA TWO. CUT TO SHAN.
I CAN SEE EVERYTHING.

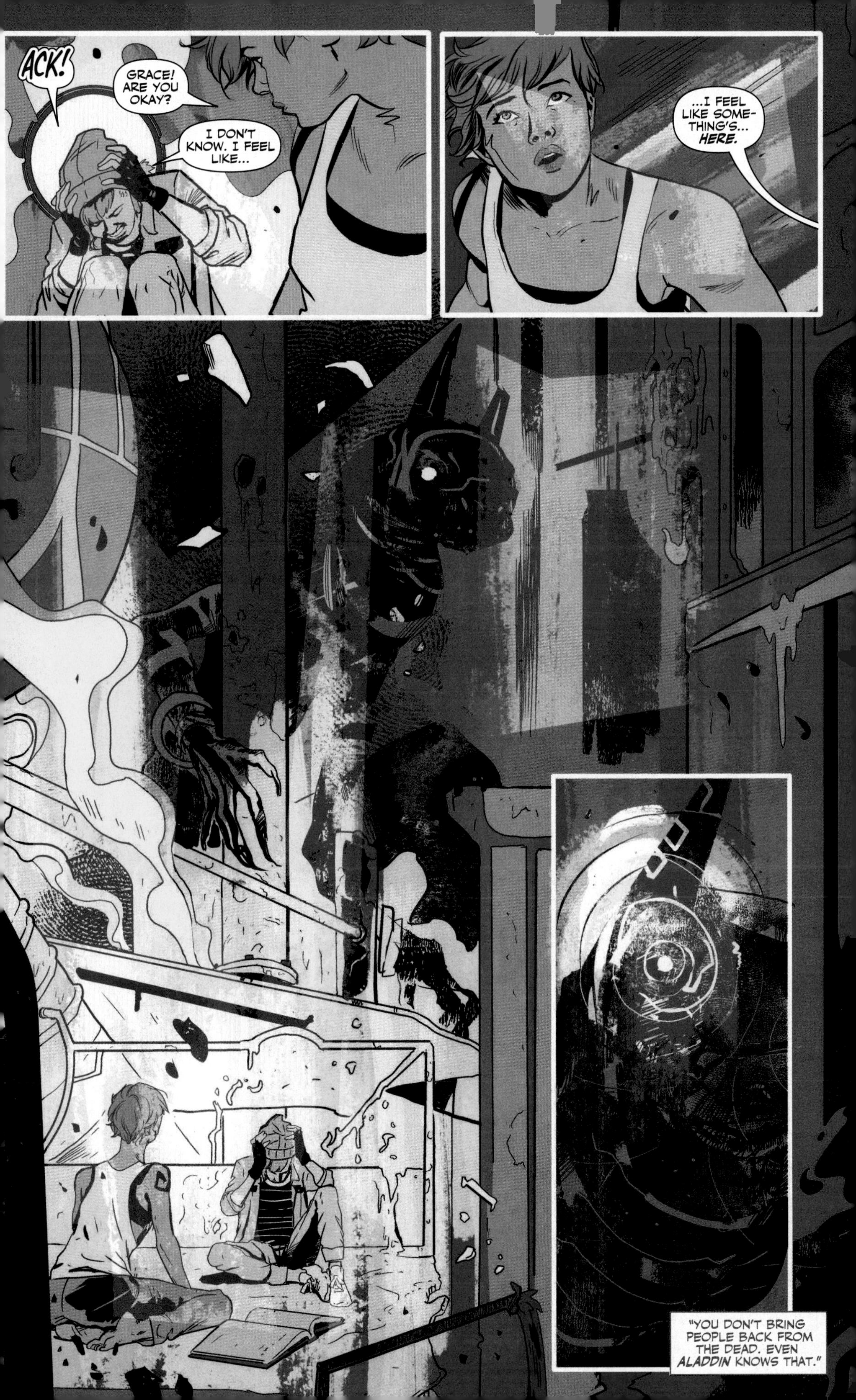
ACK!
GRACE! ARE YOU OKAY?
I DON'T KNOW. I FEEL LIKE...
...I FEEL LIKE SOME-THING'S... HERE.
"YOU DON'T BRING PEOPLE BACK FROM THE DEAD. EVEN ALADDIN KNOWS THAT."

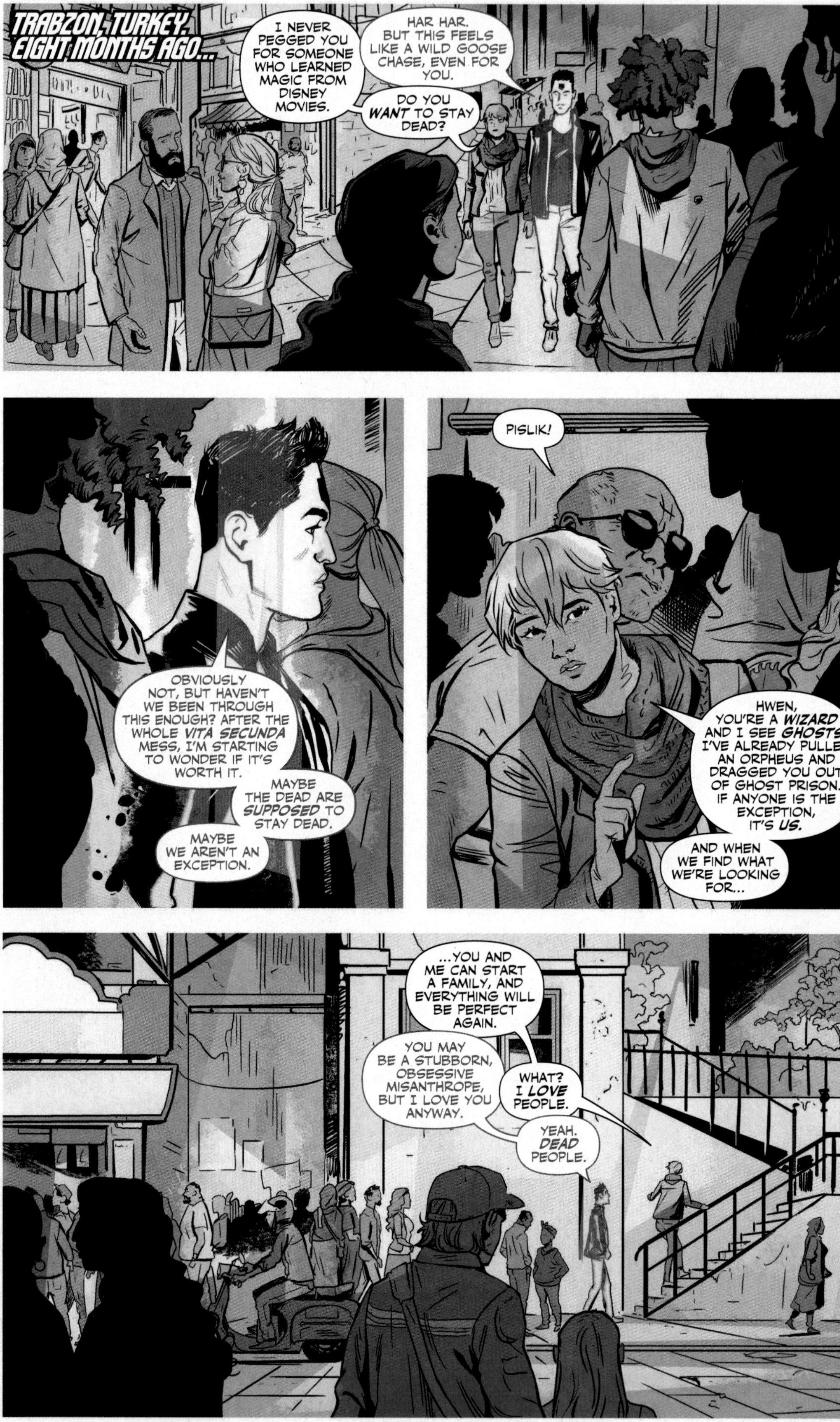
TRABZON, TURKEY. EIGHT MONTHS AGO...
I NEVER PEGGED YOU FOR SOMEONE WHO LEARNED MAGIC FROM DISNEY MOVIES.
HAR HAR. BUT THIS FEELS LIKE A WILD GOOSE CHASE, EVEN FOR YOU.
DO YOU WANT TO STAY DEAD?
OBVIOUSLY NOT, BUT HAVEN'T WE BEEN THROUGH THIS ENOUGH? AFTER THE WHOLE VITA SECUNDA MESS, I'M STARTING TO WONDER IF IT'S WORTH IT.
MAYBE THE DEAD ARE SUPPOSED TO STAY DEAD.
MAYBE WE AREN'T AN EXCEPTION.
PISLIK!
HWEN, YOU'RE A WIZARD AND I SEE GHOSTS. I'VE ALREADY PULLED AN ORPHEUS AND DRAGGED YOU OUT OF GHOST PRISON. IF ANYONE IS THE EXCEPTION, IT'S US.
AND WHEN WE FIND WHAT WE'RE LOOKING FOR...
...YOU AND ME CAN START A FAMILY, AND EVERYTHING WILL BE PERFECT AGAIN.
YOU MAY BE A STUBBORN, OBSESSIVE MISANTHROPE, BUT I LOVE YOU ANYWAY.
WHAT? I LOVE PEOPLE.
YEAH. DEAD PEOPLE.

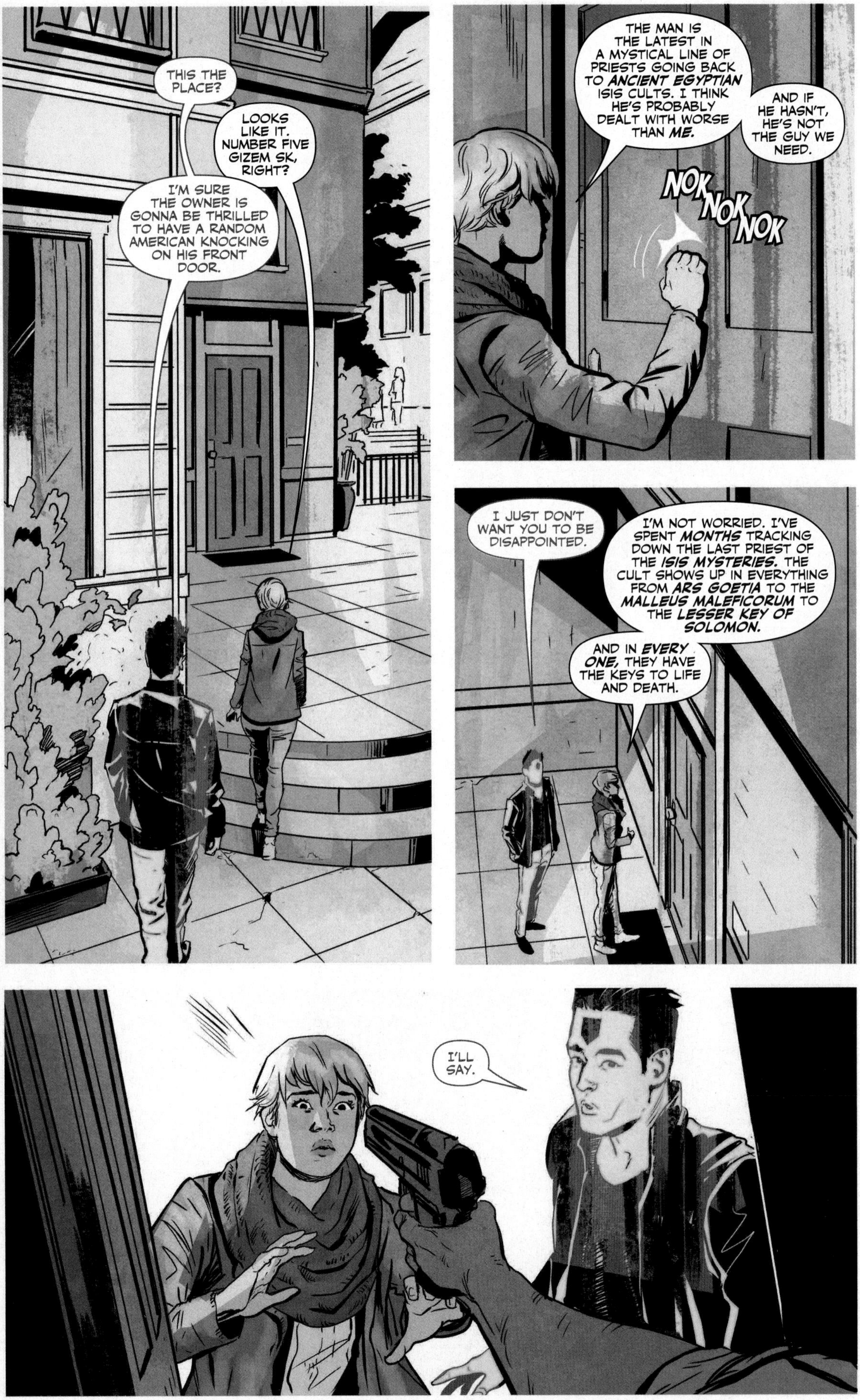
THIS THE PLACE?
LOOKS LIKE IT. NUMBER FIVE GIZEM SK, RIGHT?
I'M SURE THE OWNER IS GONNA BE THRILLED TO HAVE A RANDOM AMERICAN KNOCKING ON HIS FRONT DOOR.
THE MAN IS THE LATEST IN A MYSTICAL LINE OF PRIESTS GOING BACK TO *ANCIENT EGYPTIAN* ISIS CULTS. I THINK HE'S PROBABLY DEALT WITH WORSE THAN *ME.*
AND IF HE HASN'T, HE'S NOT THE GUY WE NEED.
NOK NOK NOK
I JUST DON'T WANT YOU TO BE DISAPPOINTED.
I'M NOT WORRIED. I'VE SPENT *MONTHS* TRACKING DOWN THE LAST PRIEST OF THE *ISIS MYSTERIES.* THE CULT SHOWS UP IN EVERYTHING FROM *ARS GOETIA* TO THE *MALLEUS MALEFICORUM* TO THE *LESSER KEY OF SOLOMON.*
AND IN *EVERY ONE,* THEY HAVE THE KEYS TO LIFE AND DEATH.
I'LL SAY.

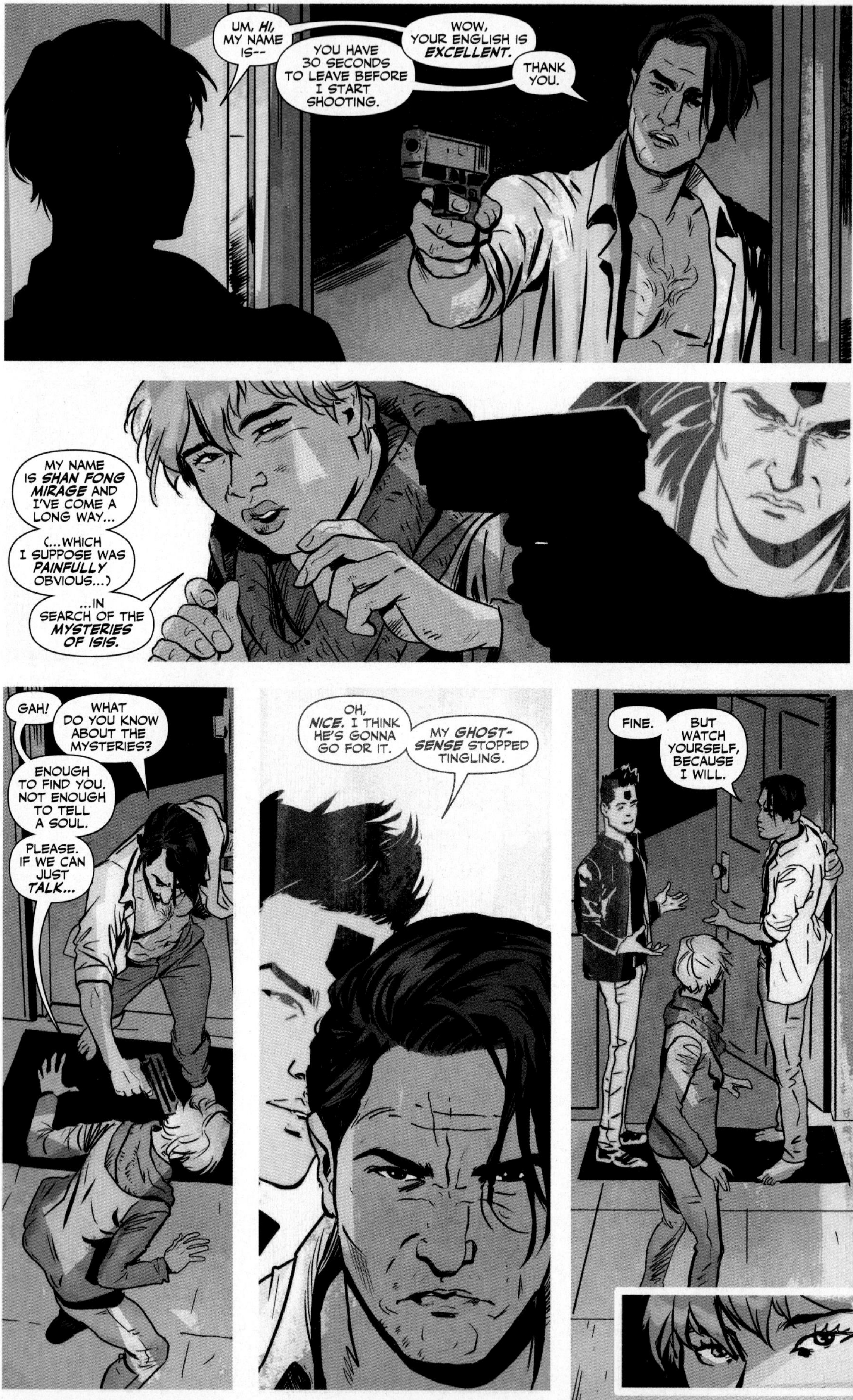
UM, HI, MY NAME IS--
YOU HAVE 30 SECONDS TO LEAVE BEFORE I START SHOOTING.
WOW, YOUR ENGLISH IS EXCELLENT.
THANK YOU.
MY NAME IS SHAN FONG MIRAGE AND I'VE COME A LONG WAY...
(...WHICH I SUPPOSE WAS PAINFULLY OBVIOUS...)
...IN SEARCH OF THE MYSTERIES OF ISIS.
GAH!
WHAT DO YOU KNOW ABOUT THE MYSTERIES?
ENOUGH TO FIND YOU. NOT ENOUGH TO TELL A SOUL.
PLEASE. IF WE CAN JUST TALK...
OH, NICE. I THINK HE'S GONNA GO FOR IT.
MY GHOST-SENSE STOPPED TINGLING.
FINE.
BUT WATCH YOURSELF, BECAUSE I WILL.

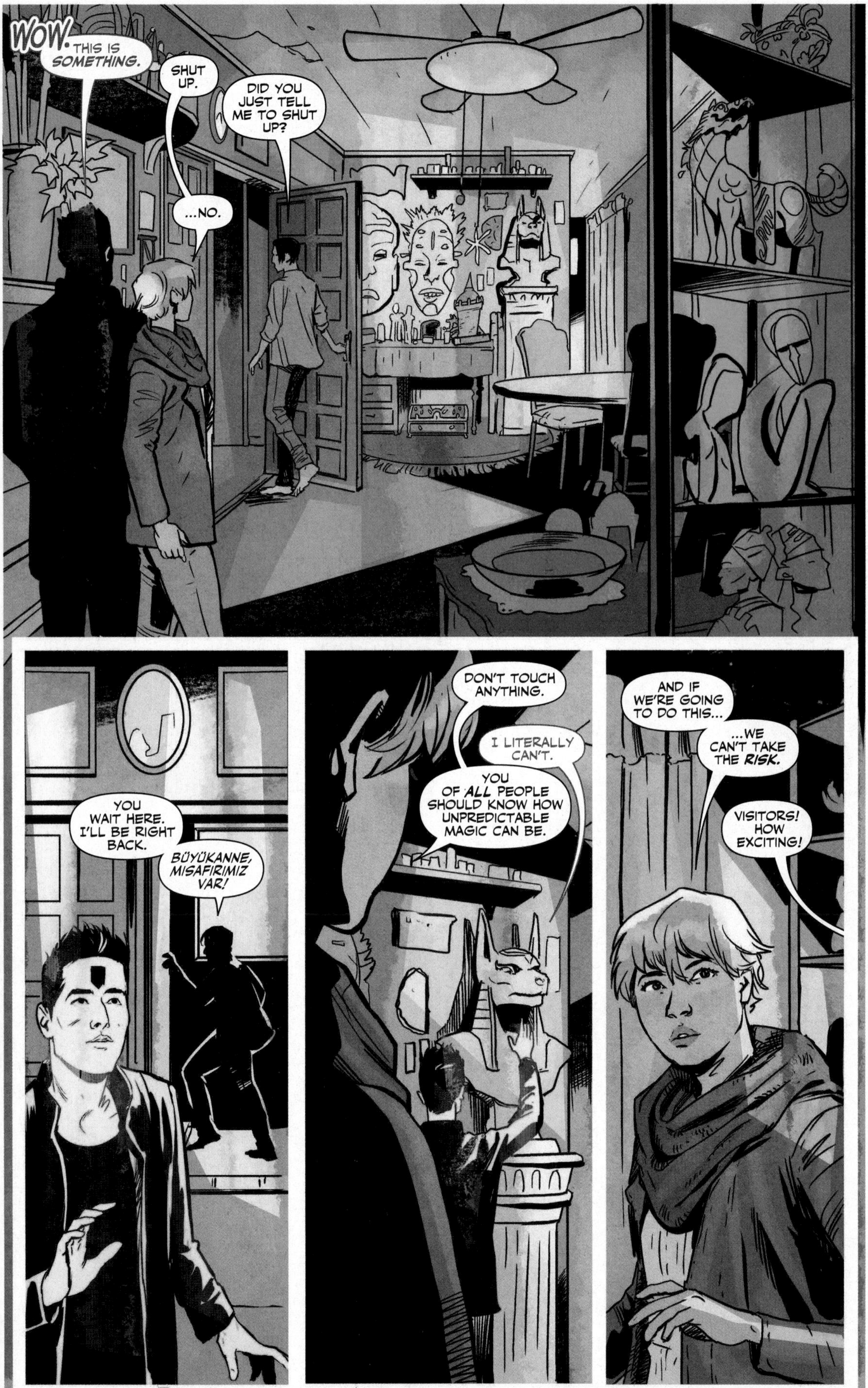
WOW. THIS IS SOMETHING.
SHUT UP.
DID YOU JUST TELL ME TO SHUT UP?
...NO.
YOU WAIT HERE. I'LL BE RIGHT BACK.
BÜYÜKANNE, MISAFIRIMIZ VAR!
DON'T TOUCH ANYTHING.
I LITERALLY CAN'T.
YOU OF ALL PEOPLE SHOULD KNOW HOW UNPREDICTABLE MAGIC CAN BE.
AND IF WE'RE GOING TO DO THIS...
...WE CAN'T TAKE THE RISK.
VISITORS! HOW EXCITING!

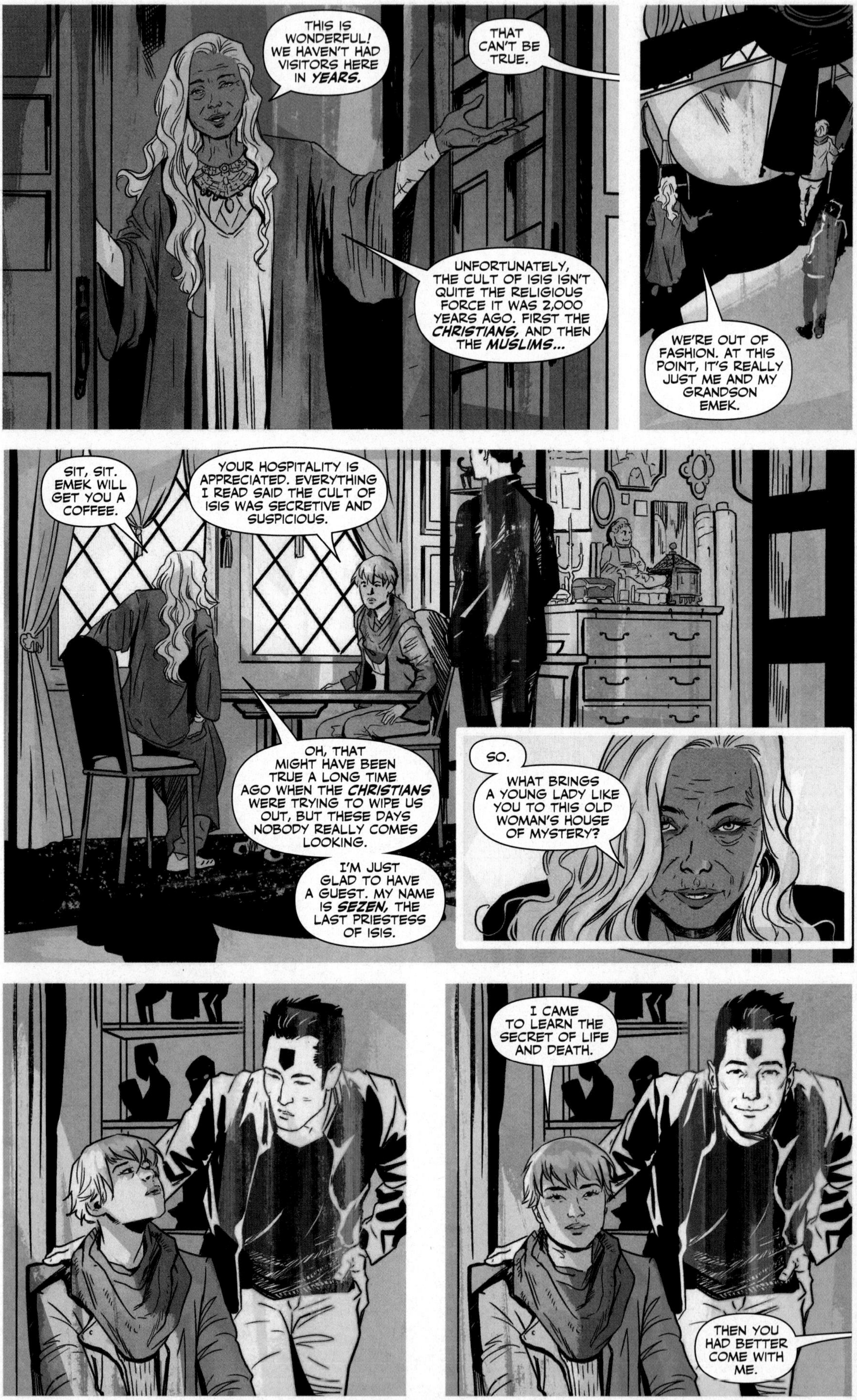
THIS IS WONDERFUL! WE HAVEN'T HAD VISITORS HERE IN YEARS.
THAT CAN'T BE TRUE.
UNFORTUNATELY, THE CULT OF ISIS ISN'T QUITE THE RELIGIOUS FORCE IT WAS 2,000 YEARS AGO. FIRST THE CHRISTIANS, AND THEN THE MUSLIMS...
WE'RE OUT OF FASHION. AT THIS POINT, IT'S REALLY JUST ME AND MY GRANDSON EMEK.
SIT, SIT. EMEK WILL GET YOU A COFFEE.
YOUR HOSPITALITY IS APPRECIATED. EVERYTHING I READ SAID THE CULT OF ISIS WAS SECRETIVE AND SUSPICIOUS.
OH, THAT MIGHT HAVE BEEN TRUE A LONG TIME AGO WHEN THE CHRISTIANS WERE TRYING TO WIPE US OUT, BUT THESE DAYS NOBODY REALLY COMES LOOKING.
I'M JUST GLAD TO HAVE A GUEST. MY NAME IS SEZEN, THE LAST PRIESTESS OF ISIS.
SO.
WHAT BRINGS A YOUNG LADY LIKE YOU TO THIS OLD WOMAN'S HOUSE OF MYSTERY?
I CAME TO LEARN THE SECRET OF LIFE AND DEATH.
THEN YOU HAD BETTER COME WITH ME.

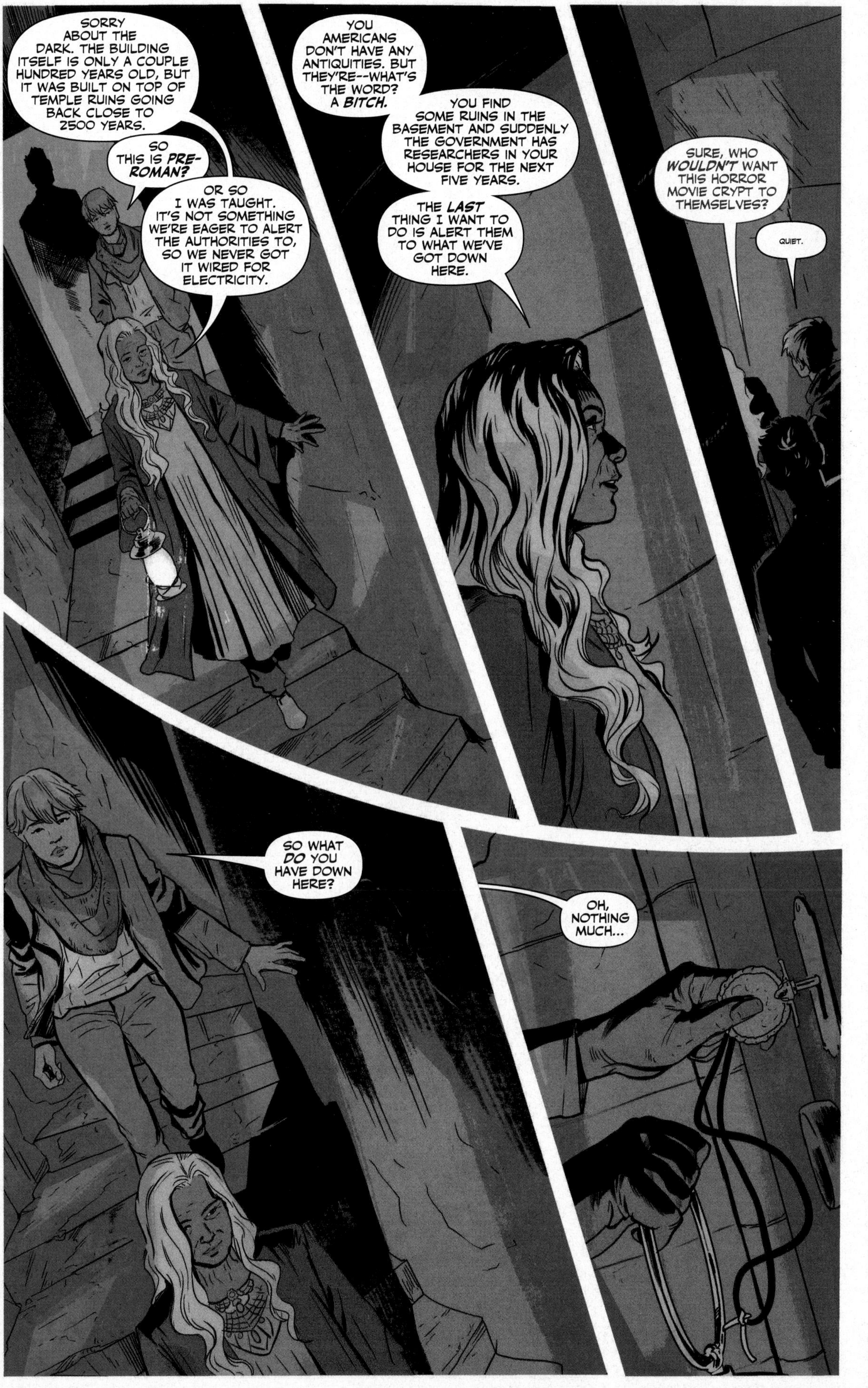
SORRY ABOUT THE DARK. THE BUILDING ITSELF IS ONLY A COUPLE HUNDRED YEARS OLD, BUT IT WAS BUILT ON TOP OF TEMPLE RUINS GOING BACK CLOSE TO 2500 YEARS.
SO THIS IS PRE-ROMAN?
OR SO I WAS TAUGHT. IT'S NOT SOMETHING WE'RE EAGER TO ALERT THE AUTHORITIES TO, SO WE NEVER GOT IT WIRED FOR ELECTRICITY.
YOU AMERICANS DON'T HAVE ANY ANTIQUITIES. BUT THEY'RE--WHAT'S THE WORD? A BITCH.
YOU FIND SOME RUINS IN THE BASEMENT AND SUDDENLY THE GOVERNMENT HAS RESEARCHERS IN YOUR HOUSE FOR THE NEXT FIVE YEARS.
THE LAST THING I WANT TO DO IS ALERT THEM TO WHAT WE'VE GOT DOWN HERE.
SURE, WHO WOULDN'T WANT THIS HORROR MOVIE CRYPT TO THEMSELVES?
QUIET.
SO WHAT DO YOU HAVE DOWN HERE?
OH, NOTHING MUCH...

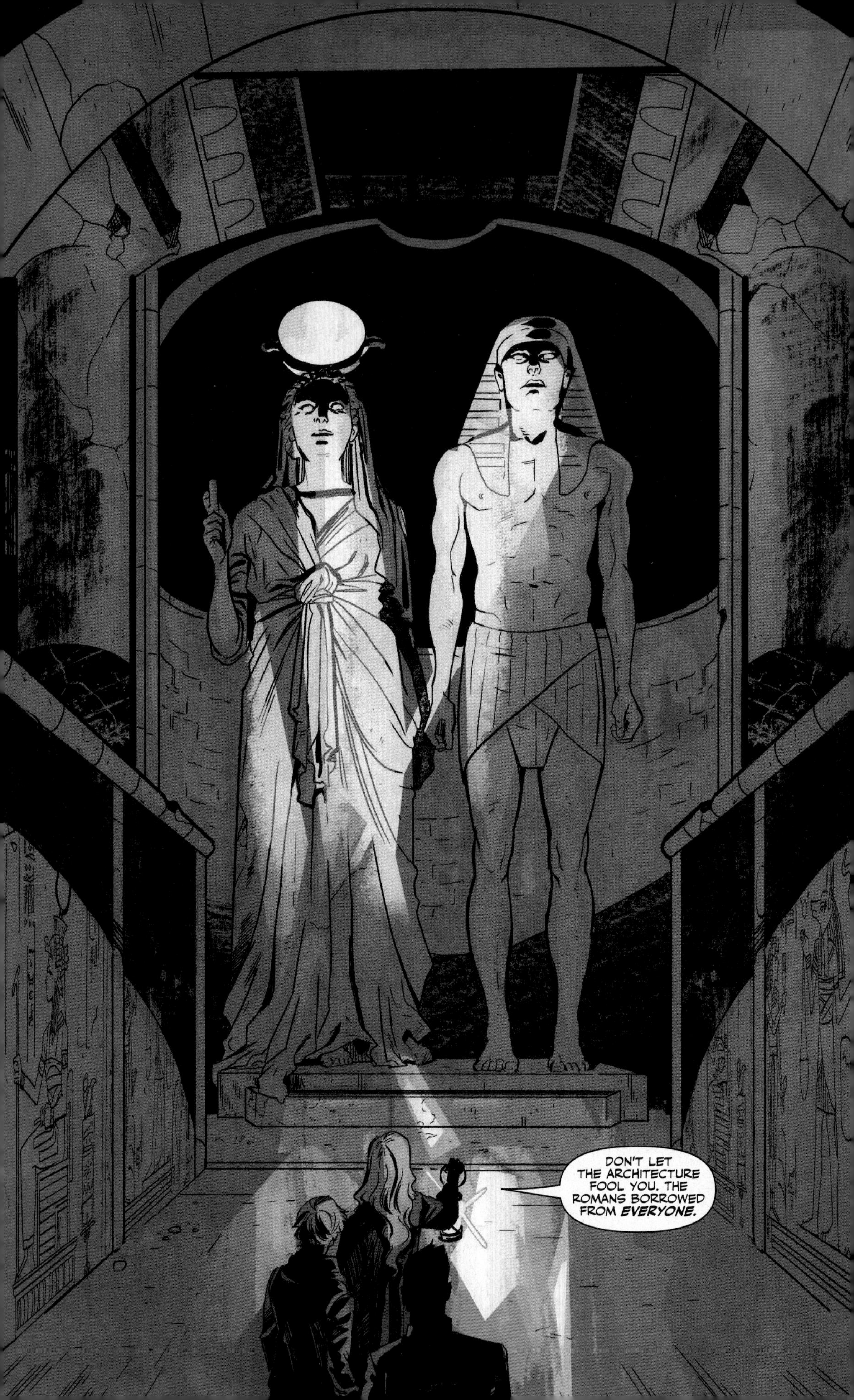
DON'T LET THE ARCHITECTURE FOOL YOU. THE ROMANS BORROWED FROM *EVERYONE.*

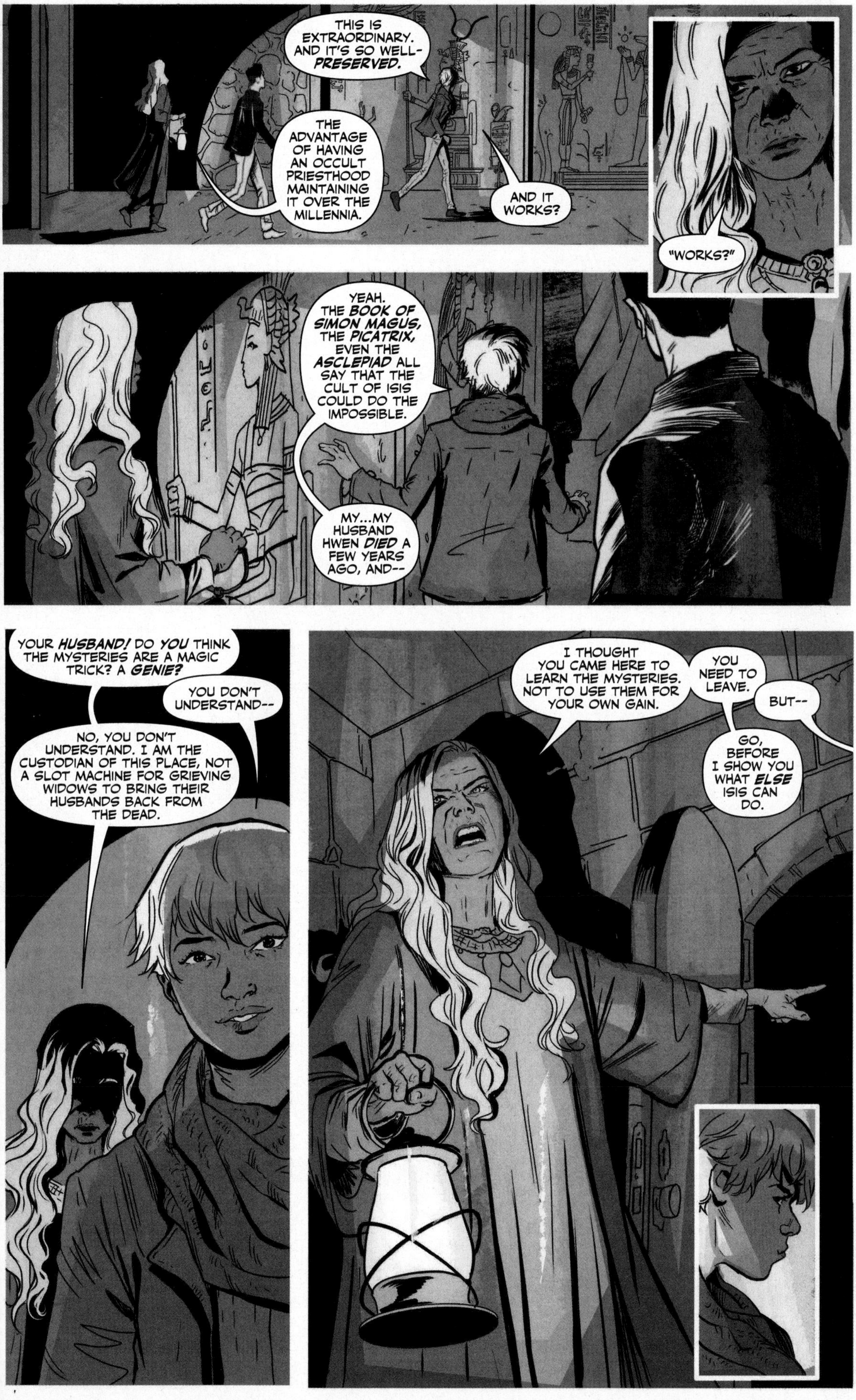

THIS IS EXTRAORDINARY. AND IT'S SO WELL-PRESERVED.
THE ADVANTAGE OF HAVING AN OCCULT PRIESTHOOD MAINTAINING IT OVER THE MILLENNIA.
AND IT WORKS?
"WORKS?"
YEAH. THE BOOK OF SIMON MAGUS, THE PICATRIX, EVEN THE ASCLEPIAD ALL SAY THAT THE CULT OF ISIS COULD DO THE IMPOSSIBLE.
MY...MY HUSBAND HWEN DIED A FEW YEARS AGO, AND--
YOUR HUSBAND! DO YOU THINK THE MYSTERIES ARE A MAGIC TRICK? A GENIE?
YOU DON'T UNDERSTAND--
NO, YOU DON'T UNDERSTAND. I AM THE CUSTODIAN OF THIS PLACE, NOT A SLOT MACHINE FOR GRIEVING WIDOWS TO BRING THEIR HUSBANDS BACK FROM THE DEAD.
I THOUGHT YOU CAME HERE TO LEARN THE MYSTERIES. NOT TO USE THEM FOR YOUR OWN GAIN.
YOU NEED TO LEAVE.
BUT--
GO, BEFORE I SHOW YOU WHAT ELSE ISIS CAN DO.

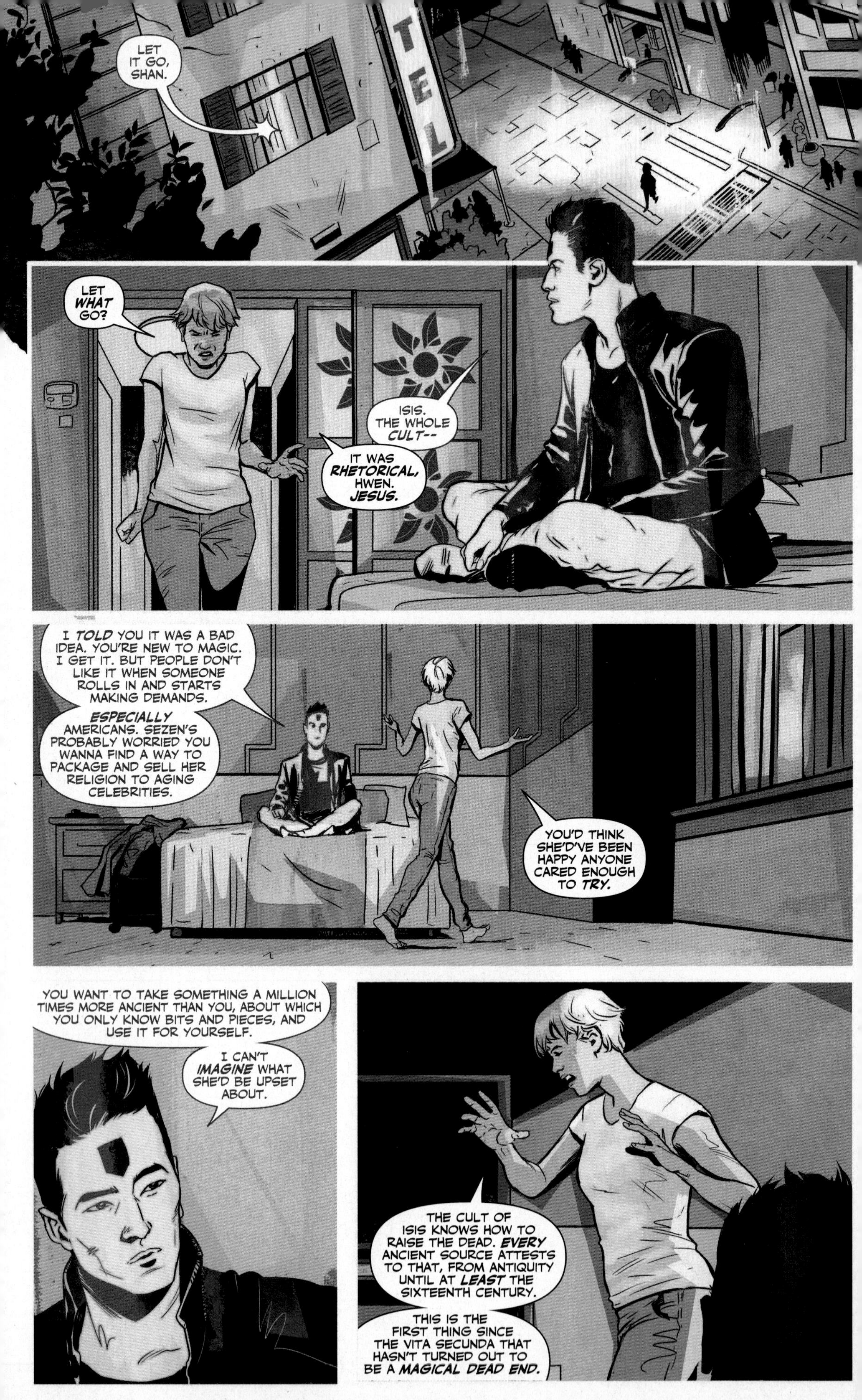
LET IT GO, SHAN.
TEL
LET WHAT GO?
ISIS. THE WHOLE CULT--
IT WAS RHETORICAL, HWEN. JESUS.
I TOLD YOU IT WAS A BAD IDEA. YOU'RE NEW TO MAGIC. I GET IT. BUT PEOPLE DON'T LIKE IT WHEN SOMEONE ROLLS IN AND STARTS MAKING DEMANDS.
ESPECIALLY AMERICANS. SEZEN'S PROBABLY WORRIED YOU WANNA FIND A WAY TO PACKAGE AND SELL HER RELIGION TO AGING CELEBRITIES.
YOU'D THINK SHE'D'VE BEEN HAPPY ANYONE CARED ENOUGH TO TRY.
YOU WANT TO TAKE SOMETHING A MILLION TIMES MORE ANCIENT THAN YOU, ABOUT WHICH YOU ONLY KNOW BITS AND PIECES, AND USE IT FOR YOURSELF.
I CAN'T IMAGINE WHAT SHE'D BE UPSET ABOUT.
THE CULT OF ISIS KNOWS HOW TO RAISE THE DEAD. EVERY ANCIENT SOURCE ATTESTS TO THAT, FROM ANTIQUITY UNTIL AT LEAST THE SIXTEENTH CENTURY.
THIS IS THE FIRST THING SINCE THE VITA SECUNDA THAT HASN'T TURNED OUT TO BE A MAGICAL DEAD END.

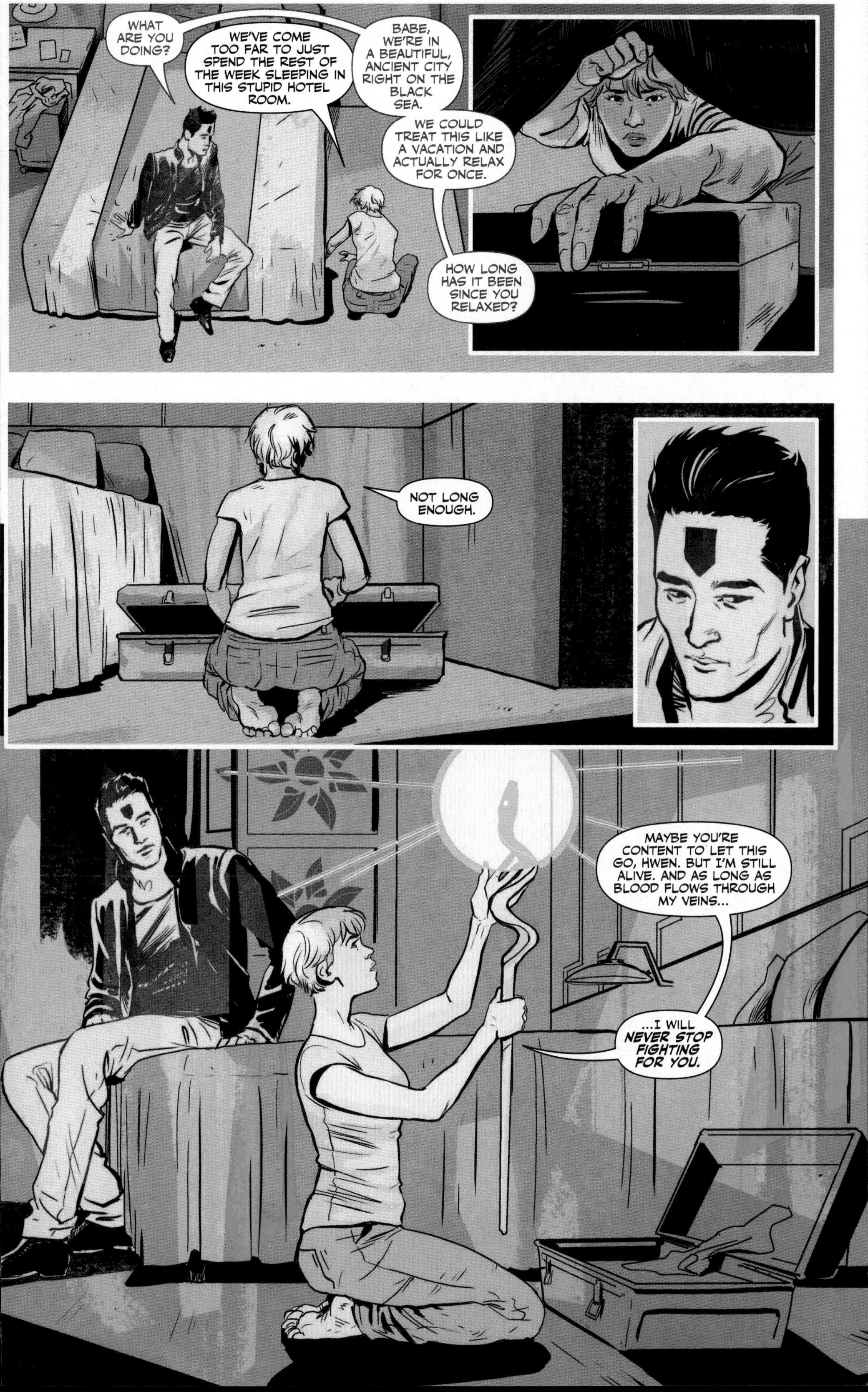
WHAT ARE YOU DOING?
WE'VE COME TOO FAR TO JUST SPEND THE REST OF THE WEEK SLEEPING IN THIS STUPID HOTEL ROOM.
BABE, WE'RE IN A BEAUTIFUL, ANCIENT CITY RIGHT ON THE BLACK SEA.
WE COULD TREAT THIS LIKE A VACATION AND ACTUALLY RELAX FOR ONCE.
HOW LONG HAS IT BEEN SINCE YOU RELAXED?
NOT LONG ENOUGH.
MAYBE YOU'RE CONTENT TO LET THIS GO, HWEN. BUT I'M STILL ALIVE. AND AS LONG AS BLOOD FLOWS THROUGH MY VEINS...
...I WILL *NEVER STOP FIGHTING FOR YOU.*

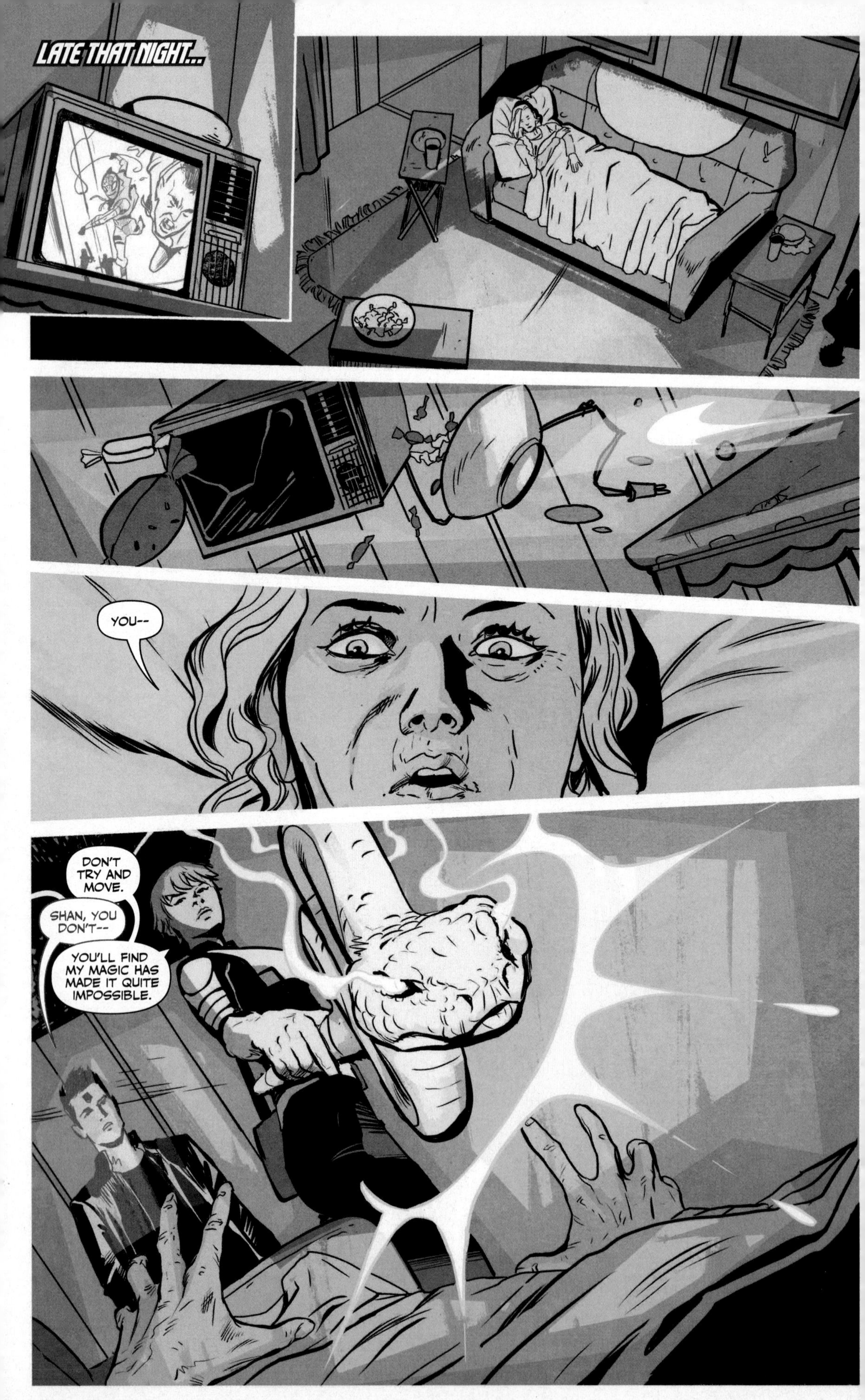
LATE THAT NIGHT...
YOU--
DON'T TRY AND MOVE.
SHAN, YOU DON'T--
YOU'LL FIND MY MAGIC HAS MADE IT QUITE IMPOSSIBLE.

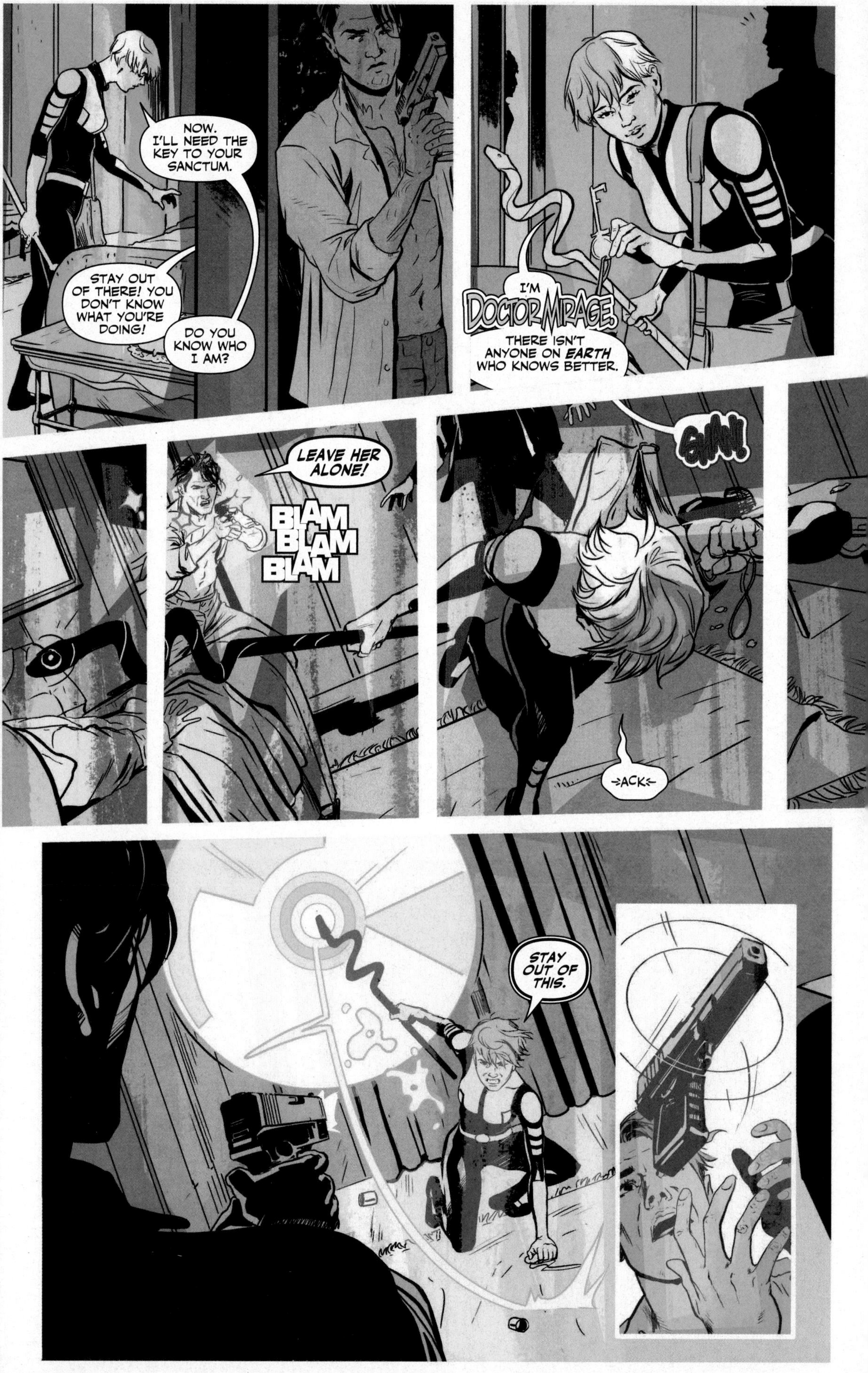
NOW. I'LL NEED THE KEY TO YOUR SANCTUM.
STAY OUT OF THERE! YOU DON'T KNOW WHAT YOU'RE DOING!
DO YOU KNOW WHO I AM?
I'M DOCTOR MIRAGE. THERE ISN'T ANYONE ON EARTH WHO KNOWS BETTER.
LEAVE HER ALONE!
BLAM BLAM BLAM
SWAN!
ACK
STAY OUT OF THIS.

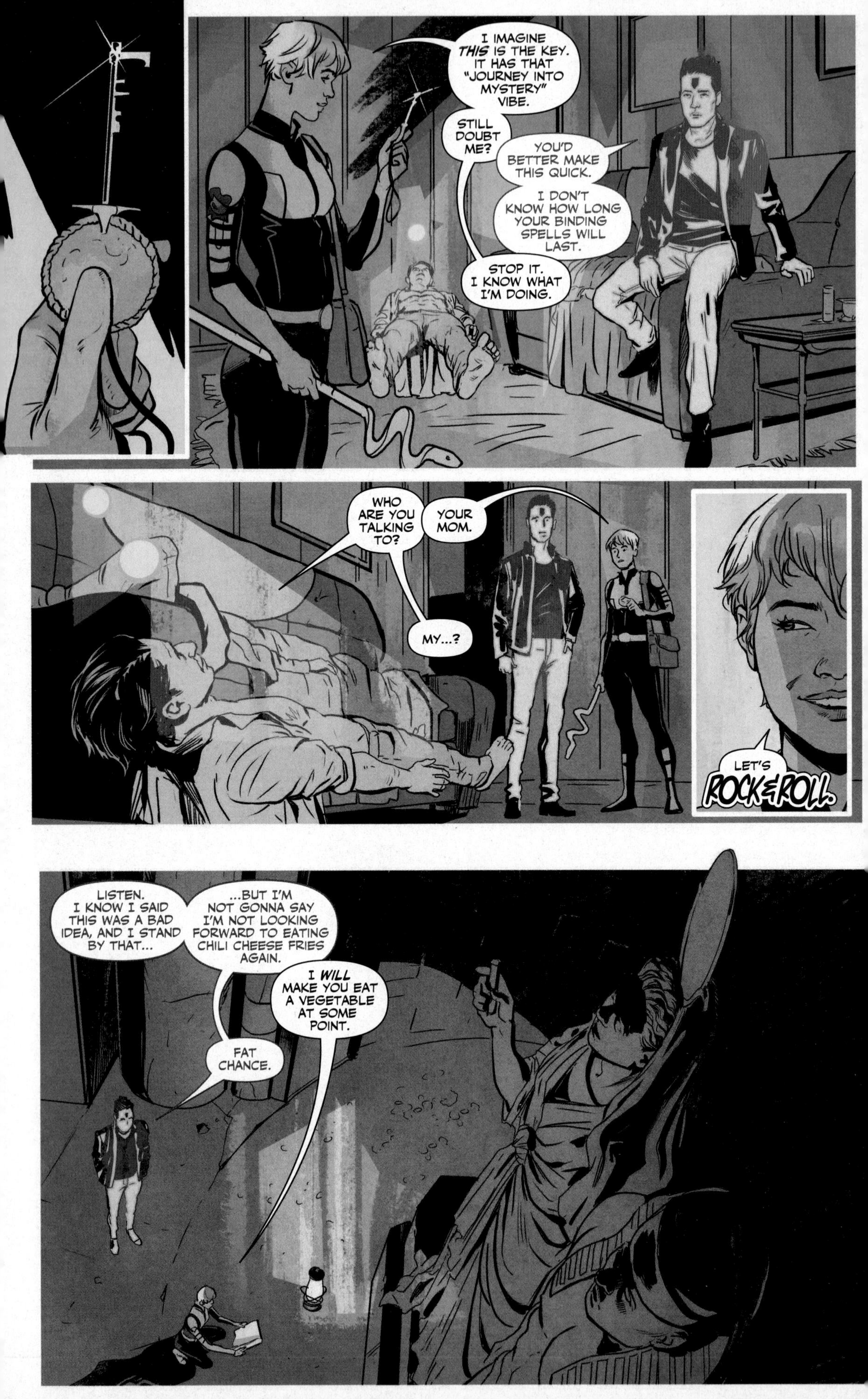

I IMAGINE THIS IS THE KEY. IT HAS THAT "JOURNEY INTO MYSTERY" VIBE.
STILL DOUBT ME?
YOU'D BETTER MAKE THIS QUICK.
I DON'T KNOW HOW LONG YOUR BINDING SPELLS WILL LAST.
STOP IT. I KNOW WHAT I'M DOING.
WHO ARE YOU TALKING TO?
YOUR MOM.
MY...?
LET'S ROCK & ROLL.
LISTEN. I KNOW I SAID THIS WAS A BAD IDEA, AND I STAND BY THAT...
...BUT I'M NOT GONNA SAY I'M NOT LOOKING FORWARD TO EATING CHILI CHEESE FRIES AGAIN.
I WILL MAKE YOU EAT A VEGETABLE AT SOME POINT.
FAT CHANCE.

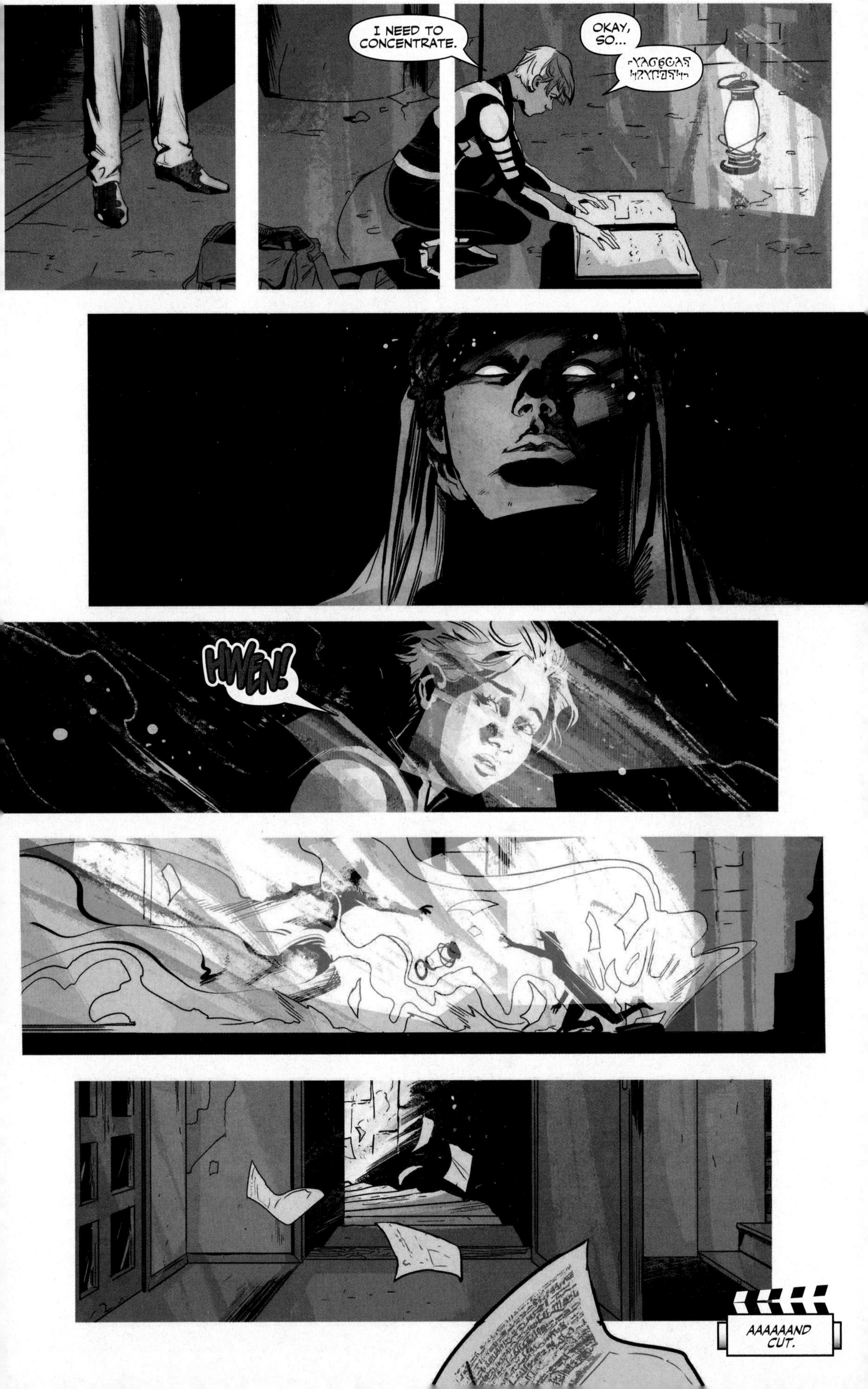
I NEED TO CONCENTRATE.
OKAY, SO...
HWEN!
AAAAAAND CUT.

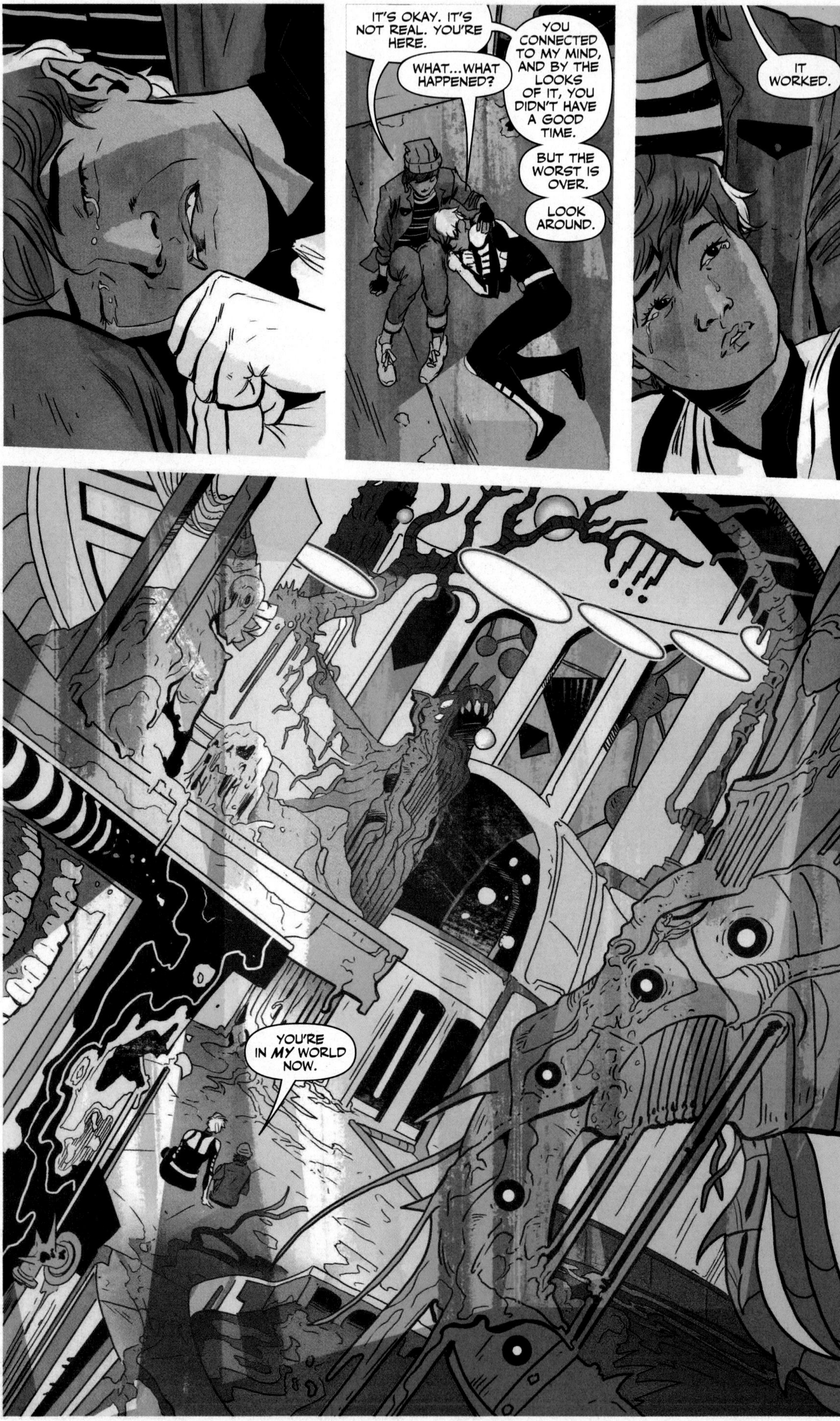

IT'S OKAY. IT'S NOT REAL. YOU'RE HERE.
WHAT...WHAT HAPPENED?
YOU CONNECTED TO MY MIND, AND BY THE LOOKS OF IT, YOU DIDN'T HAVE A GOOD TIME.
BUT THE WORST IS OVER.
LOOK AROUND.
IT WORKED.
YOU'RE IN MY WORLD NOW.

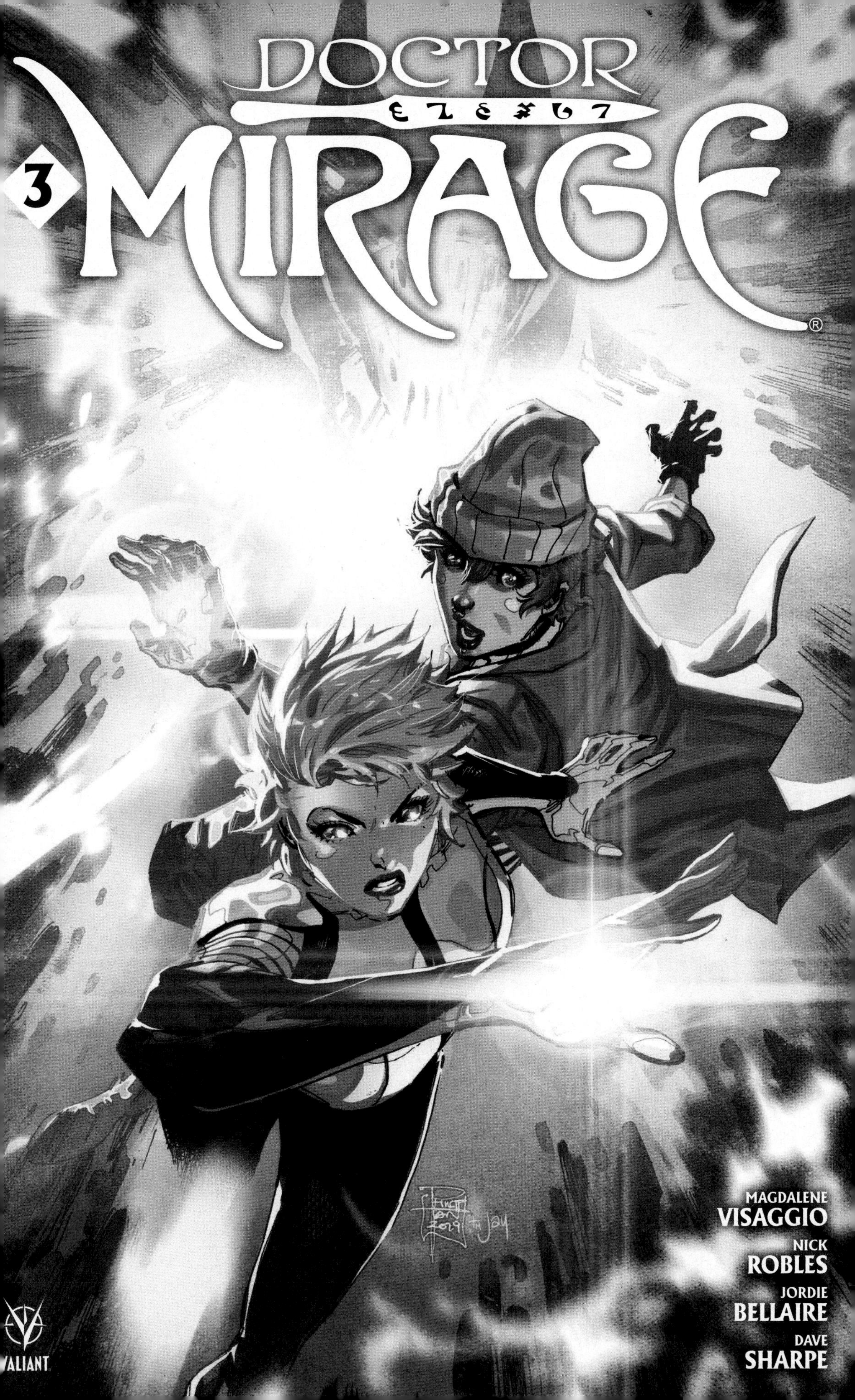

DOCTOR
MIRAGE
3
MAGDALENE
VISAGGIO
NICK
ROBLES
JORDIE
BELLAIRE
DAVE
SHARPE
VALIANT

DOCTOR MIRAGE #3

WRITER: Magdalene Visaggio
ART: Nick Robles
COLORS: Jordie Bellaire
LETTERS: Dave Sharpe
COVER ARTIST: Philip Tan with
Jay David Ramos
ASSISTANT EDITOR:
Drew Baumgartner
EDITOR: Lysa Hawkins

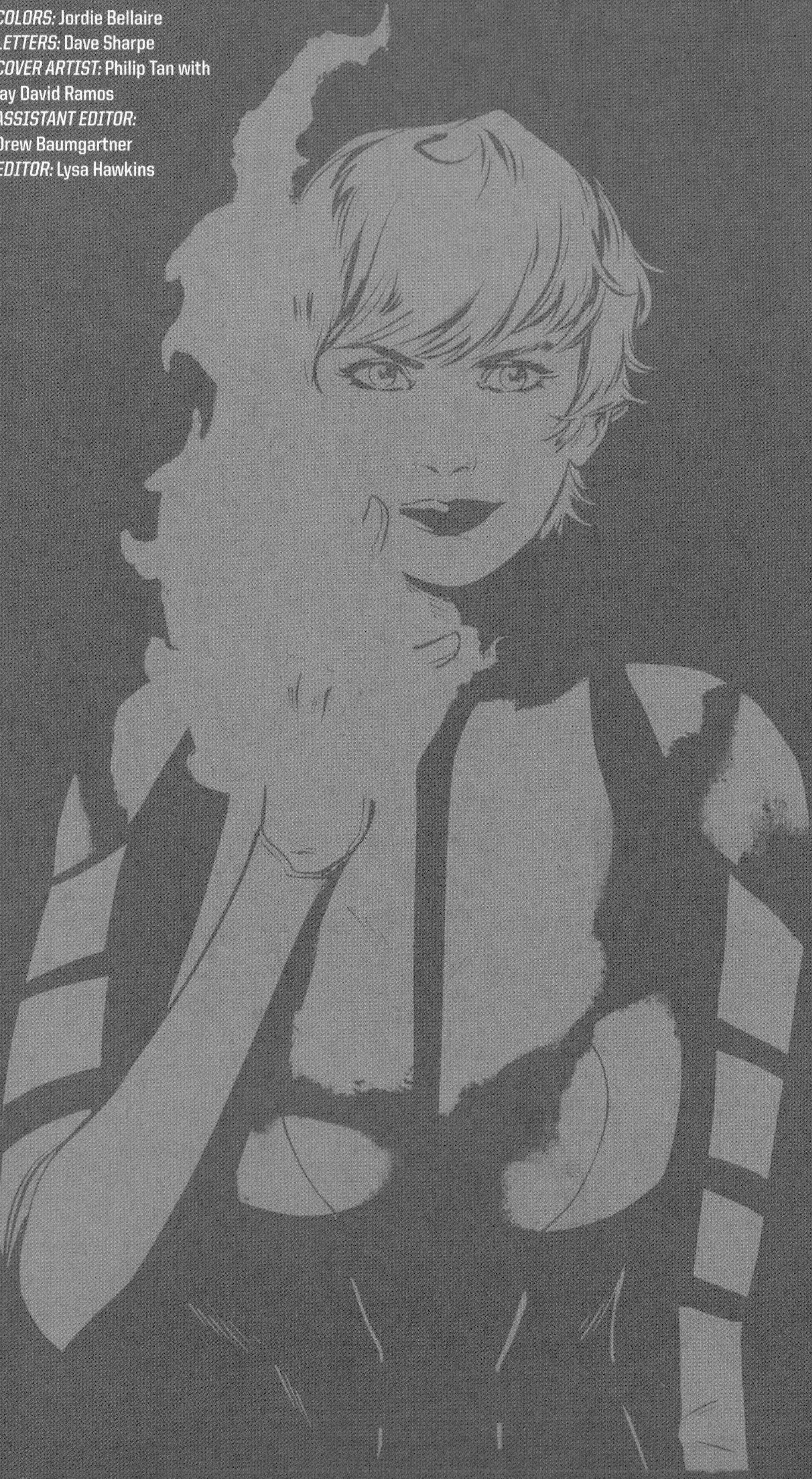

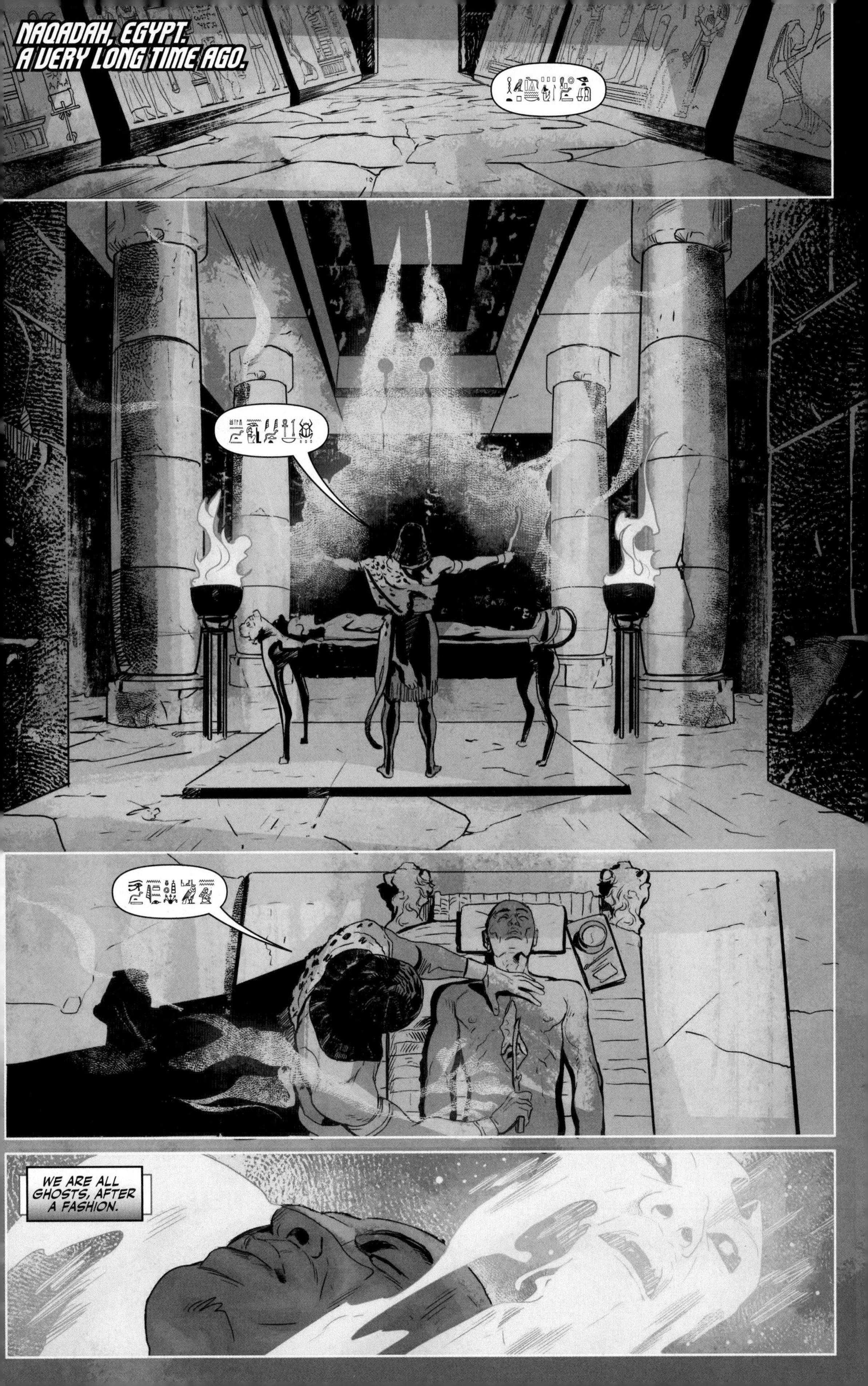
NAQADAH, EGYPT. A VERY LONG TIME AGO.
WE ARE ALL GHOSTS, AFTER A FASHION.

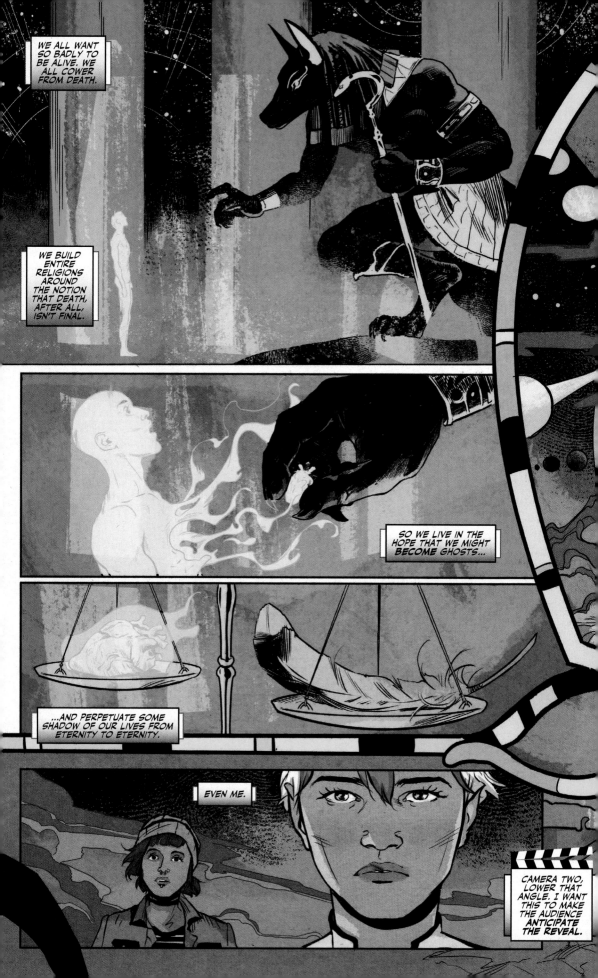

WE ALL WANT SO BADLY TO BE ALIVE. WE ALL COWER FROM DEATH.

WE BUILD ENTIRE RELIGIONS AROUND THE NOTION THAT DEATH, AFTER ALL, ISN'T FINAL.

SO WE LIVE IN THE HOPE THAT WE MIGHT BECOME GHOSTS...

...AND PERPETUATE SOME SHADOW OF OUR LIVES FROM ETERNITY TO ETERNITY.

EVEN ME.

CAMERA TWO, LOWER THAT ANGLE. I WANT THIS TO MAKE THE AUDIENCE ANTICIPATE THE REVEAL.

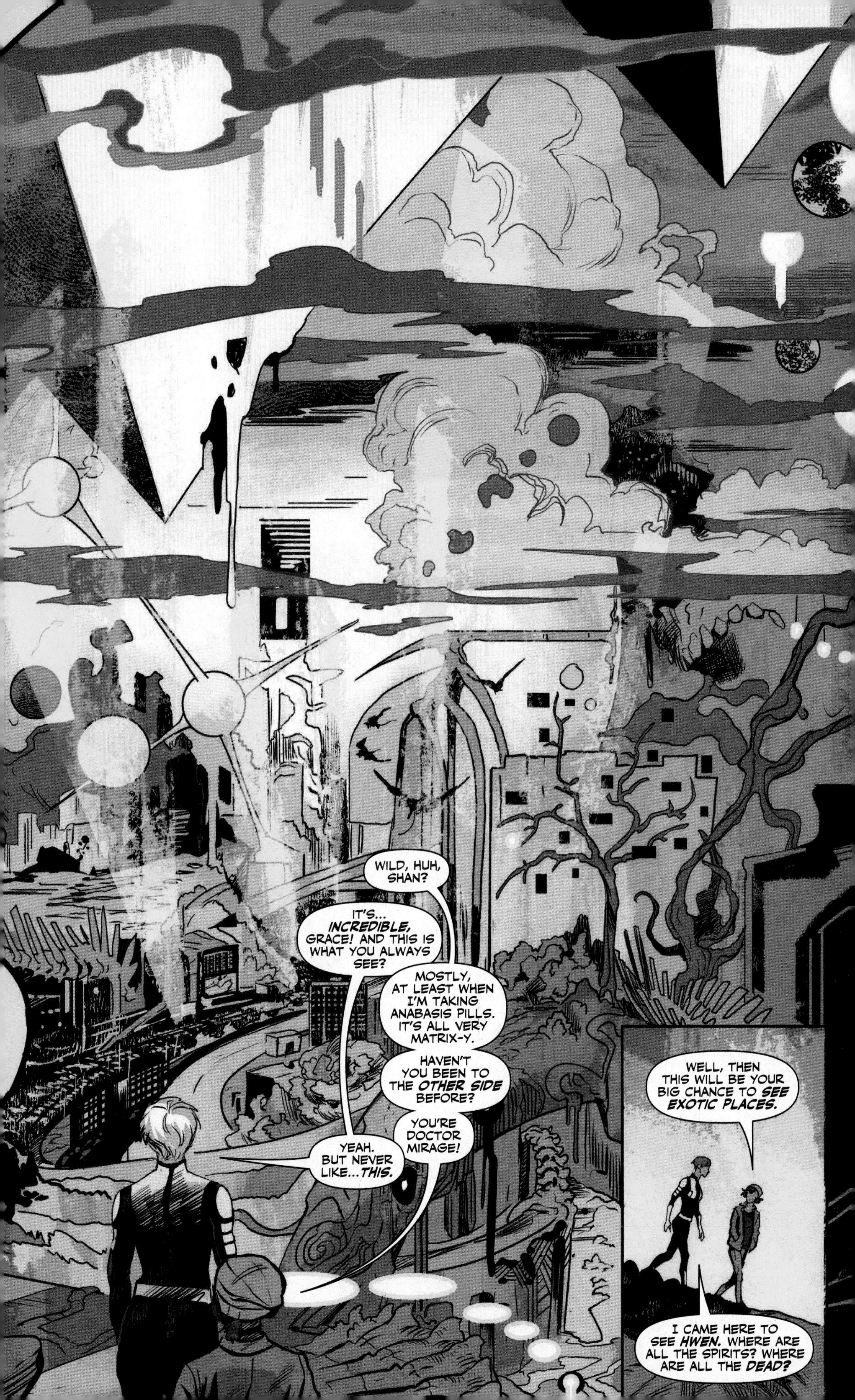
WILD, HUH, SHAN?
IT'S... ***INCREDIBLE,*** GRACE! AND THIS IS WHAT YOU ALWAYS SEE?
MOSTLY, AT LEAST WHEN I'M TAKING ANABASIS PILLS. IT'S ALL VERY MATRIX-Y.
HAVEN'T YOU BEEN TO THE ***OTHER SIDE*** BEFORE?
YOU'RE DOCTOR MIRAGE!
YEAH. BUT NEVER LIKE... ***THIS.***
WELL, THEN THIS WILL BE YOUR BIG CHANCE TO ***SEE EXOTIC PLACES.***
I CAME HERE TO SEE ***HWEN.*** WHERE ARE ALL THE SPIRITS? WHERE ARE ALL THE ***DEAD?***

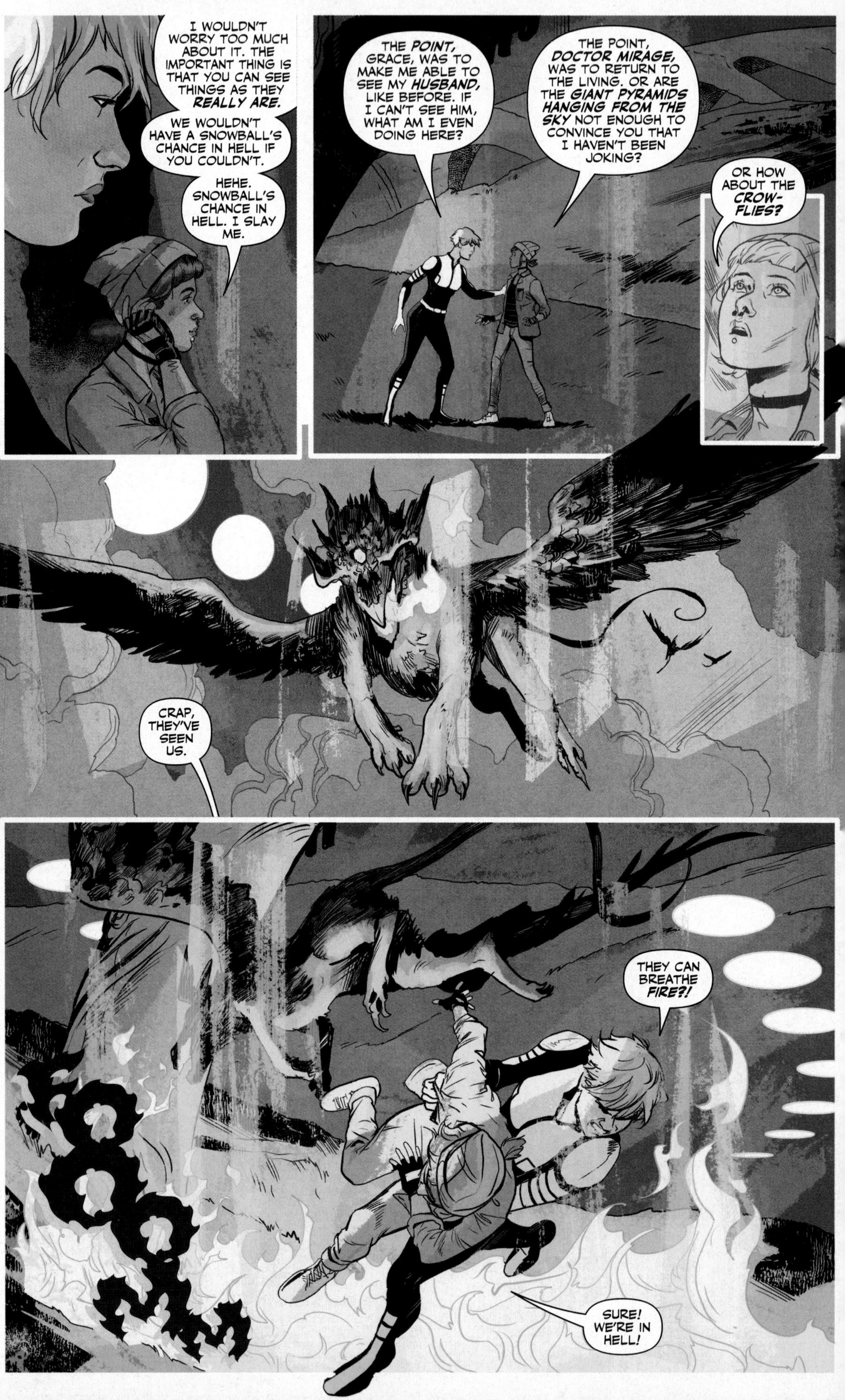
I WOULDN'T WORRY TOO MUCH ABOUT IT. THE IMPORTANT THING IS THAT YOU CAN SEE THINGS AS THEY *REALLY ARE.*
WE WOULDN'T HAVE A SNOWBALL'S CHANCE IN HELL IF YOU COULDN'T.
HEHE. SNOWBALL'S CHANCE IN HELL. I SLAY ME.
THE *POINT,* GRACE, WAS TO MAKE ME ABLE TO SEE MY *HUSBAND,* LIKE BEFORE. IF I CAN'T SEE HIM, WHAT AM I EVEN DOING HERE?
THE POINT, *DOCTOR MIRAGE,* WAS TO RETURN TO THE LIVING. OR ARE THE *GIANT PYRAMIDS HANGING FROM THE SKY* NOT ENOUGH TO CONVINCE YOU THAT I HAVEN'T BEEN JOKING?
OR HOW ABOUT THE *CROW-FLIES?*
CRAP, THEY'VE SEEN US.
THEY CAN BREATHE *FIRE?!*
SURE! WE'RE IN HELL!

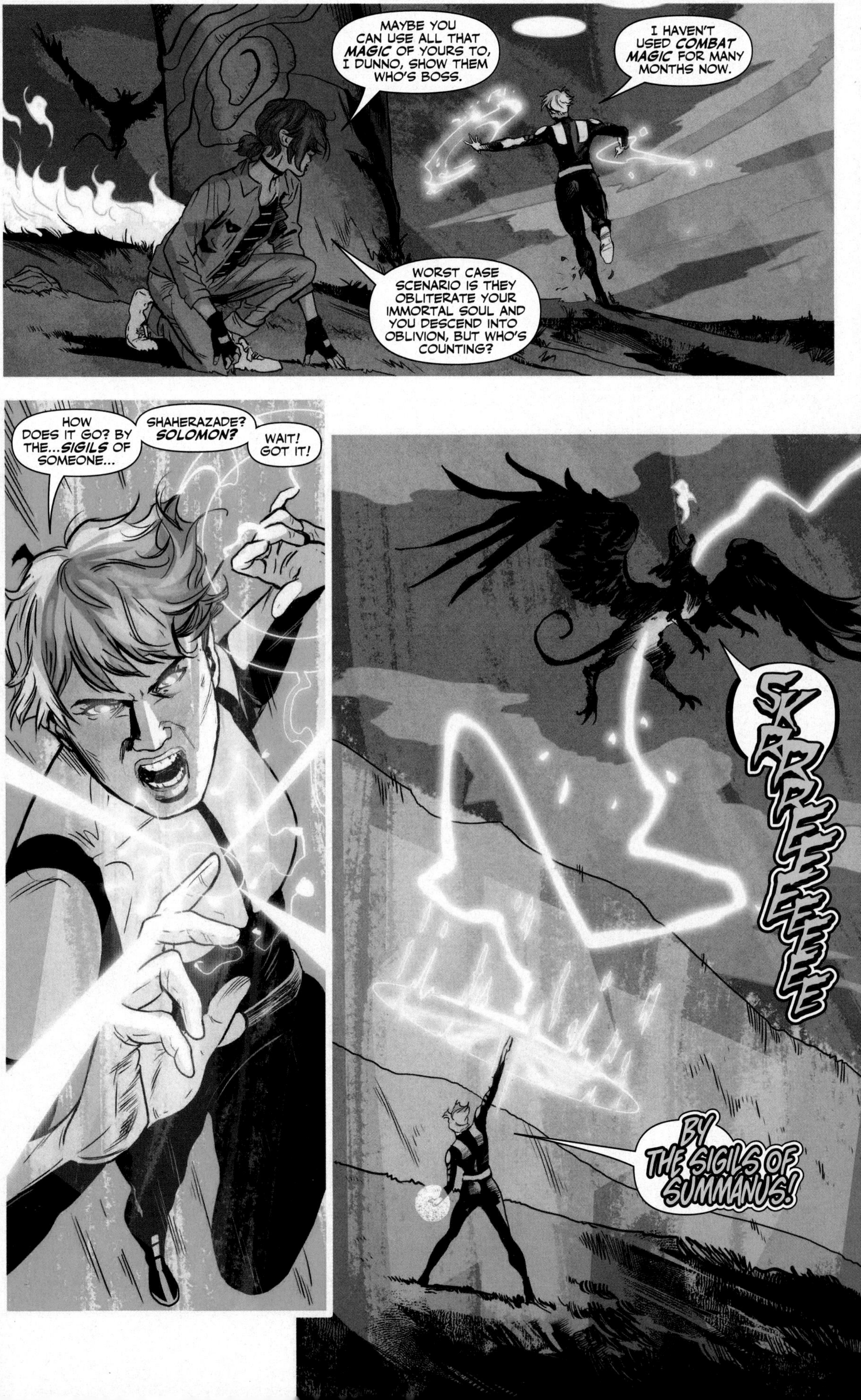
MAYBE YOU CAN USE ALL THAT MAGIC OF YOURS TO, I DUNNO, SHOW THEM WHO'S BOSS.
I HAVEN'T USED COMBAT MAGIC FOR MANY MONTHS NOW.
WORST CASE SCENARIO IS THEY OBLITERATE YOUR IMMORTAL SOUL AND YOU DESCEND INTO OBLIVION, BUT WHO'S COUNTING?
HOW DOES IT GO? BY THE...SIGILS OF SOMEONE...
SHAHERAZADE? SOLOMON?
WAIT! GOT IT!
SKRREEEEEEE
BY THE SIGILS OF SUMMANUS!

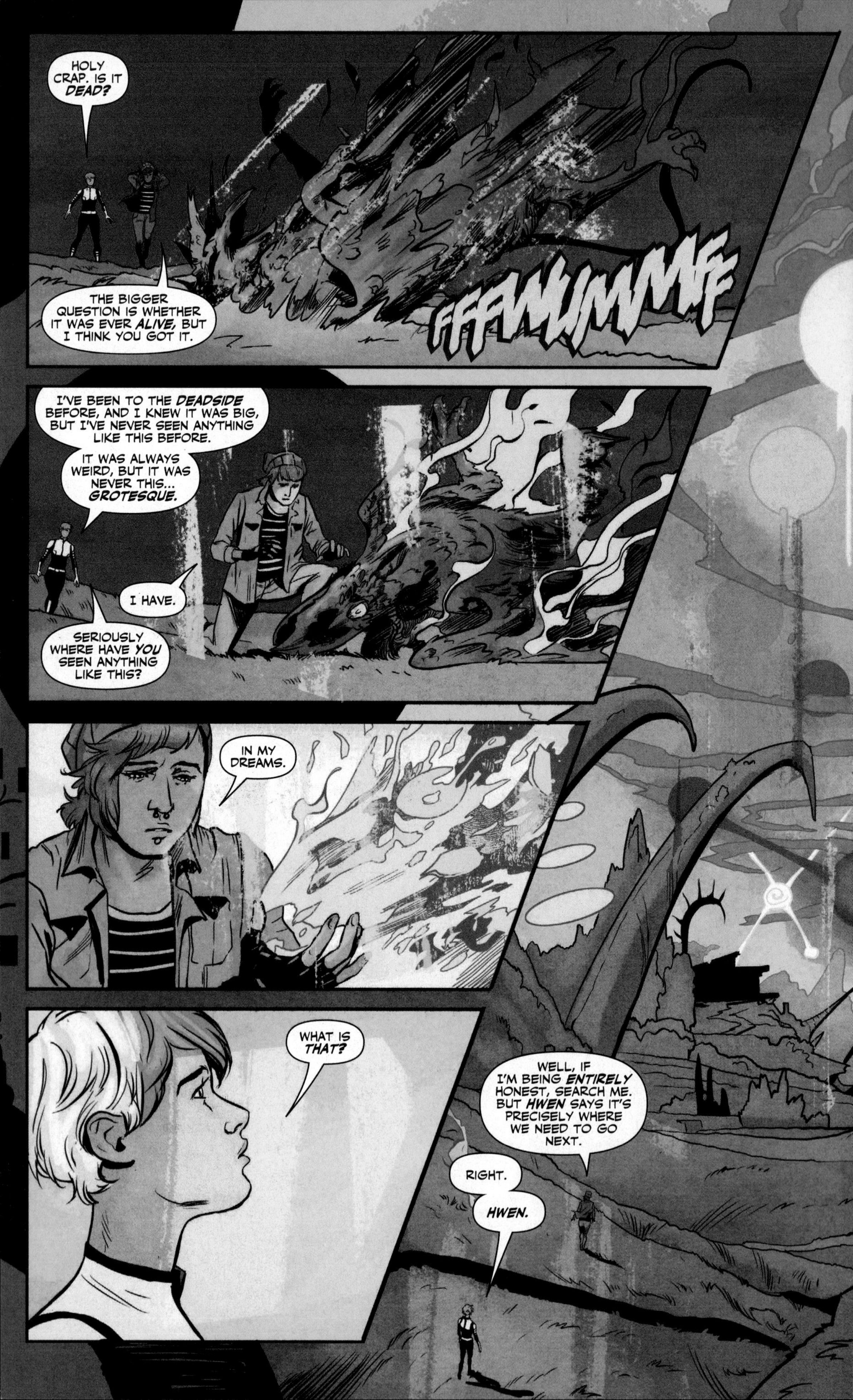

HOLY CRAP. IS IT *DEAD?*
THE BIGGER QUESTION IS WHETHER IT WAS EVER *ALIVE,* BUT I THINK YOU GOT IT.
FFFWUMMFF
I'VE BEEN TO THE *DEADSIDE* BEFORE, AND I KNEW IT WAS BIG, BUT I'VE NEVER SEEN ANYTHING LIKE THIS BEFORE.
IT WAS ALWAYS WEIRD, BUT IT WAS NEVER THIS... *GROTESQUE.*
I HAVE.
SERIOUSLY WHERE HAVE *YOU* SEEN ANYTHING LIKE THIS?
IN MY DREAMS.
WHAT IS *THAT?*
WELL, IF I'M BEING *ENTIRELY* HONEST, SEARCH ME. BUT *HWEN* SAYS IT'S PRECISELY WHERE WE NEED TO GO NEXT.
RIGHT.
HWEN.

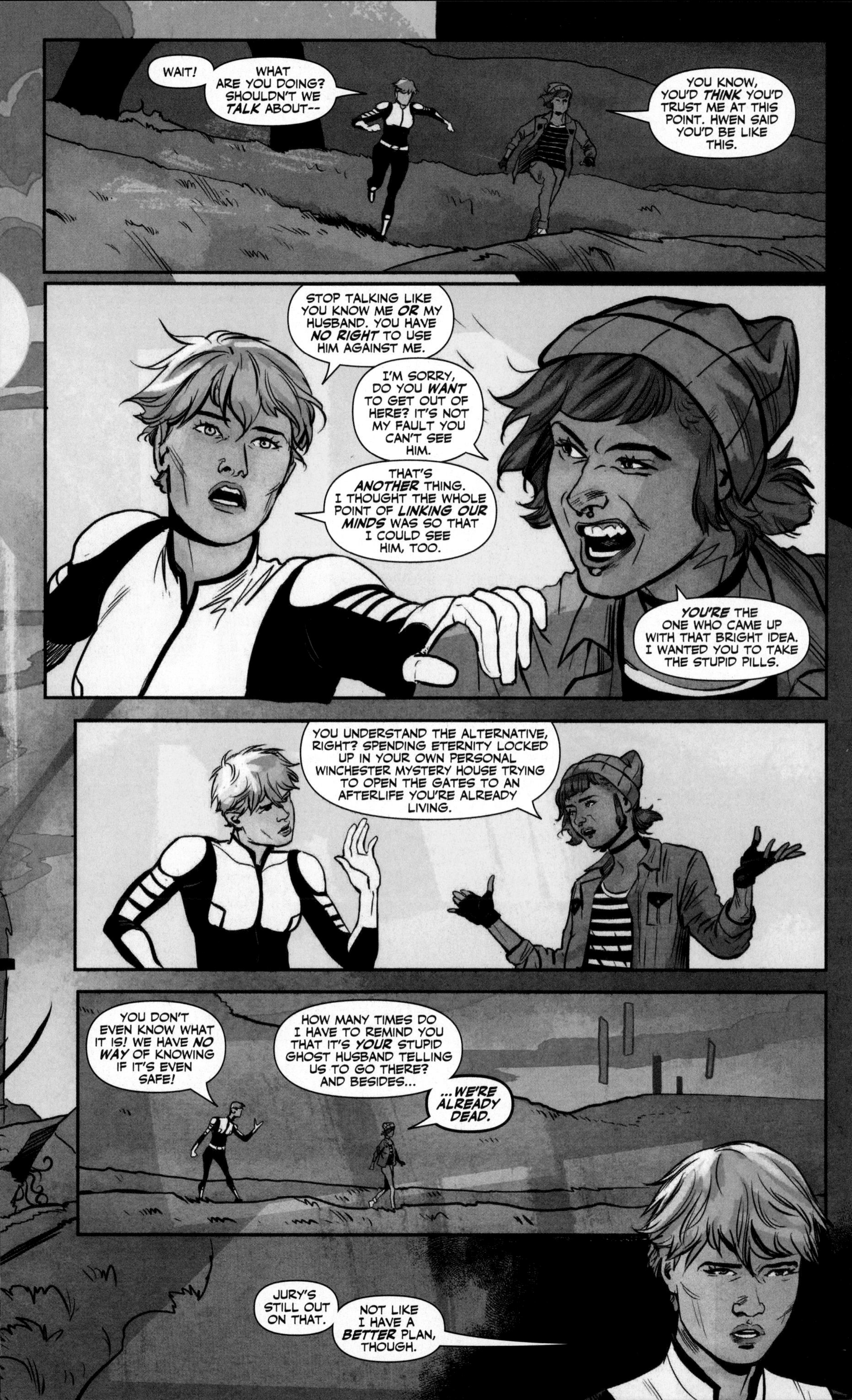
WAIT!
WHAT ARE YOU DOING? SHOULDN'T WE TALK ABOUT--
YOU KNOW, YOU'D THINK YOU'D TRUST ME AT THIS POINT. HWEN SAID YOU'D BE LIKE THIS.
STOP TALKING LIKE YOU KNOW ME OR MY HUSBAND. YOU HAVE NO RIGHT TO USE HIM AGAINST ME.
I'M SORRY, DO YOU WANT TO GET OUT OF HERE? IT'S NOT MY FAULT YOU CAN'T SEE HIM.
THAT'S ANOTHER THING. I THOUGHT THE WHOLE POINT OF LINKING OUR MINDS WAS SO THAT I COULD SEE HIM, TOO.
YOU'RE THE ONE WHO CAME UP WITH THAT BRIGHT IDEA. I WANTED YOU TO TAKE THE STUPID PILLS.
YOU UNDERSTAND THE ALTERNATIVE, RIGHT? SPENDING ETERNITY LOCKED UP IN YOUR OWN PERSONAL WINCHESTER MYSTERY HOUSE TRYING TO OPEN THE GATES TO AN AFTERLIFE YOU'RE ALREADY LIVING.
YOU DON'T EVEN KNOW WHAT IT IS! WE HAVE NO WAY OF KNOWING IF IT'S EVEN SAFE!
HOW MANY TIMES DO I HAVE TO REMIND YOU THAT IT'S YOUR STUPID GHOST HUSBAND TELLING US TO GO THERE? AND BESIDES...
...WE'RE ALREADY DEAD.
JURY'S STILL OUT ON THAT.
NOT LIKE I HAVE A BETTER PLAN, THOUGH.

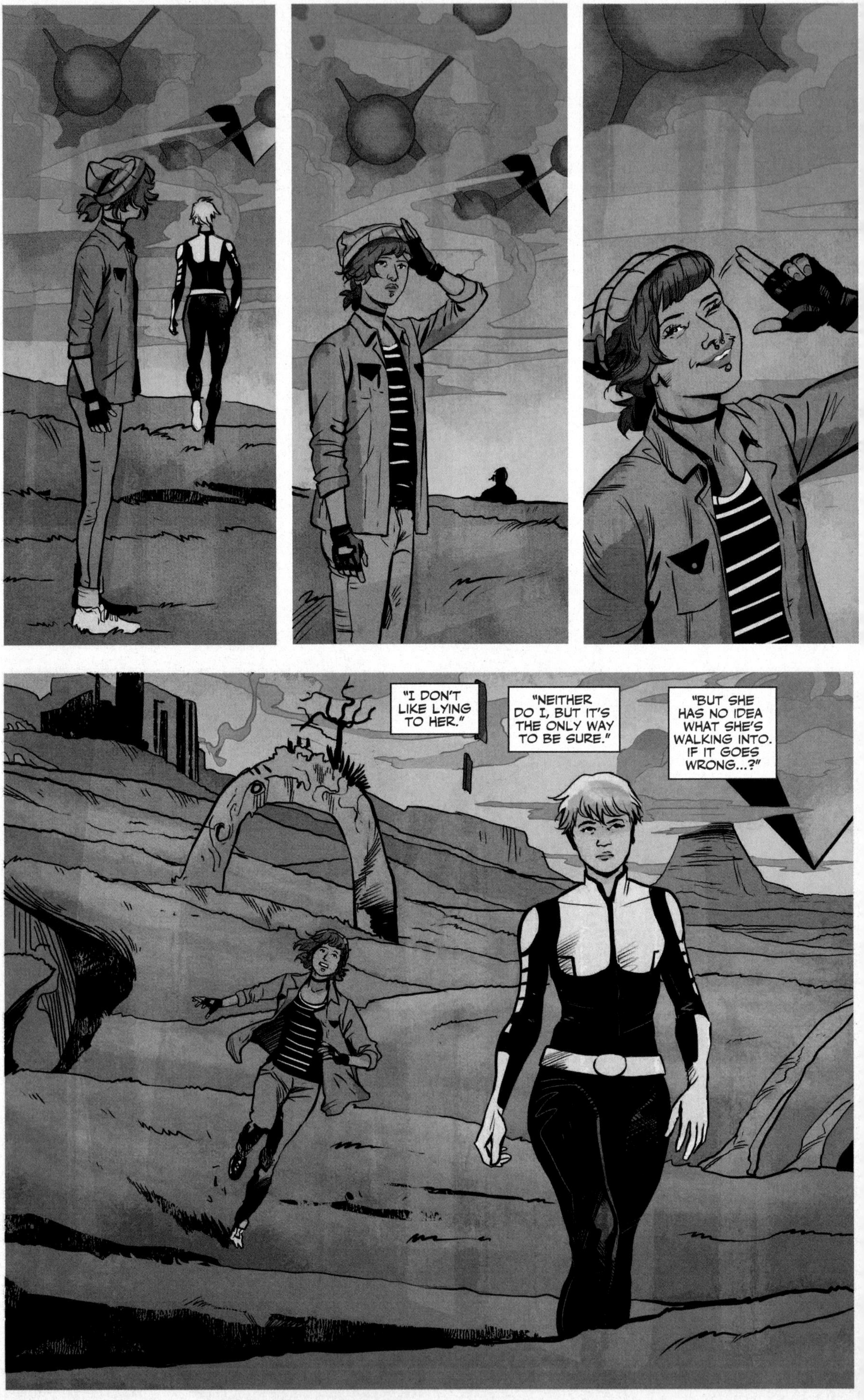
"I DON'T LIKE LYING TO HER."
"NEITHER DO I, BUT IT'S THE ONLY WAY TO BE SURE."
"BUT SHE HAS NO IDEA WHAT SHE'S WALKING INTO. IF IT GOES WRONG...?"

IF IT GOES WRONG, THERE'S NOT ANYTHING WE CAN DO.

"WE POINTED HER IN THE RIGHT DIRECTION.

"IT'S UP TO HER NOW."

YOU EXCITED?

CURIOUS, MOSTLY. I WONDER WHAT WE'LL FIND?

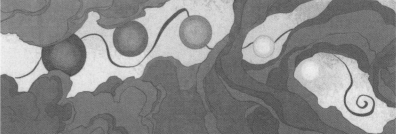

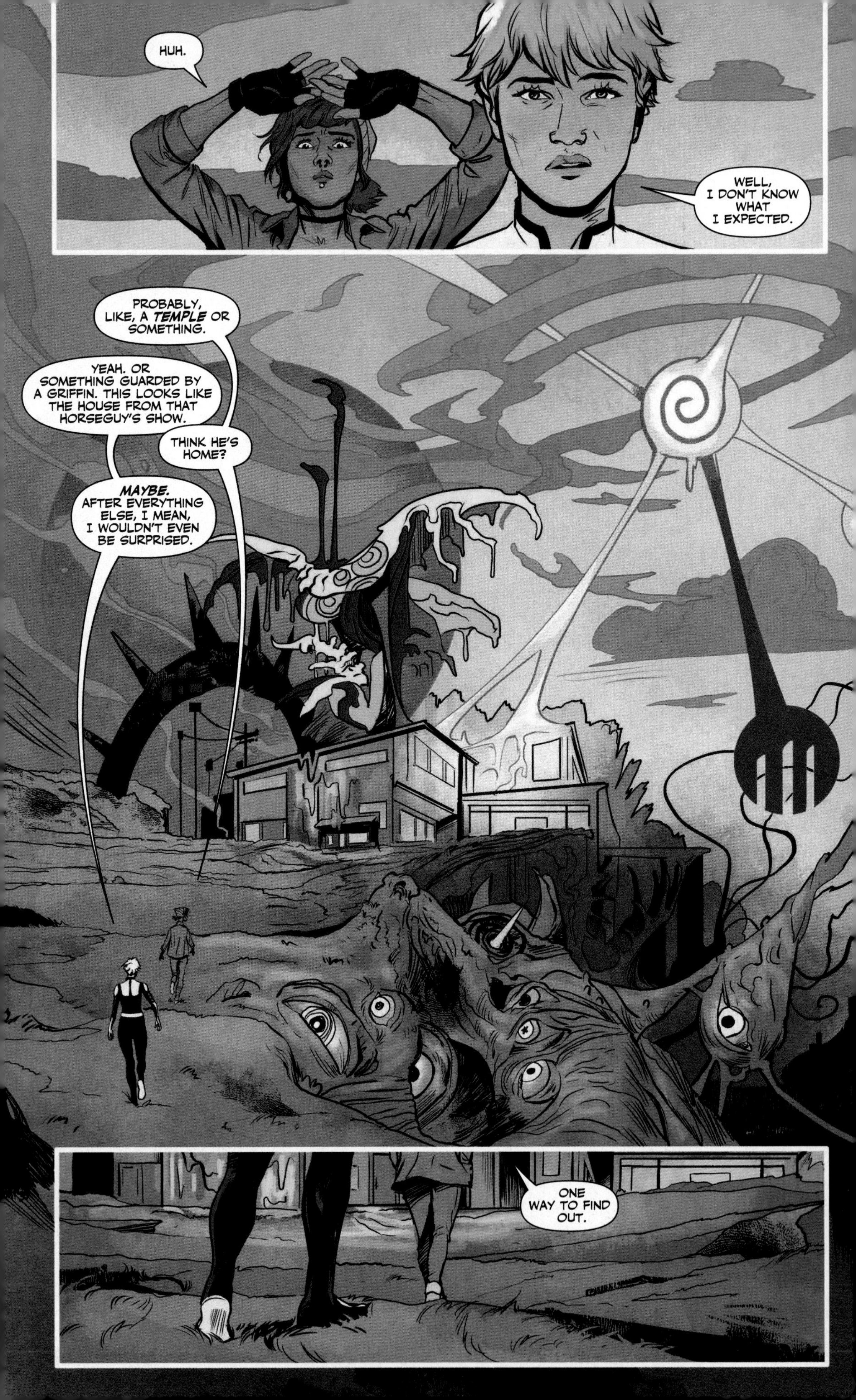
HUH.
WELL, I DON'T KNOW WHAT I EXPECTED.
PROBABLY, LIKE, A *TEMPLE* OR SOMETHING.
YEAH. OR SOMETHING GUARDED BY A GRIFFIN. THIS LOOKS LIKE THE HOUSE FROM THAT HORSEGUY'S SHOW.
THINK HE'S HOME?
MAYBE. AFTER EVERYTHING ELSE, I MEAN, I WOULDN'T EVEN BE SURPRISED.
ONE WAY TO FIND OUT.

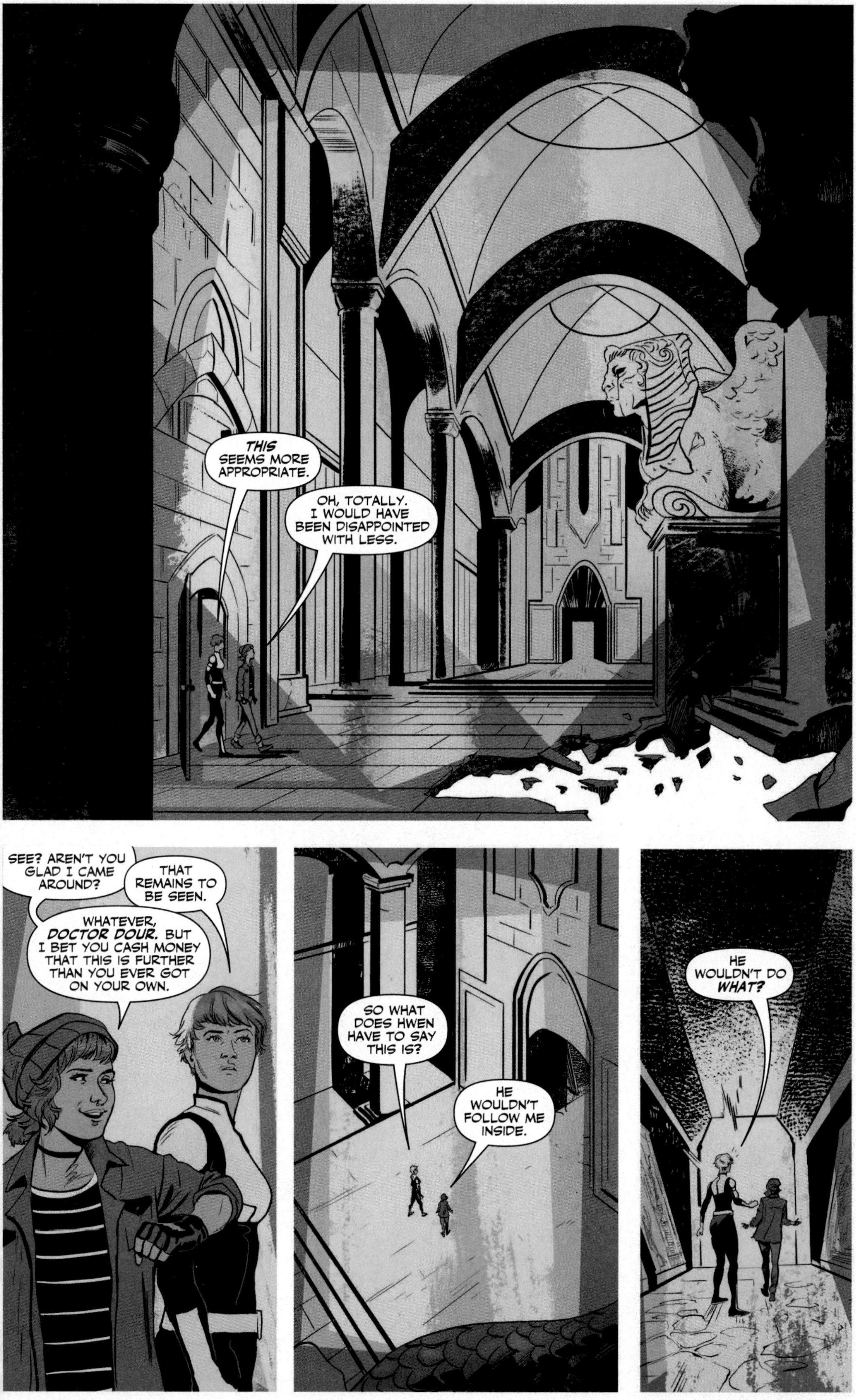
THIS SEEMS MORE APPROPRIATE.
OH, TOTALLY. I WOULD HAVE BEEN DISAPPOINTED WITH LESS.
SEE? AREN'T YOU GLAD I CAME AROUND?
THAT REMAINS TO BE SEEN.
WHATEVER, DOCTOR DOUR. BUT I BET YOU CASH MONEY THAT THIS IS FURTHER THAN YOU EVER GOT ON YOUR OWN.
SO WHAT DOES HWEN HAVE TO SAY THIS IS?
HE WOULDN'T FOLLOW ME INSIDE.
HE WOULDN'T DO WHAT?

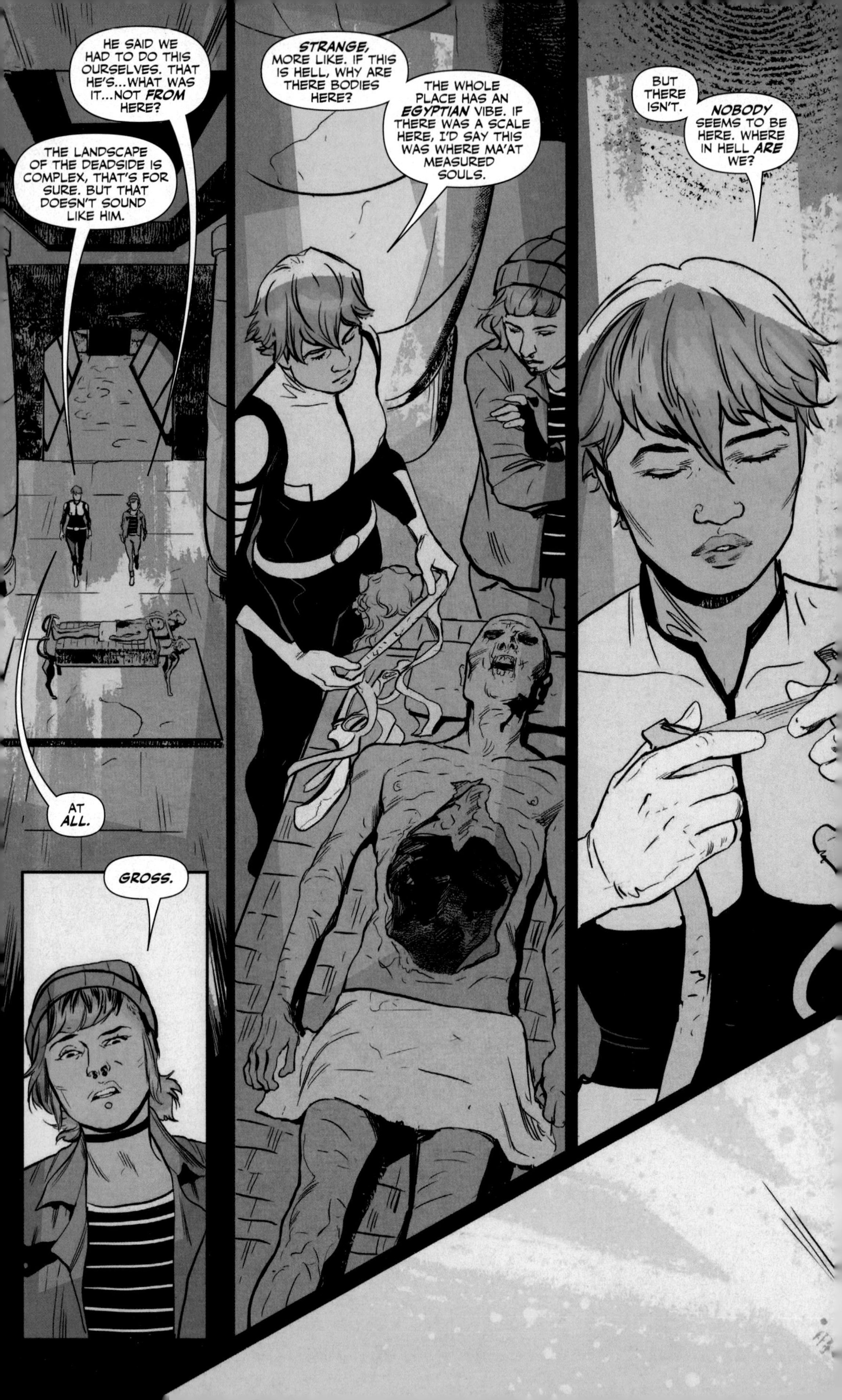
HE SAID WE HAD TO DO THIS OURSELVES. THAT HE'S...WHAT WAS IT...NOT FROM HERE?
THE LANDSCAPE OF THE DEADSIDE IS COMPLEX, THAT'S FOR SURE. BUT THAT DOESN'T SOUND LIKE HIM.
AT ALL.
GROSS.
STRANGE, MORE LIKE. IF THIS IS HELL, WHY ARE THERE BODIES HERE?
THE WHOLE PLACE HAS AN EGYPTIAN VIBE. IF THERE WAS A SCALE HERE, I'D SAY THIS WAS WHERE MA'AT MEASURED SOULS.
BUT THERE ISN'T.
NOBODY SEEMS TO BE HERE. WHERE IN HELL ARE WE?

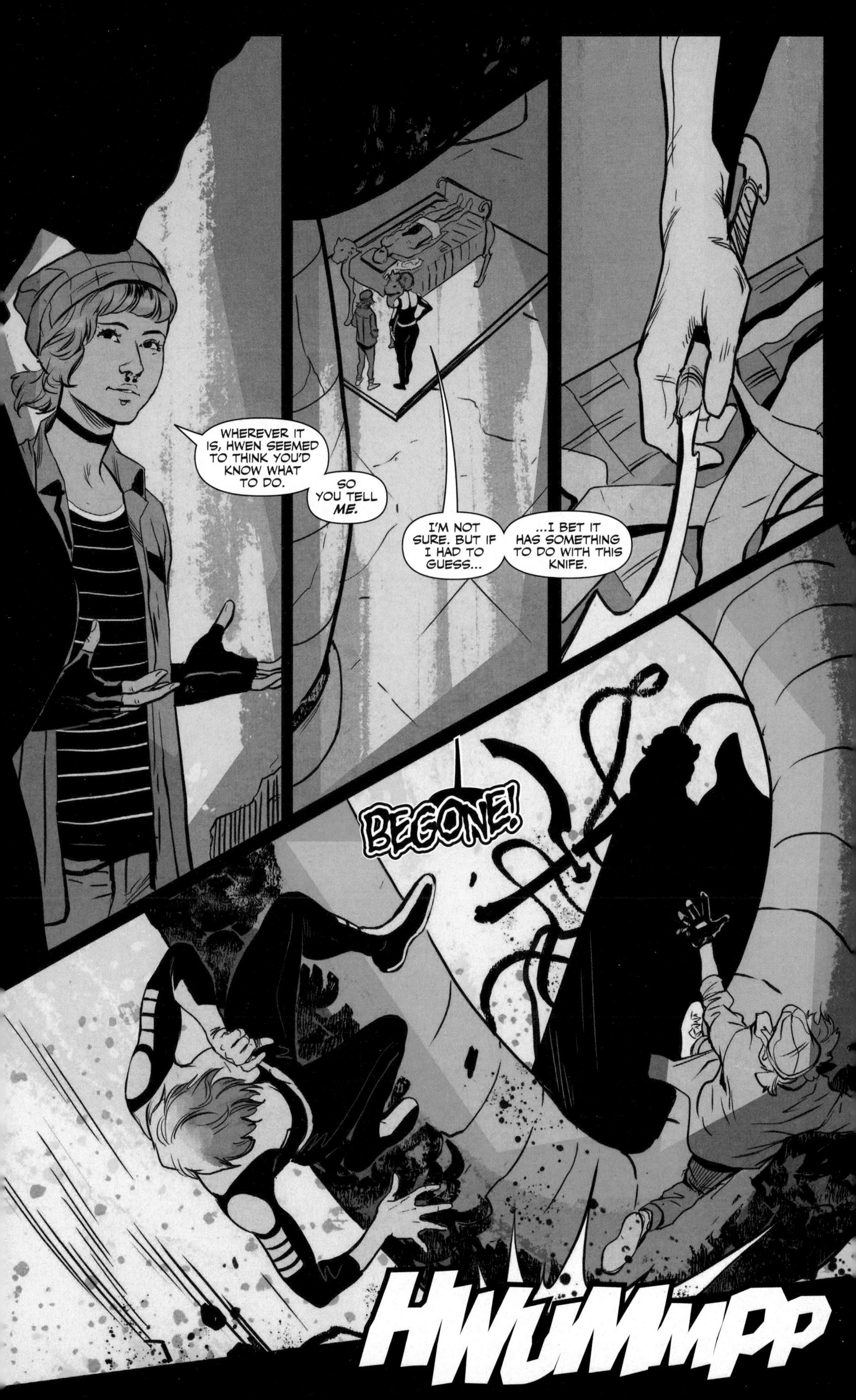
WHEREVER IT IS, HWEN SEEMED TO THINK YOU'D KNOW WHAT TO DO.
SO YOU TELL *ME.*
I'M NOT SURE. BUT IF I HAD TO GUESS...
...I BET IT HAS SOMETHING TO DO WITH THIS KNIFE.
BEGONE!
HWUMMPP

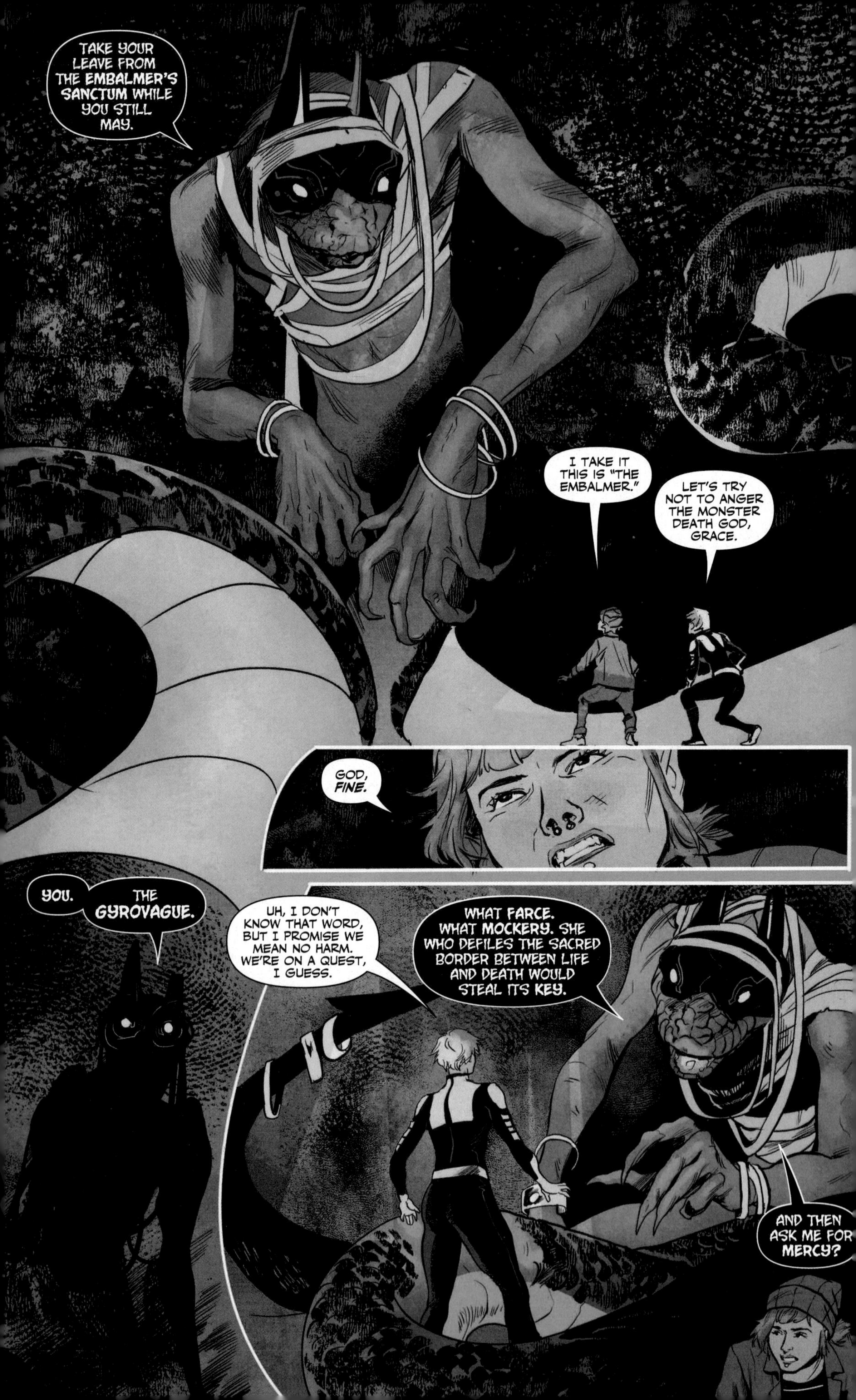
TAKE YOUR LEAVE FROM THE EMBALMER'S SANCTUM WHILE YOU STILL MAY.
I TAKE IT THIS IS "THE EMBALMER."
LET'S TRY NOT TO ANGER THE MONSTER DEATH GOD, GRACE.
GOD, FINE.
YOU.
THE GYROVAGUE.
UH, I DON'T KNOW THAT WORD, BUT I PROMISE WE MEAN NO HARM. WE'RE ON A QUEST, I GUESS.
WHAT FARCE. WHAT MOCKERY. SHE WHO DEFILES THE SACRED BORDER BETWEEN LIFE AND DEATH WOULD STEAL ITS KEY.
AND THEN ASK ME FOR MERCY?

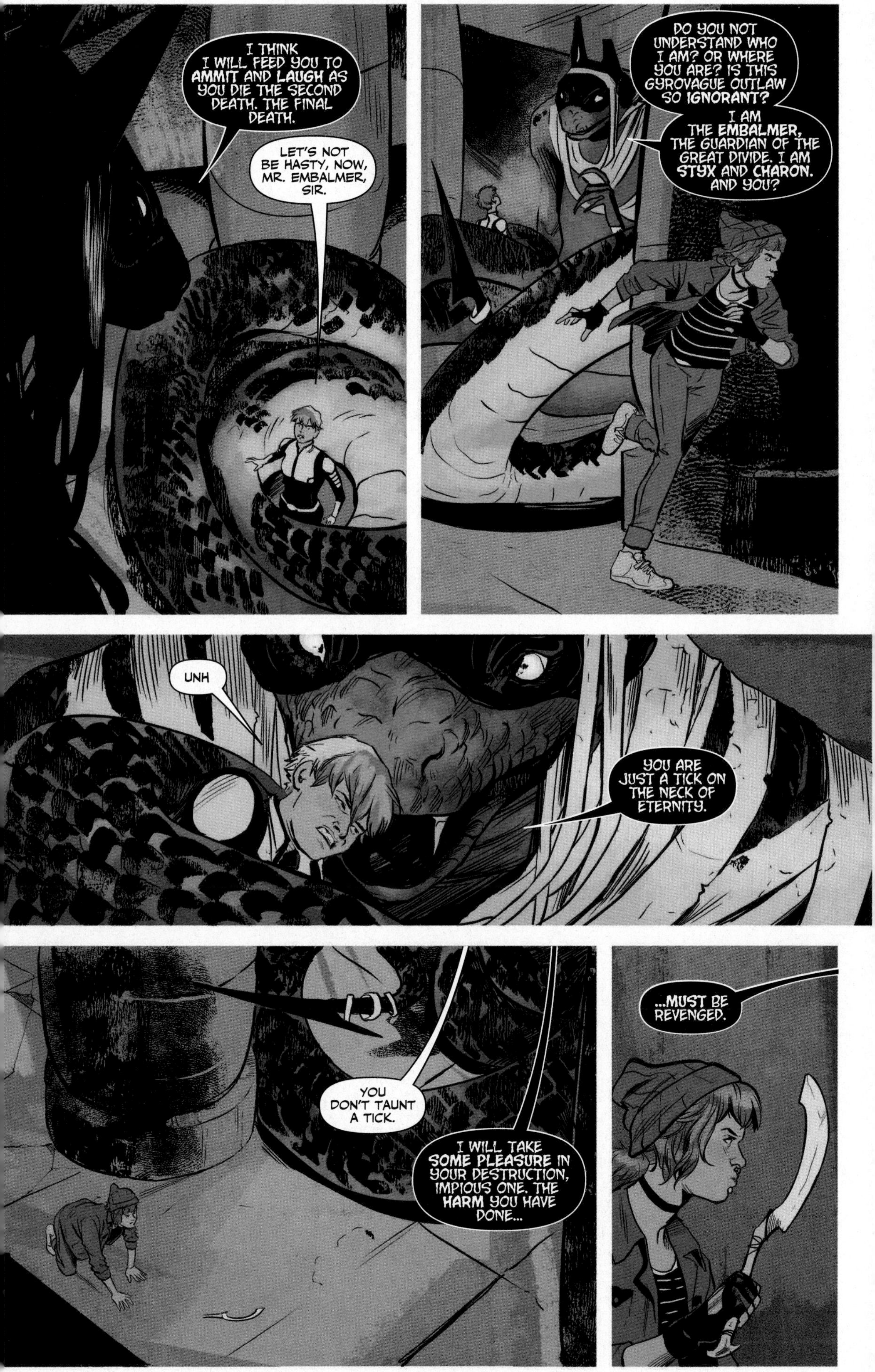
I THINK I WILL FEED YOU TO AMMIT AND LAUGH AS YOU DIE THE SECOND DEATH. THE FINAL DEATH.
LET'S NOT BE HASTY, NOW, MR. EMBALMER, SIR.
DO YOU NOT UNDERSTAND WHO I AM? OR WHERE YOU ARE? IS THIS GYROVAGUE OUTLAW SO IGNORANT?
I AM THE EMBALMER, THE GUARDIAN OF THE GREAT DIVIDE. I AM STYX AND CHARON. AND YOU?
UNH
YOU ARE JUST A TICK ON THE NECK OF ETERNITY.
YOU DON'T TAUNT A TICK.
I WILL TAKE SOME PLEASURE IN YOUR DESTRUCTION, IMPIOUS ONE. THE HARM YOU HAVE DONE...
...MUST BE REVENGED.

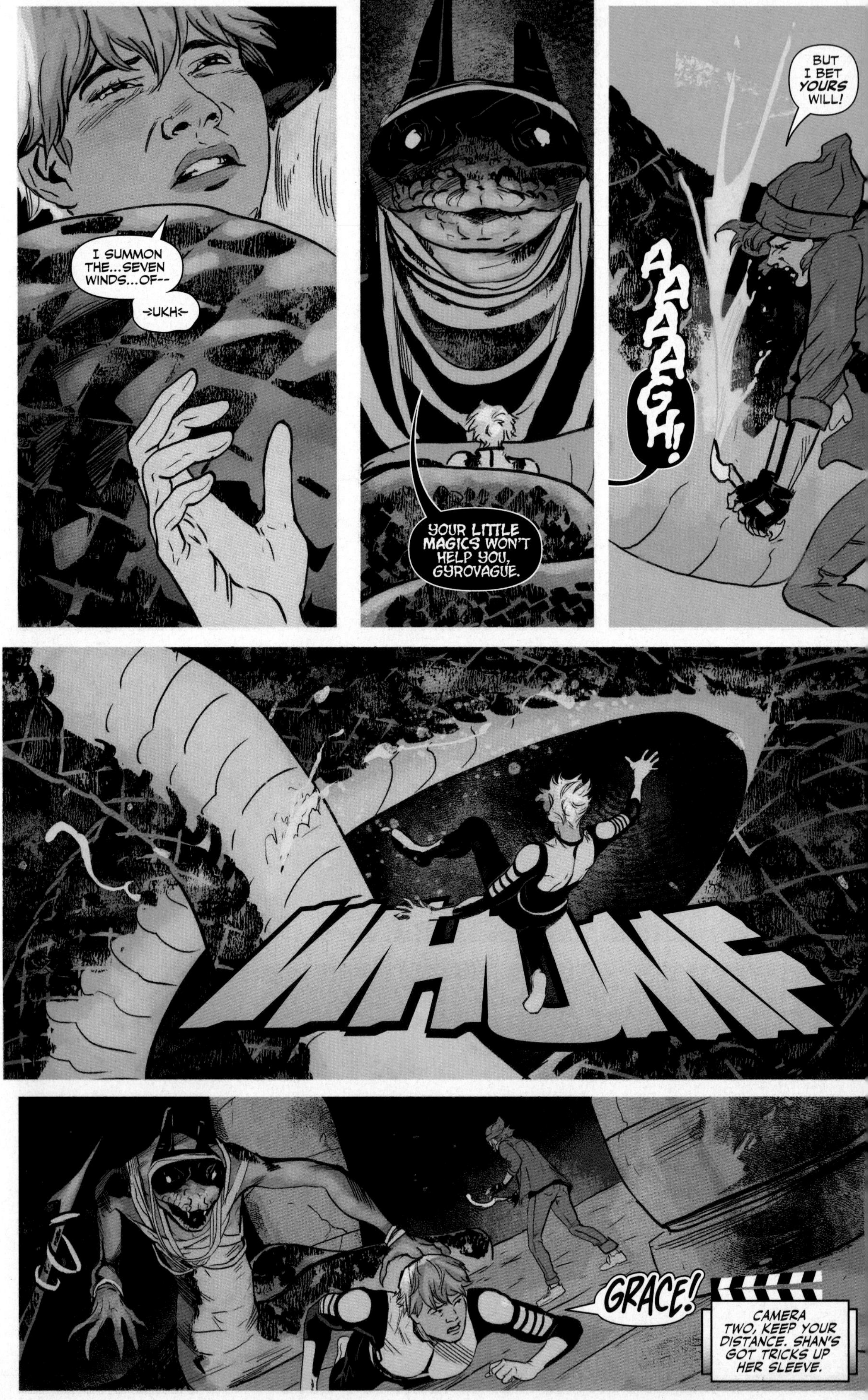
I SUMMON THE...SEVEN WINDS...OF--
UKH
YOUR LITTLE MAGICS WON'T HELP YOU, GYROVAGUE.
BUT I BET YOURS WILL!
AAAAGH!
WHUMF
GRACE!
CAMERA TWO, KEEP YOUR DISTANCE. SHAN'S GOT TRICKS UP HER SLEEVE.

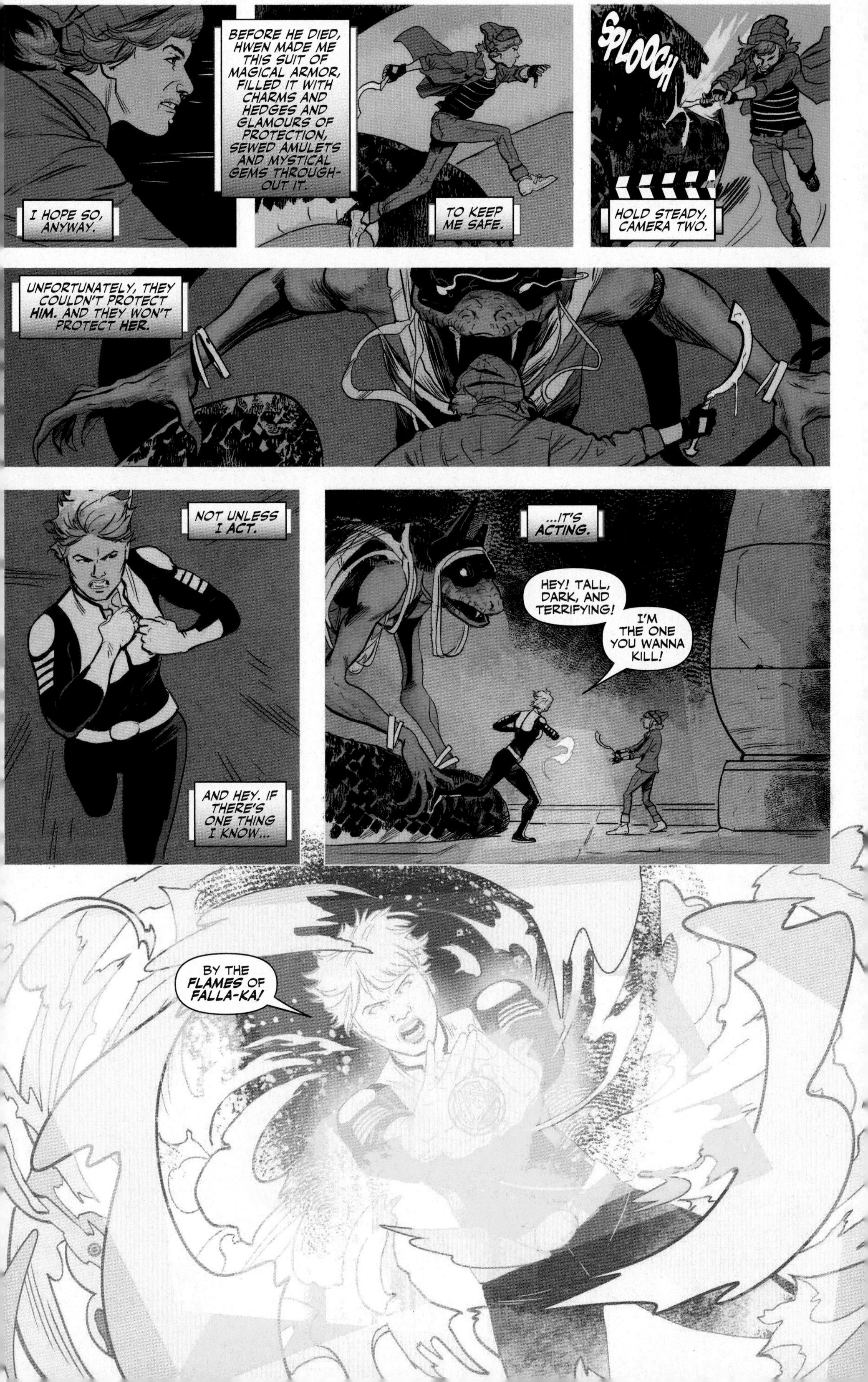
I HOPE SO, ANYWAY.
BEFORE HE DIED, HWEN MADE ME THIS SUIT OF MAGICAL ARMOR, FILLED IT WITH CHARMS AND HEDGES AND GLAMOURS OF PROTECTION, SEWED AMULETS AND MYSTICAL GEMS THROUGHOUT IT.
TO KEEP ME SAFE.
SPLOOCH
HOLD STEADY, CAMERA TWO.
UNFORTUNATELY, THEY COULDN'T PROTECT HIM. AND THEY WON'T PROTECT HER.
NOT UNLESS I ACT.
AND HEY. IF THERE'S ONE THING I KNOW...
...IT'S ACTING.
HEY! TALL, DARK, AND TERRIFYING!
I'M THE ONE YOU WANNA KILL!
BY THE FLAMES OF FALLA-KA!

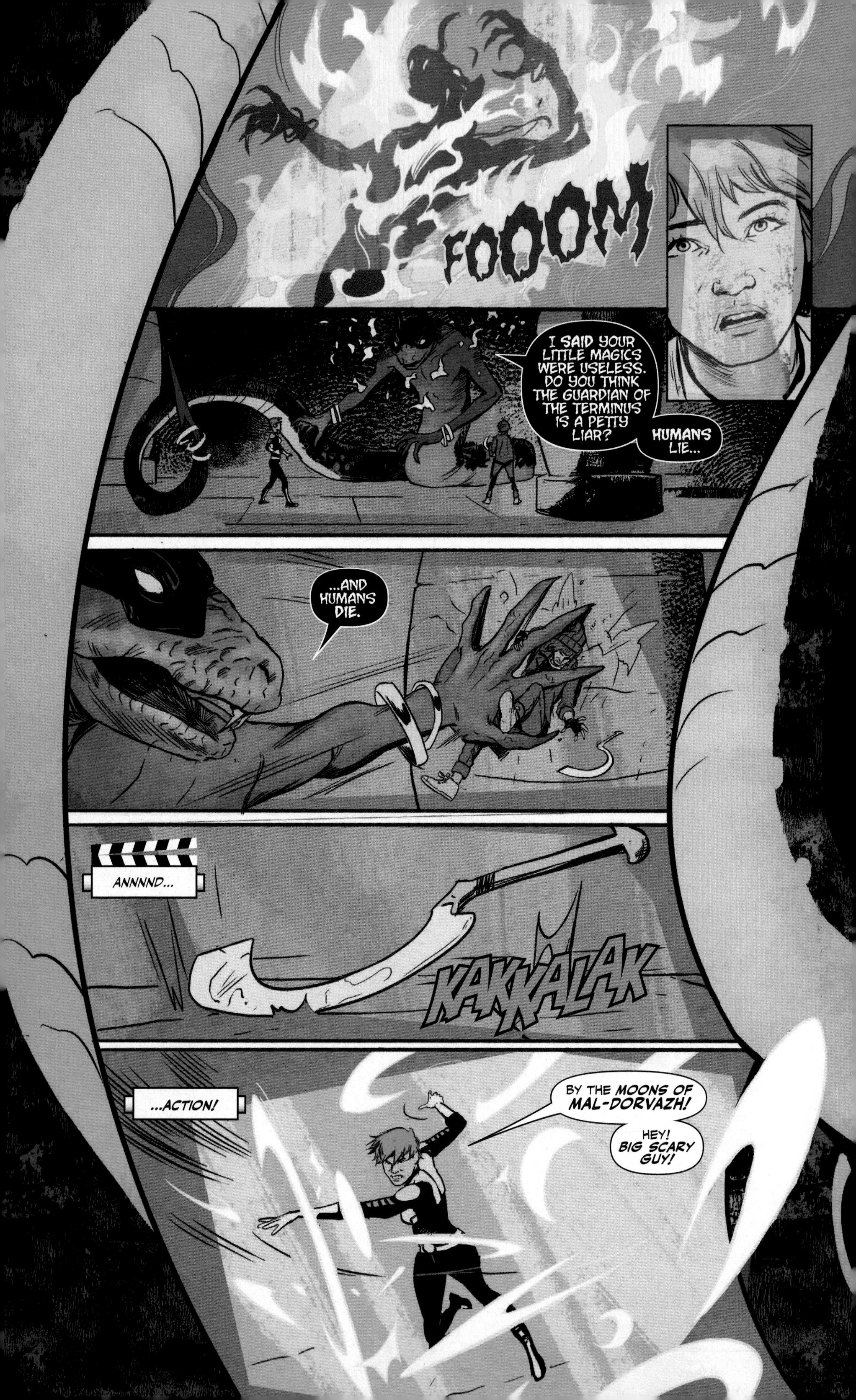
FOOOM
I SAID YOUR LITTLE MAGICS WERE USELESS. DO YOU THINK THE GUARDIAN OF THE TERMINUS IS A PETTY LIAR?
HUMANS LIE...
...AND HUMANS DIE.
ANNNND...
KAKKALAK
...ACTION!
BY THE MOONS OF MAL-DORVAZH!
HEY! BIG SCARY GUY!

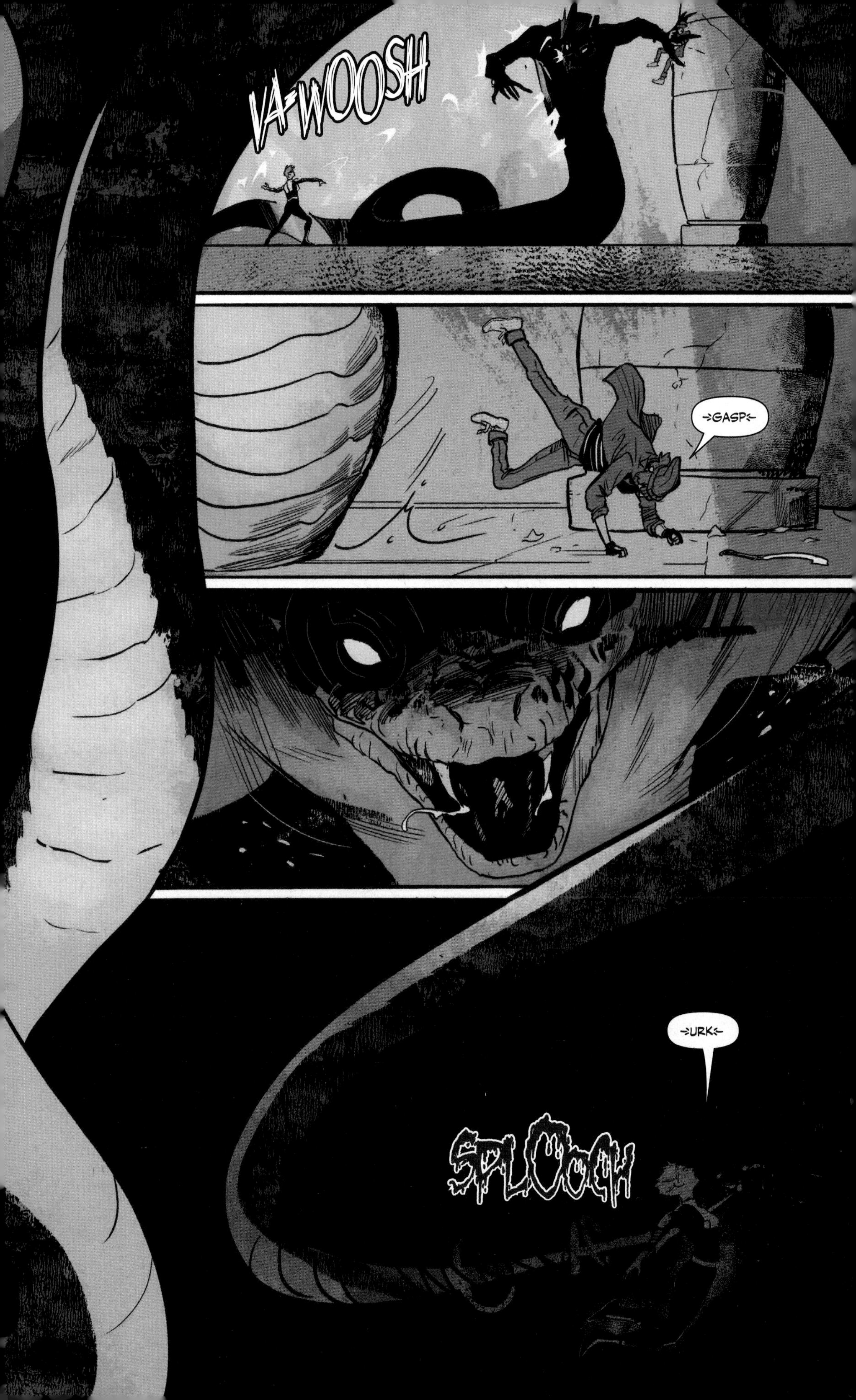
VA-WOOSH
GASP
SPLOOCH
URK

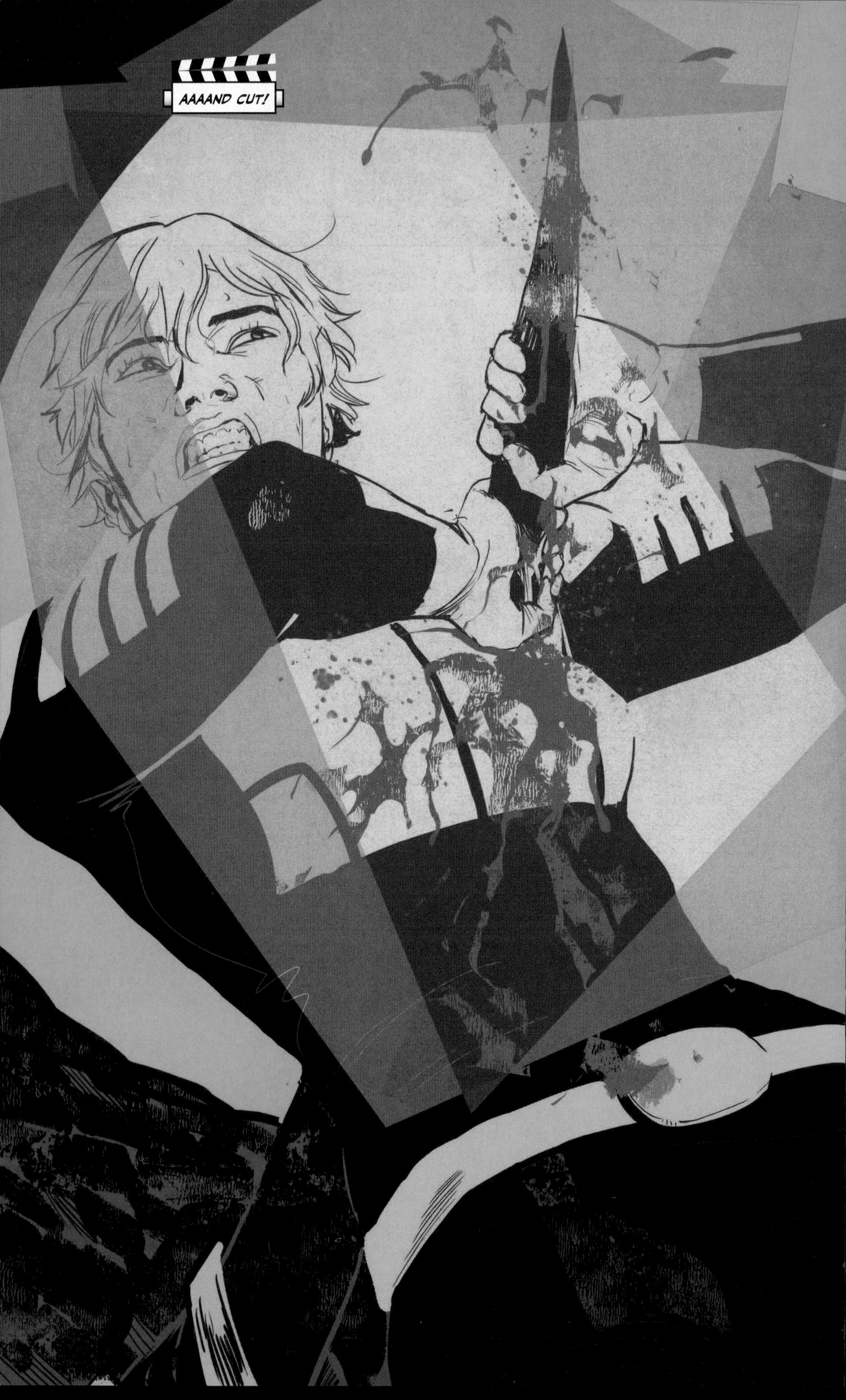
AAAAND CUT!

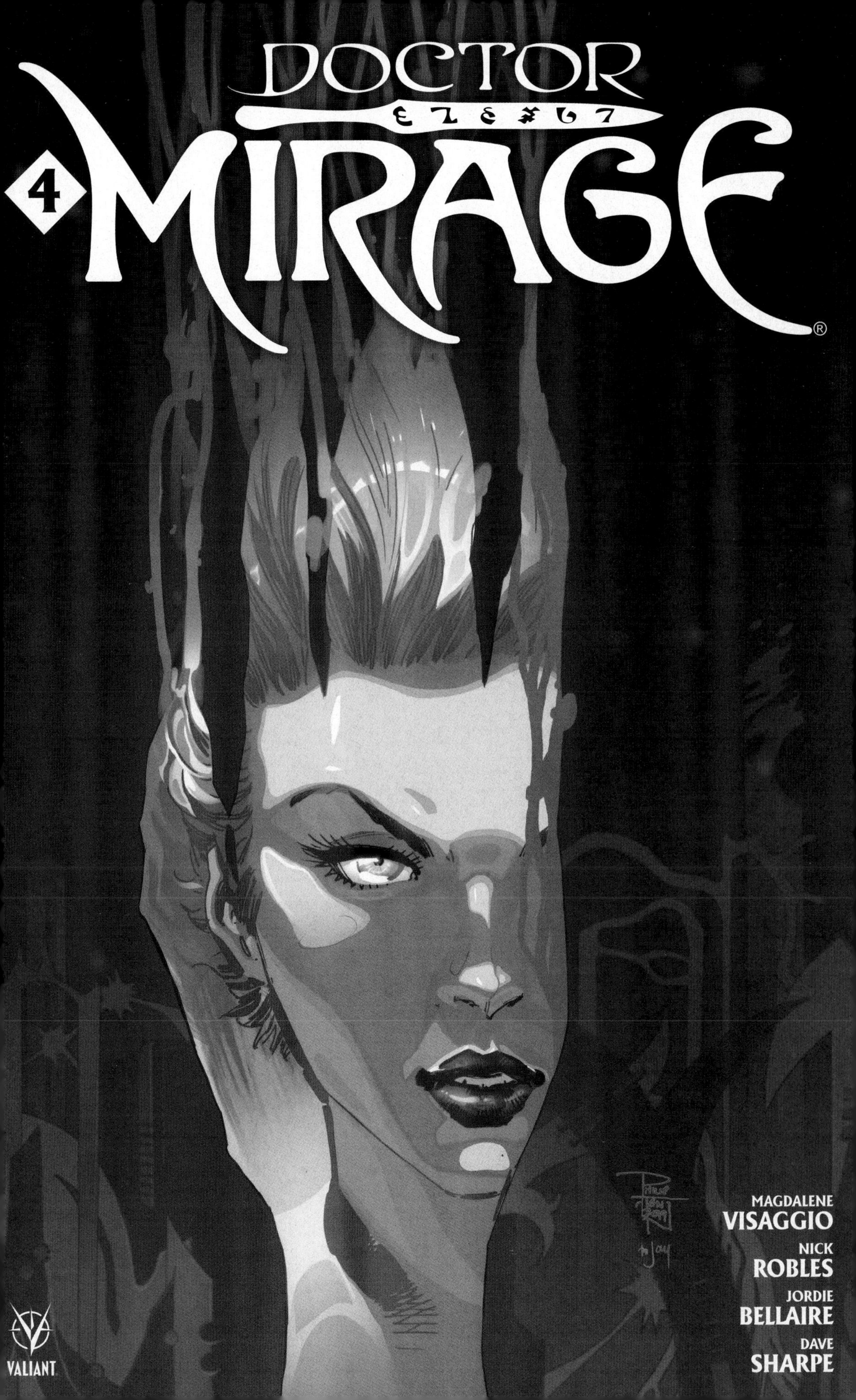
DOCTOR
MIRAGE
4
MAGDALENE
VISAGGIO
NICK
ROBLES
JORDIE
BELLAIRE
DAVE
SHARPE
VALIANT

DOCTOR MIRAGE #4

WRITER: Magdalene Visaggio
ART: Nick Robles
COLORS: Jordie Bellaire
LETTERS: Dave Sharpe
COVER ARTIST: Philip Tan
with Jay David Ramos
ASSISTANT EDITOR:
Drew Baumgartner
EDITOR: Lysa Hawkins

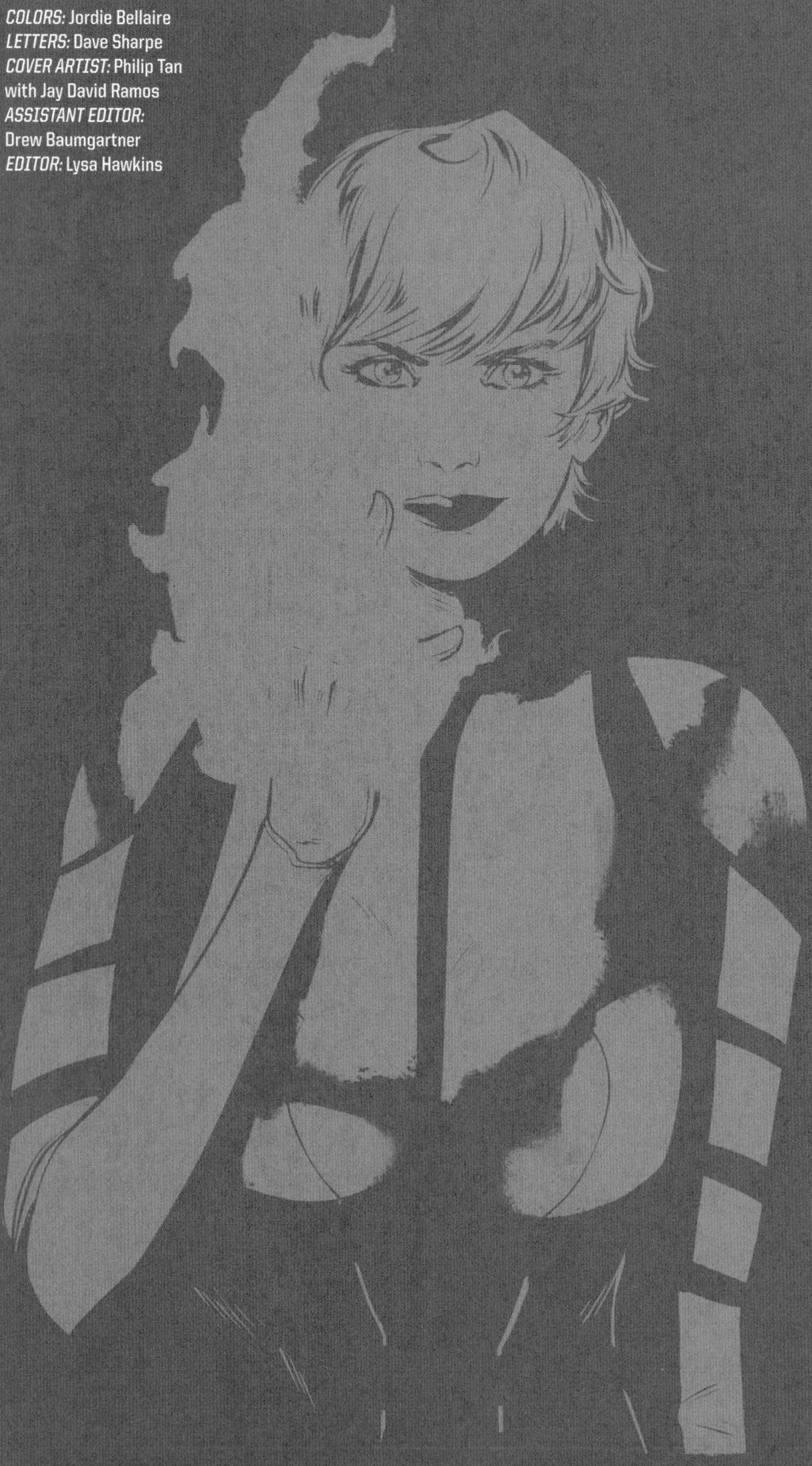

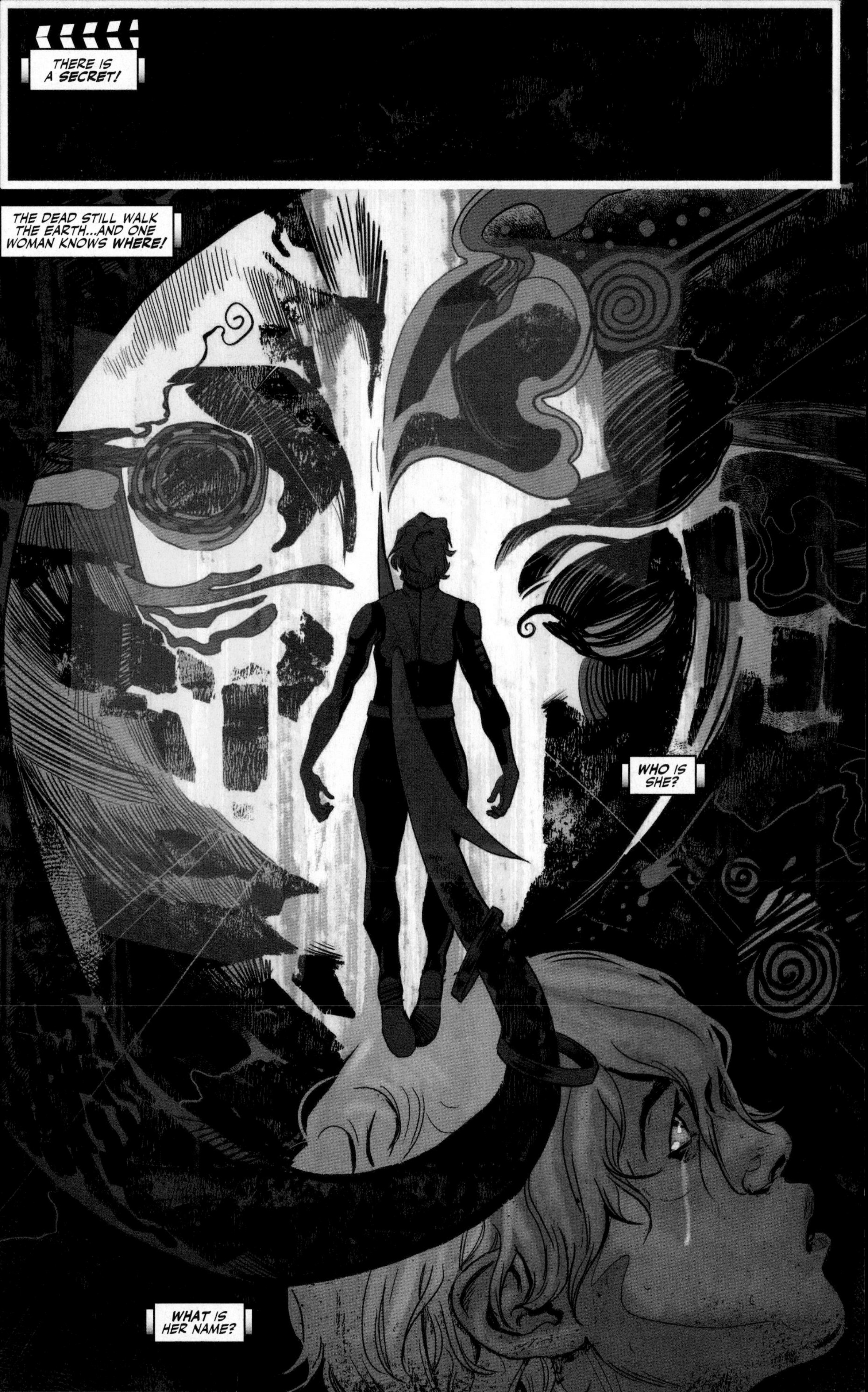
THERE IS A SECRET!
THE DEAD STILL WALK THE EARTH...AND ONE WOMAN KNOWS WHERE!
WHO IS SHE?
WHAT IS HER NAME?

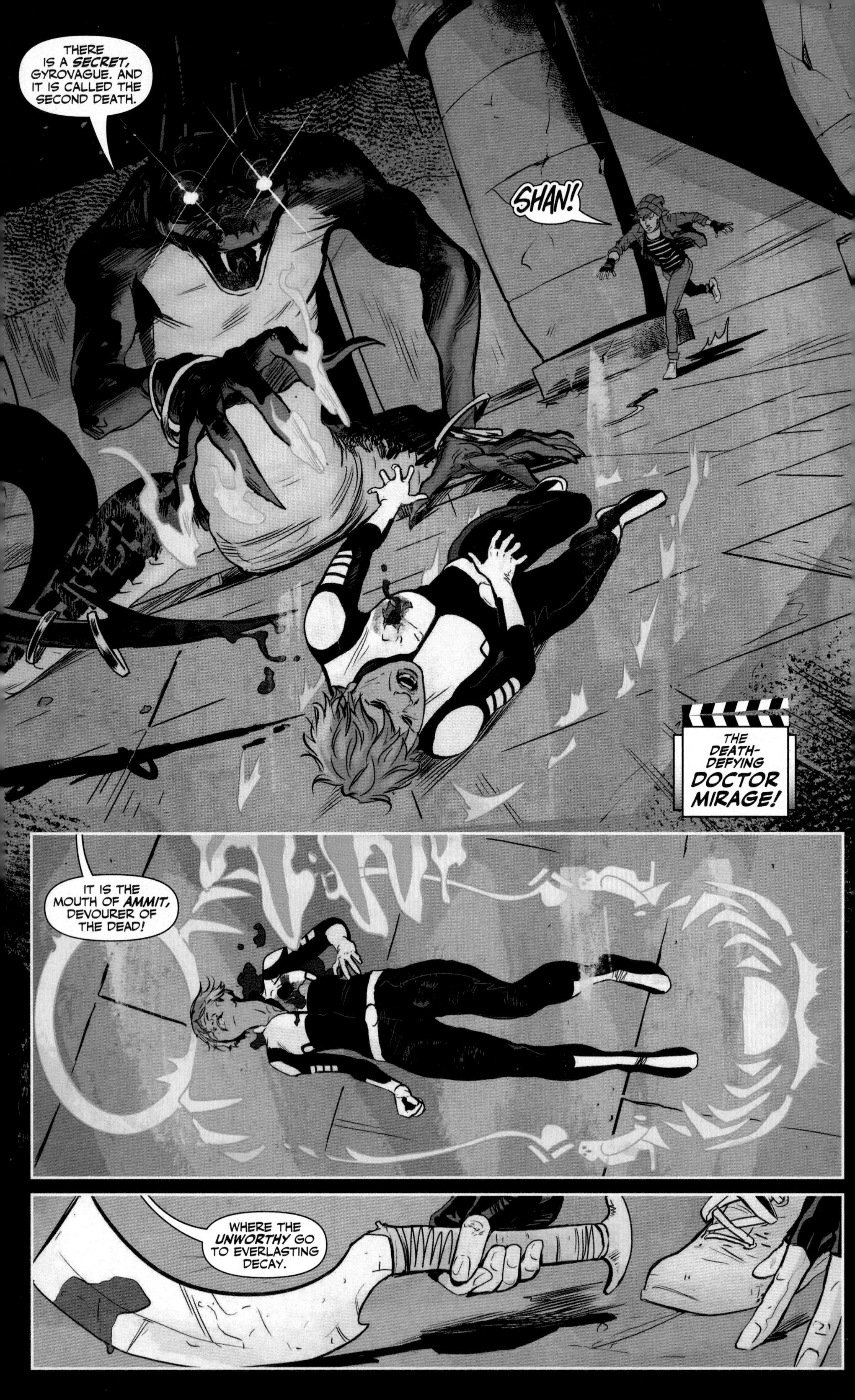
THERE IS A SECRET, GYROVAGUE. AND IT IS CALLED THE SECOND DEATH.
SHAN!
THE DEATH-DEFYING DOCTOR MIRAGE!
IT IS THE MOUTH OF AMMIT, DEVOURER OF THE DEAD!
WHERE THE UNWORTHY GO TO EVERLASTING DECAY.

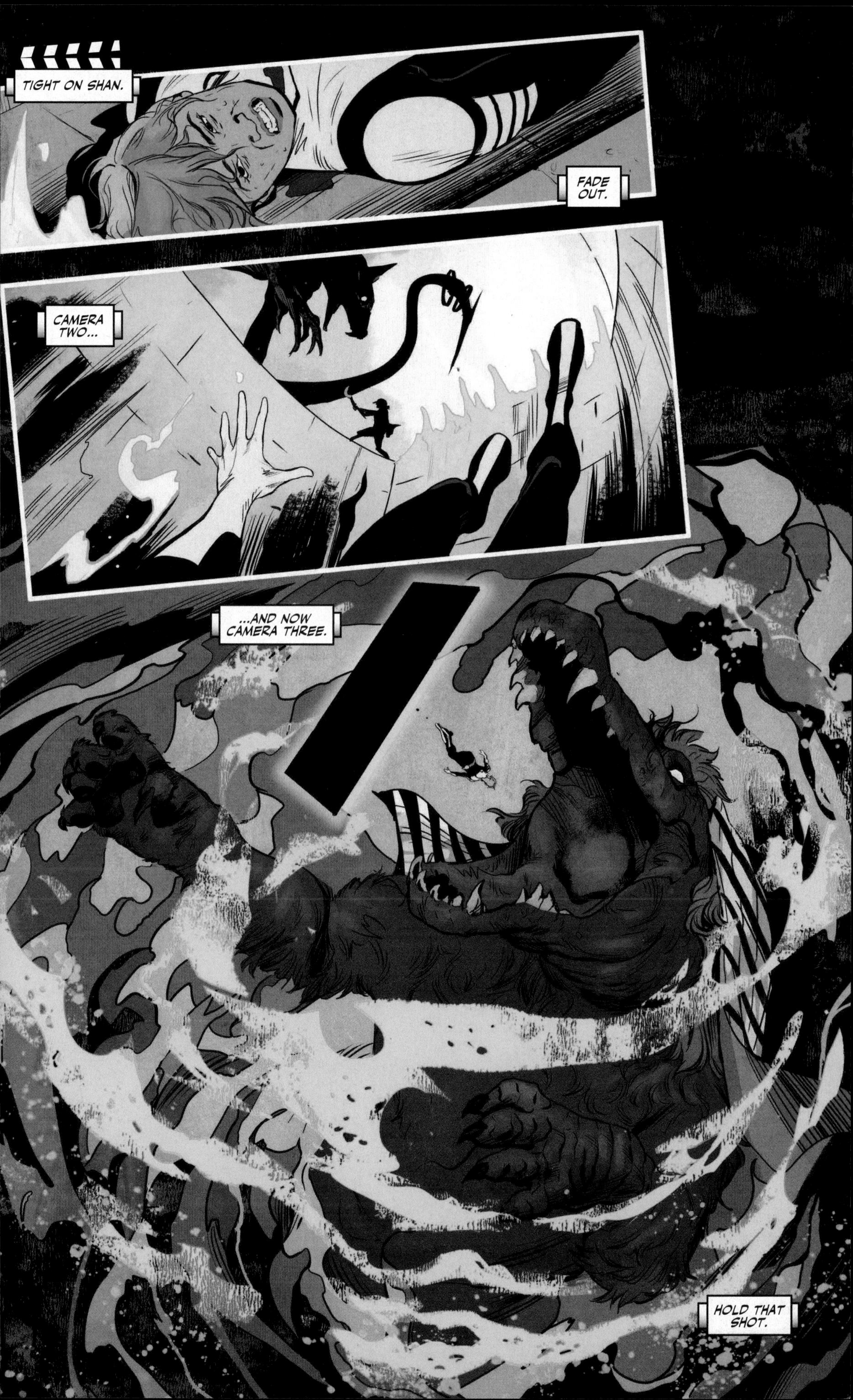
TIGHT ON SHAN.
FADE OUT.
CAMERA TWO...
...AND NOW CAMERA THREE.
HOLD THAT SHOT.

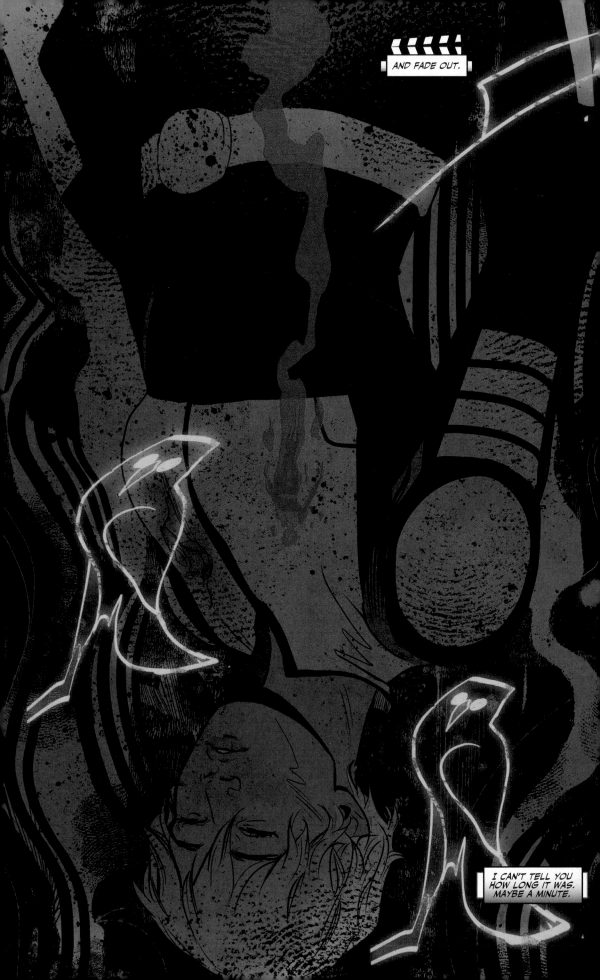

AND FADE OUT.

I CAN'T TELL YOU HOW LONG IT WAS. MAYBE A MINUTE.

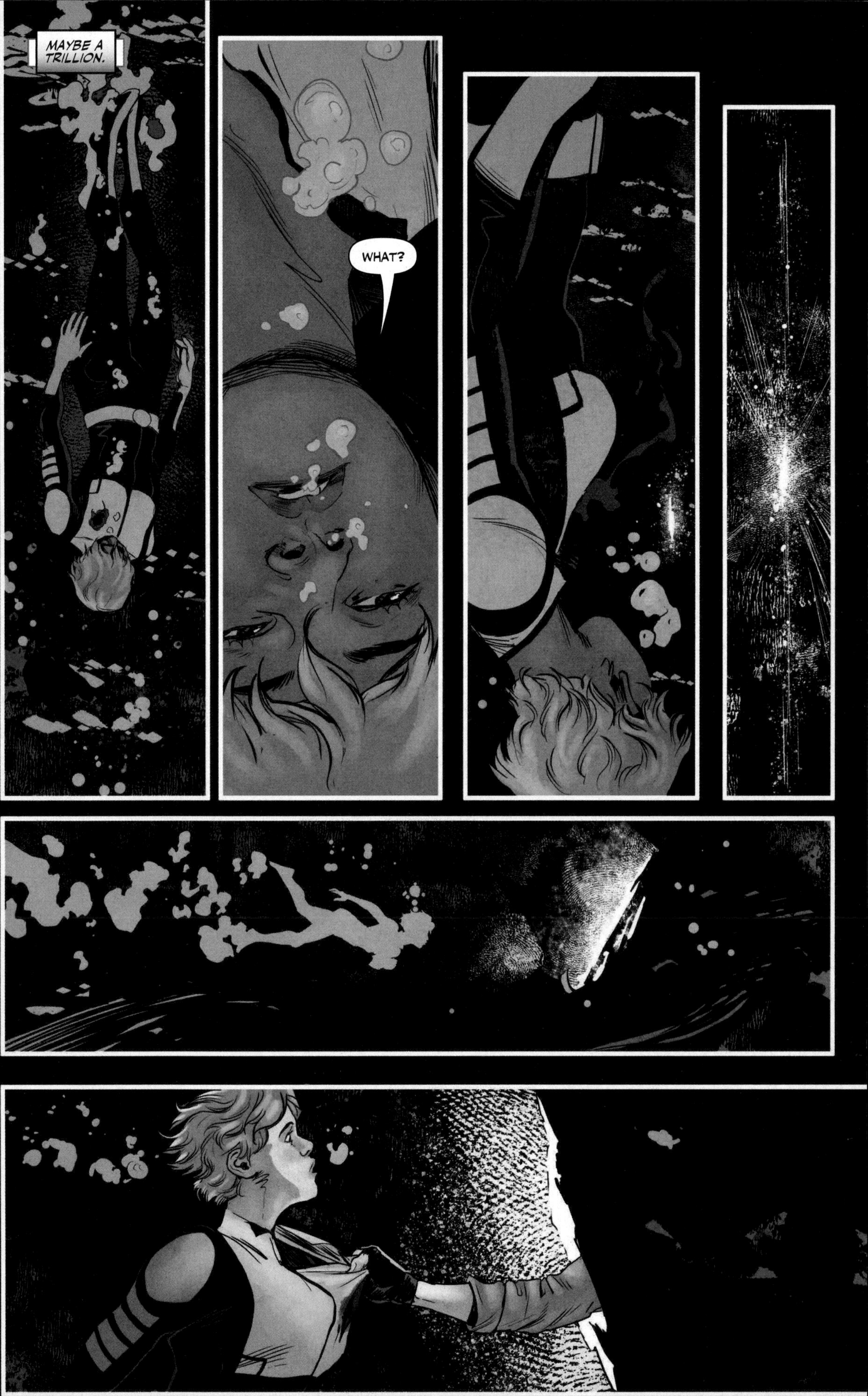
MAYBE A TRILLION.
WHAT?

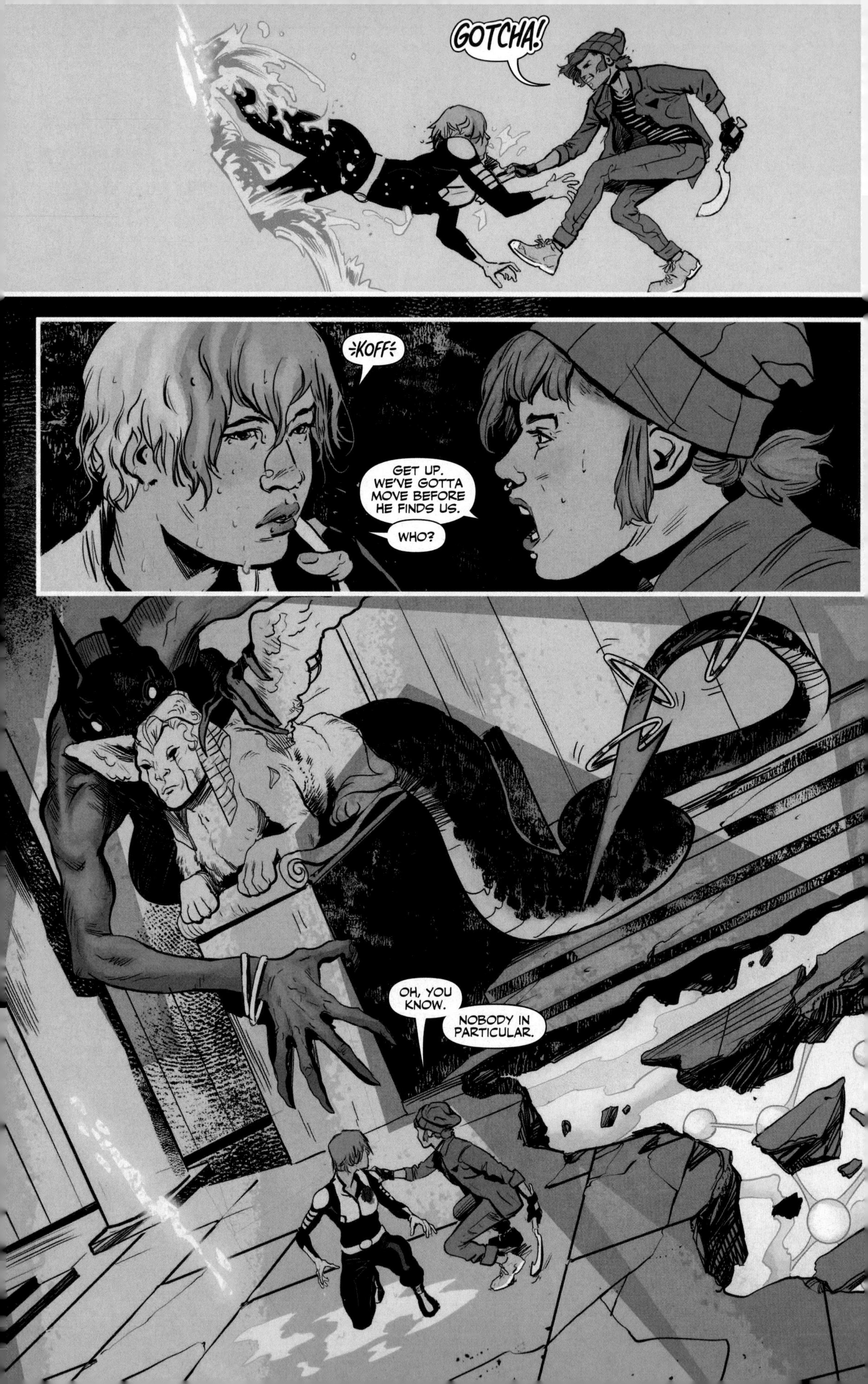
GOTCHA!
KOFF
GET UP. WE'VE GOTTA MOVE BEFORE HE FINDS US.
WHO?
OH, YOU KNOW.
NOBODY IN PARTICULAR.

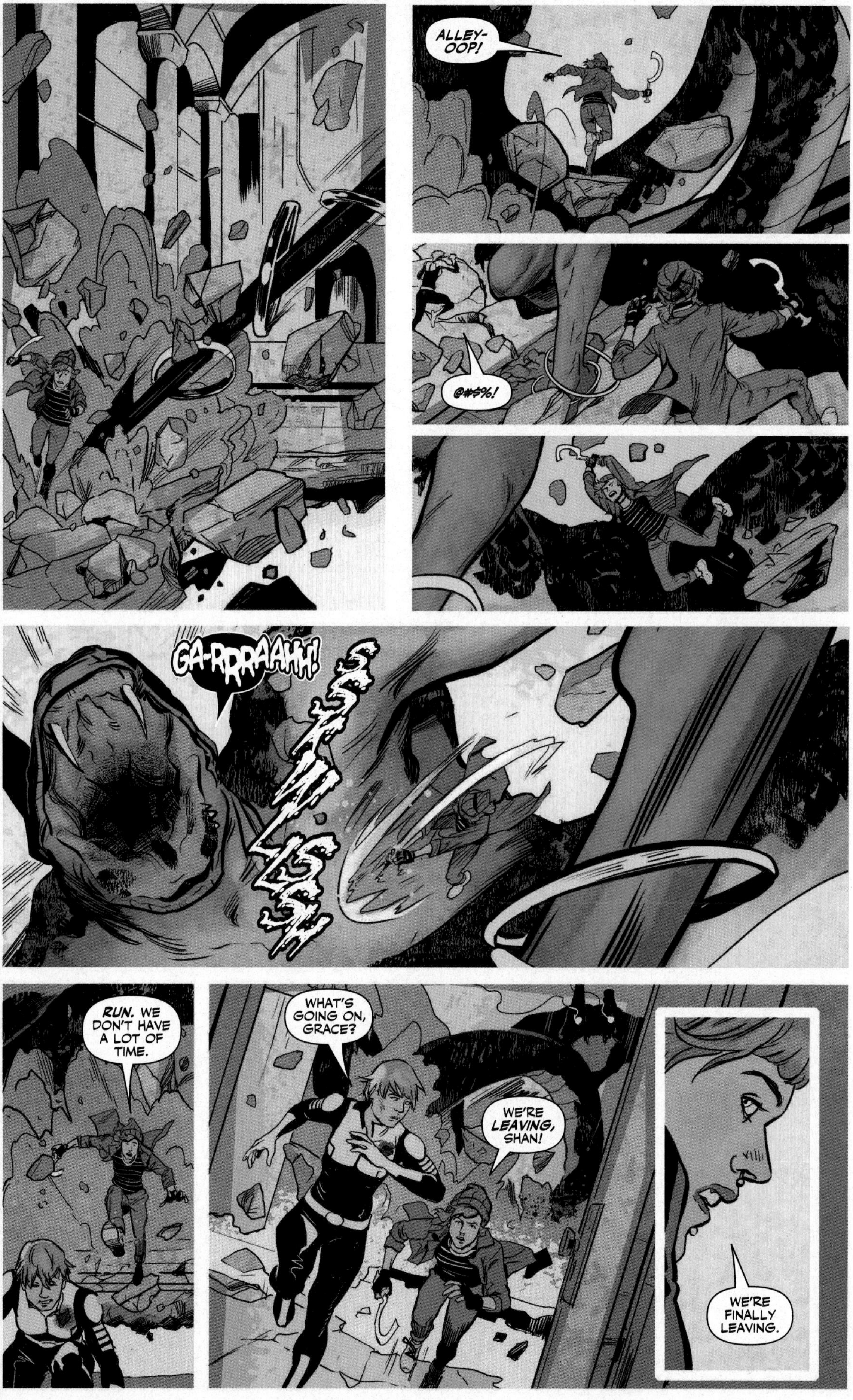
ALLEY-OOP!
@#$%!
GA-RRRAAHH!
SSSHHLLSSSH
RUN. WE DON'T HAVE A LOT OF TIME.
WHAT'S GOING ON, GRACE?
WE'RE LEAVING, SHAN!
WE'RE FINALLY LEAVING.

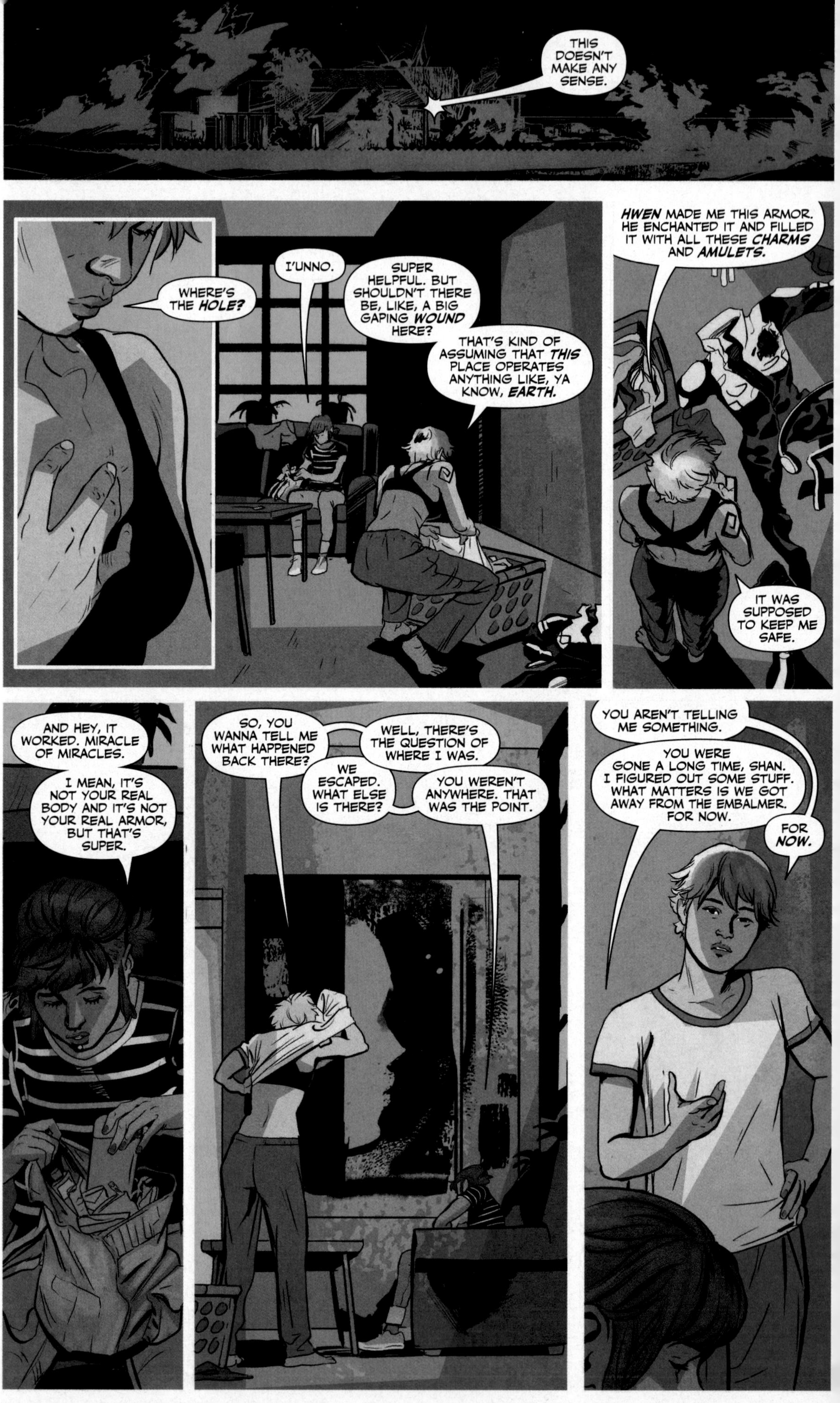
THIS DOESN'T MAKE ANY SENSE.
WHERE'S THE HOLE?
I'UNNO.
SUPER HELPFUL. BUT SHOULDN'T THERE BE, LIKE, A BIG GAPING WOUND HERE?
THAT'S KIND OF ASSUMING THAT THIS PLACE OPERATES ANYTHING LIKE, YA KNOW, EARTH.
HWEN MADE ME THIS ARMOR. HE ENCHANTED IT AND FILLED IT WITH ALL THESE CHARMS AND AMULETS.
IT WAS SUPPOSED TO KEEP ME SAFE.
AND HEY, IT WORKED. MIRACLE OF MIRACLES.
I MEAN, IT'S NOT YOUR REAL BODY AND IT'S NOT YOUR REAL ARMOR, BUT THAT'S SUPER.
SO, YOU WANNA TELL ME WHAT HAPPENED BACK THERE?
WE ESCAPED. WHAT ELSE IS THERE?
WELL, THERE'S THE QUESTION OF WHERE I WAS.
YOU WEREN'T ANYWHERE. THAT WAS THE POINT.
YOU AREN'T TELLING ME SOMETHING.
YOU WERE GONE A LONG TIME, SHAN. I FIGURED OUT SOME STUFF. WHAT MATTERS IS WE GOT AWAY FROM THE EMBALMER. FOR NOW.
FOR NOW.

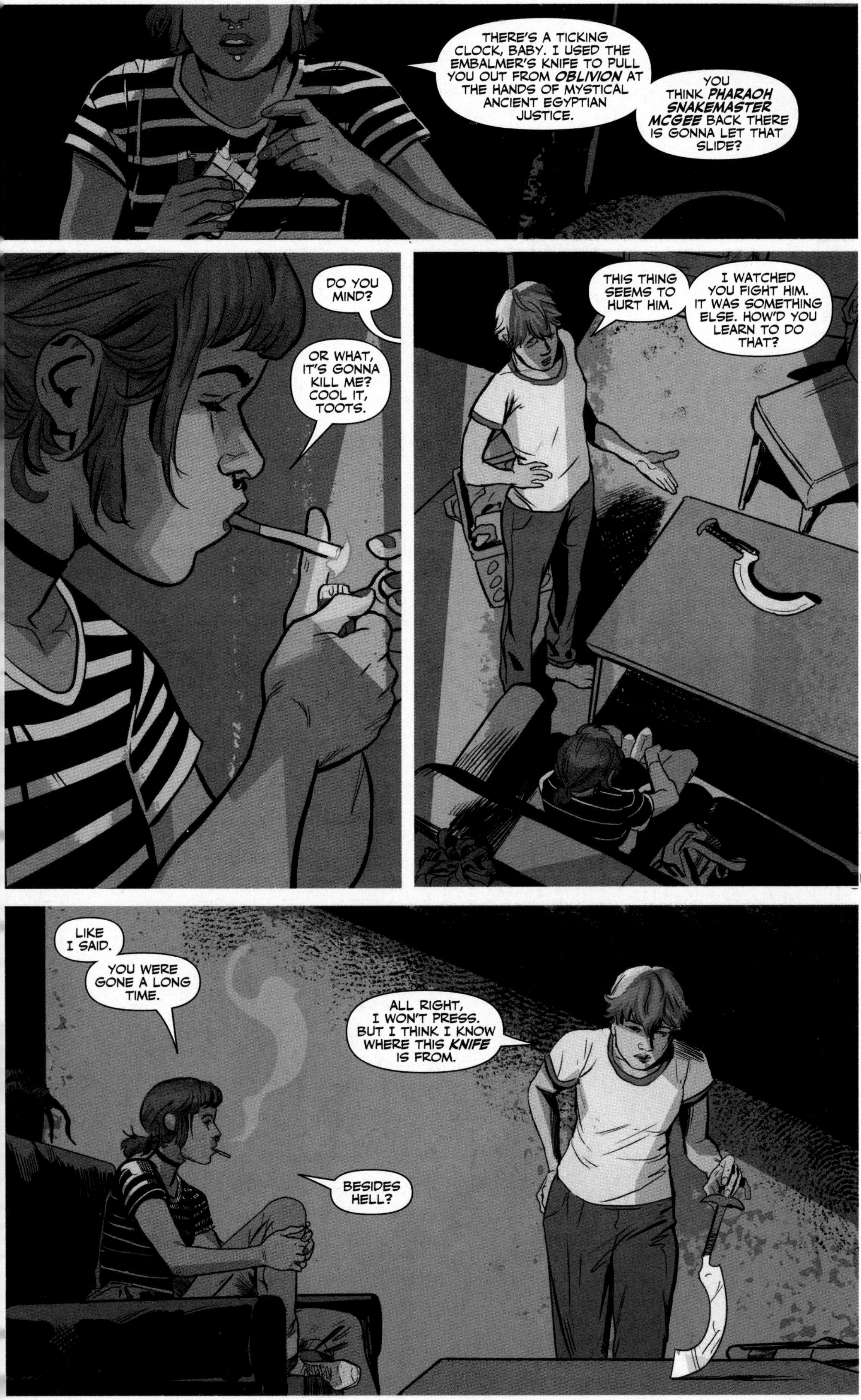
THERE'S A TICKING CLOCK, BABY. I USED THE EMBALMER'S KNIFE TO PULL YOU OUT FROM *OBLIVION* AT THE HANDS OF MYSTICAL ANCIENT EGYPTIAN JUSTICE.
YOU THINK ***PHARAOH SNAKEMASTER MCGEE*** BACK THERE IS GONNA LET THAT SLIDE?
DO YOU MIND?
OR WHAT, IT'S GONNA KILL ME? COOL IT, TOOTS.
THIS THING SEEMS TO HURT HIM.
I WATCHED YOU FIGHT HIM. IT WAS SOMETHING ELSE. HOW'D YOU LEARN TO DO THAT?
LIKE I SAID.
YOU WERE GONE A LONG TIME.
ALL RIGHT, I WON'T PRESS. BUT I THINK I KNOW WHERE THIS *KNIFE* IS FROM.
BESIDES HELL?

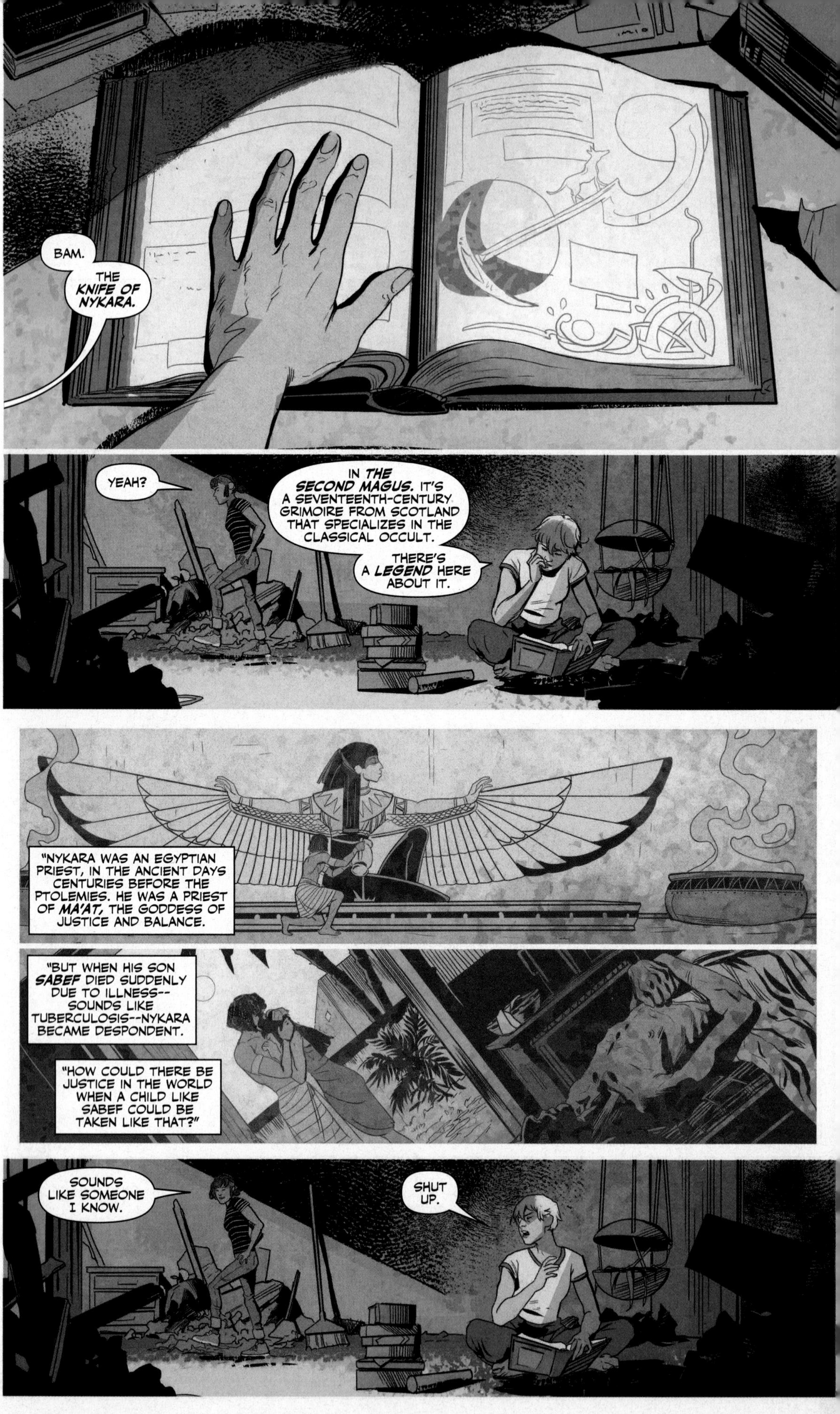
BAM.
THE KNIFE OF NYKARA.
YEAH?
IN THE SECOND MAGUS. IT'S A SEVENTEENTH-CENTURY GRIMOIRE FROM SCOTLAND THAT SPECIALIZES IN THE CLASSICAL OCCULT.
THERE'S A LEGEND HERE ABOUT IT.
"NYKARA WAS AN EGYPTIAN PRIEST, IN THE ANCIENT DAYS CENTURIES BEFORE THE PTOLEMIES. HE WAS A PRIEST OF MA'AT, THE GODDESS OF JUSTICE AND BALANCE.
"BUT WHEN HIS SON SABEF DIED SUDDENLY DUE TO ILLNESS-- SOUNDS LIKE TUBERCULOSIS--NYKARA BECAME DESPONDENT.
"HOW COULD THERE BE JUSTICE IN THE WORLD WHEN A CHILD LIKE SABEF COULD BE TAKEN LIKE THAT?"
SOUNDS LIKE SOMEONE I KNOW.
SHUT UP.

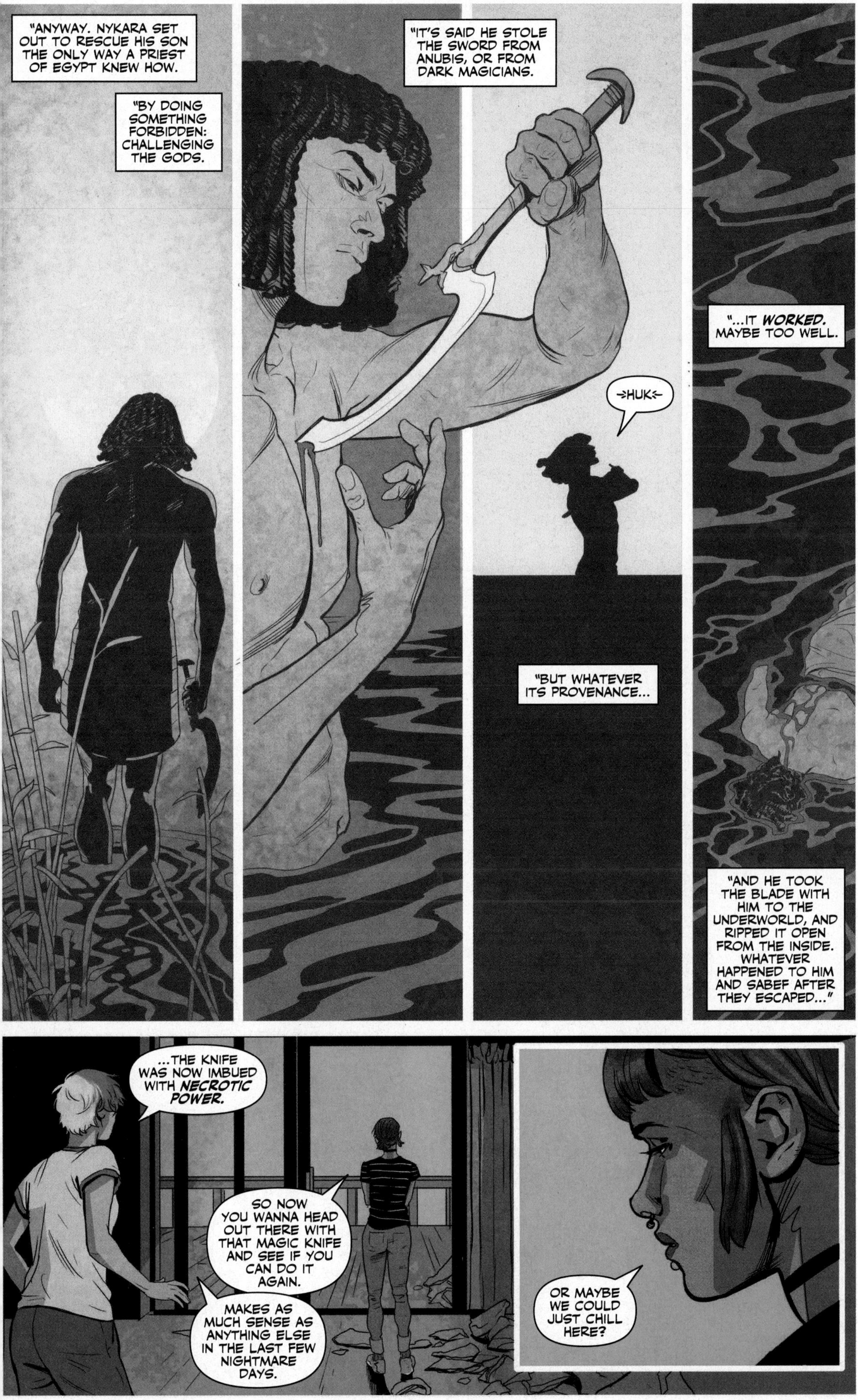
"ANYWAY. NYKARA SET OUT TO RESCUE HIS SON THE ONLY WAY A PRIEST OF EGYPT KNEW HOW.
"BY DOING SOMETHING FORBIDDEN: CHALLENGING THE GODS.
"IT'S SAID HE STOLE THE SWORD FROM ANUBIS, OR FROM DARK MAGICIANS.
HUK
"BUT WHATEVER ITS PROVENANCE...
"...IT WORKED. MAYBE TOO WELL.
"AND HE TOOK THE BLADE WITH HIM TO THE UNDERWORLD, AND RIPPED IT OPEN FROM THE INSIDE. WHATEVER HAPPENED TO HIM AND SABEF AFTER THEY ESCAPED..."
...THE KNIFE WAS NOW IMBUED WITH NECROTIC POWER.
SO NOW YOU WANNA HEAD OUT THERE WITH THAT MAGIC KNIFE AND SEE IF YOU CAN DO IT AGAIN.
MAKES AS MUCH SENSE AS ANYTHING ELSE IN THE LAST FEW NIGHTMARE DAYS.
OR MAYBE WE COULD JUST CHILL HERE?

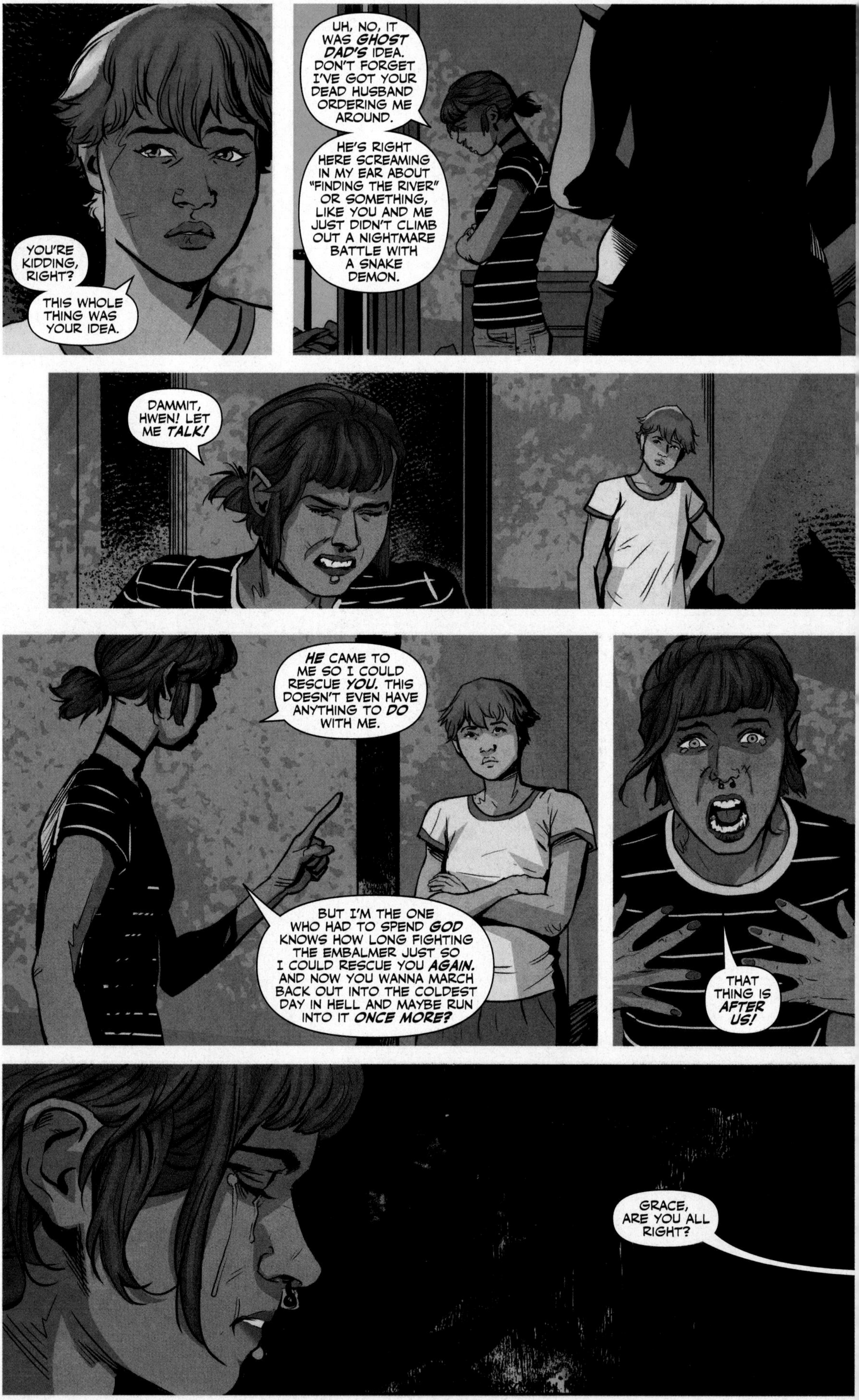
YOU'RE KIDDING, RIGHT?
THIS WHOLE THING WAS YOUR IDEA.
UH, NO, IT WAS GHOST DAD'S IDEA. DON'T FORGET I'VE GOT YOUR DEAD HUSBAND ORDERING ME AROUND.
HE'S RIGHT HERE SCREAMING IN MY EAR ABOUT "FINDING THE RIVER" OR SOMETHING, LIKE YOU AND ME JUST DIDN'T CLIMB OUT A NIGHTMARE BATTLE WITH A SNAKE DEMON.
DAMMIT, HWEN! LET ME TALK!
HE CAME TO ME SO I COULD RESCUE YOU. THIS DOESN'T EVEN HAVE ANYTHING TO DO WITH ME.
BUT I'M THE ONE WHO HAD TO SPEND GOD KNOWS HOW LONG FIGHTING THE EMBALMER JUST SO I COULD RESCUE YOU AGAIN. AND NOW YOU WANNA MARCH BACK OUT INTO THE COLDEST DAY IN HELL AND MAYBE RUN INTO IT ONCE MORE?
THAT THING IS AFTER US!
GRACE, ARE YOU ALL RIGHT?

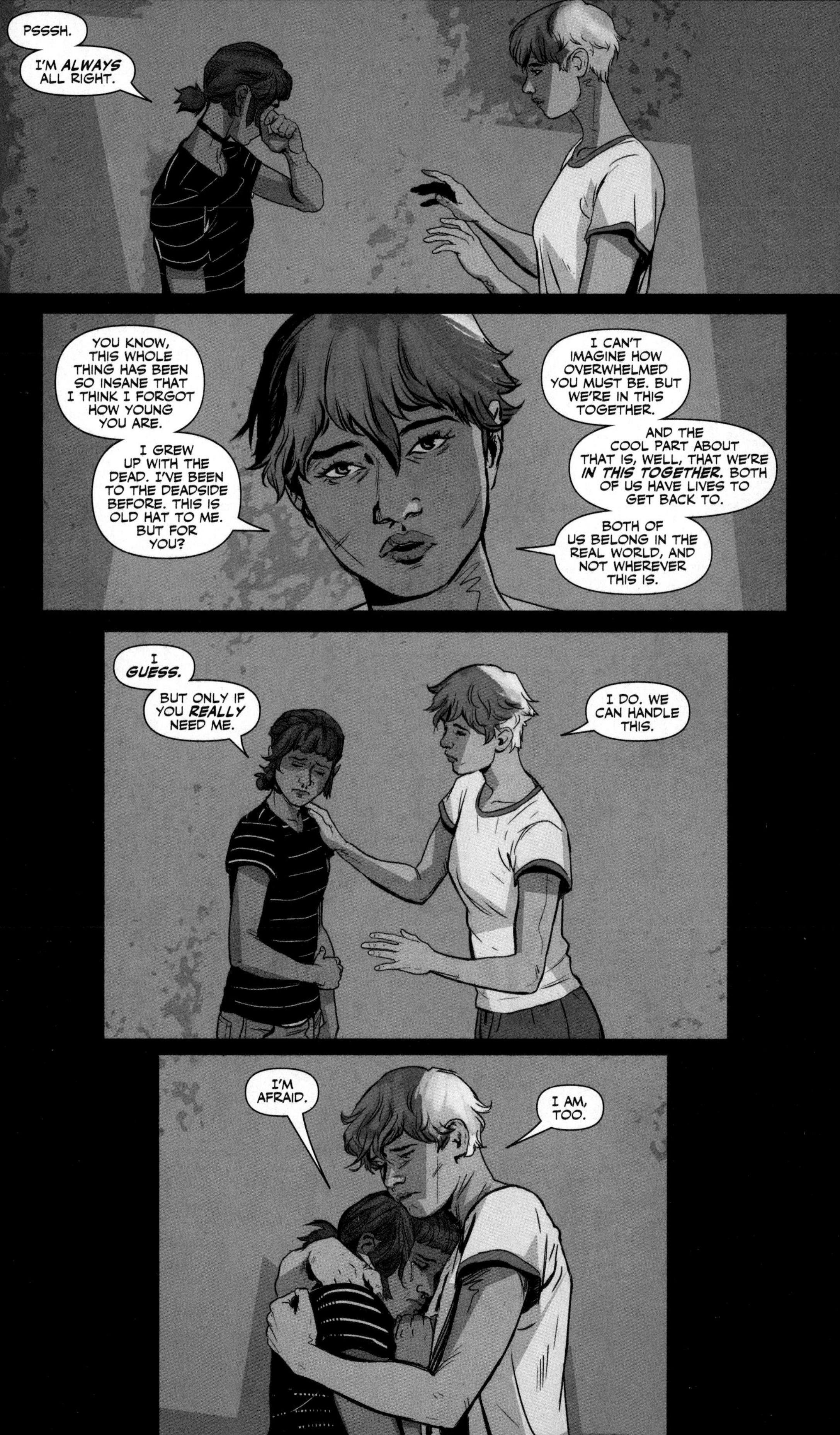
PSSSH.
I'M ALWAYS ALL RIGHT.
YOU KNOW, THIS WHOLE THING HAS BEEN SO INSANE THAT I THINK I FORGOT HOW YOUNG YOU ARE.
I GREW UP WITH THE DEAD. I'VE BEEN TO THE DEADSIDE BEFORE. THIS IS OLD HAT TO ME. BUT FOR YOU?
I CAN'T IMAGINE HOW OVERWHELMED YOU MUST BE. BUT WE'RE IN THIS TOGETHER.
AND THE COOL PART ABOUT THAT IS, WELL, THAT WE'RE IN THIS TOGETHER. BOTH OF US HAVE LIVES TO GET BACK TO.
BOTH OF US BELONG IN THE REAL WORLD, AND NOT WHEREVER THIS IS.
I GUESS.
BUT ONLY IF YOU REALLY NEED ME.
I DO. WE CAN HANDLE THIS.
I'M AFRAID.
I AM, TOO.

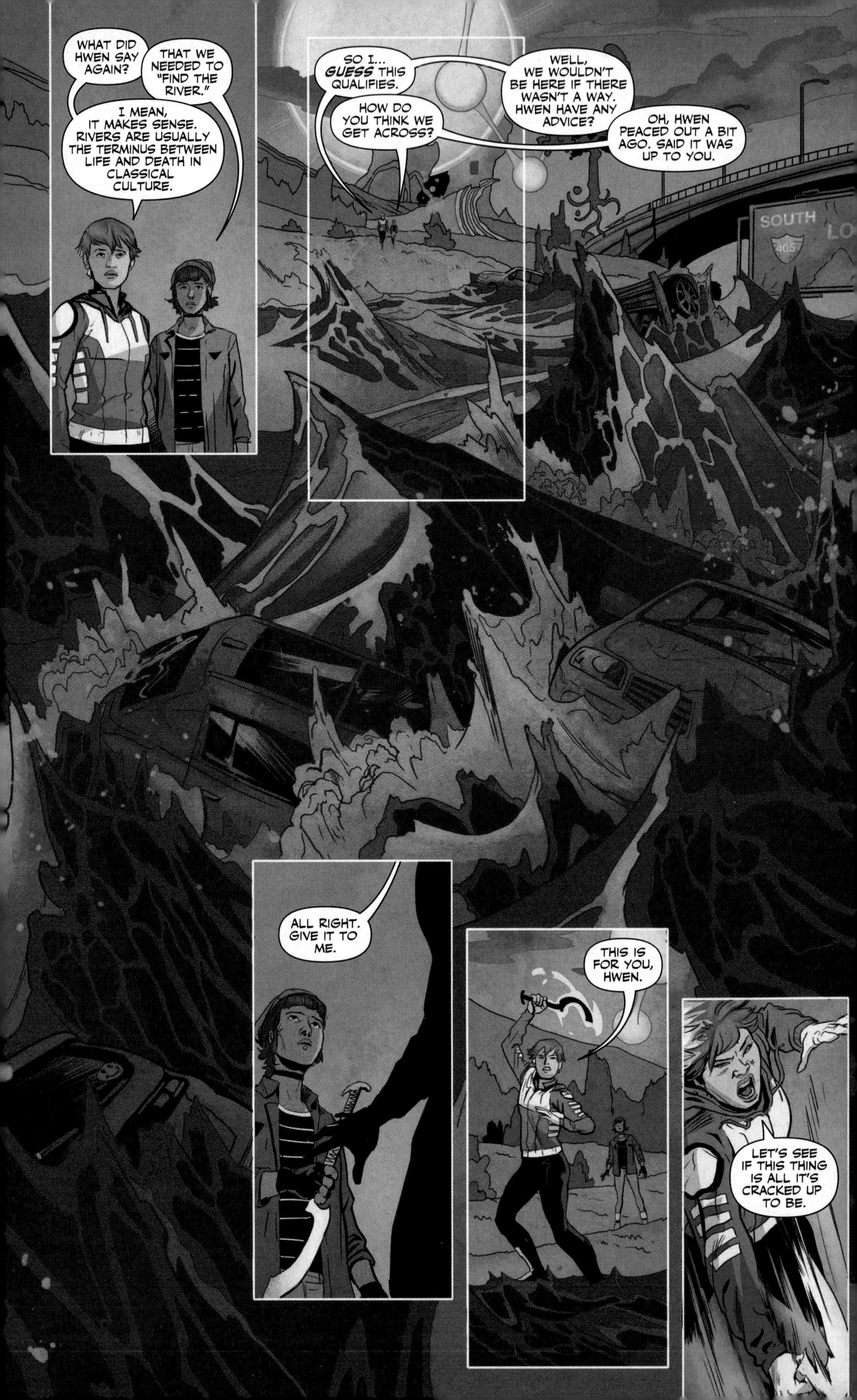
WHAT DID HWEN SAY AGAIN?
THAT WE NEEDED TO "FIND THE RIVER."
I MEAN, IT MAKES SENSE. RIVERS ARE USUALLY THE TERMINUS BETWEEN LIFE AND DEATH IN CLASSICAL CULTURE.
SO I... GUESS THIS QUALIFIES.
HOW DO YOU THINK WE GET ACROSS?
WELL, WE WOULDN'T BE HERE IF THERE WASN'T A WAY. HWEN HAVE ANY ADVICE?
OH, HWEN PEACED OUT A BIT AGO. SAID IT WAS UP TO YOU.
SOUTH
405
ALL RIGHT. GIVE IT TO ME.
THIS IS FOR YOU, HWEN.
LET'S SEE IF THIS THING IS ALL IT'S CRACKED UP TO BE.

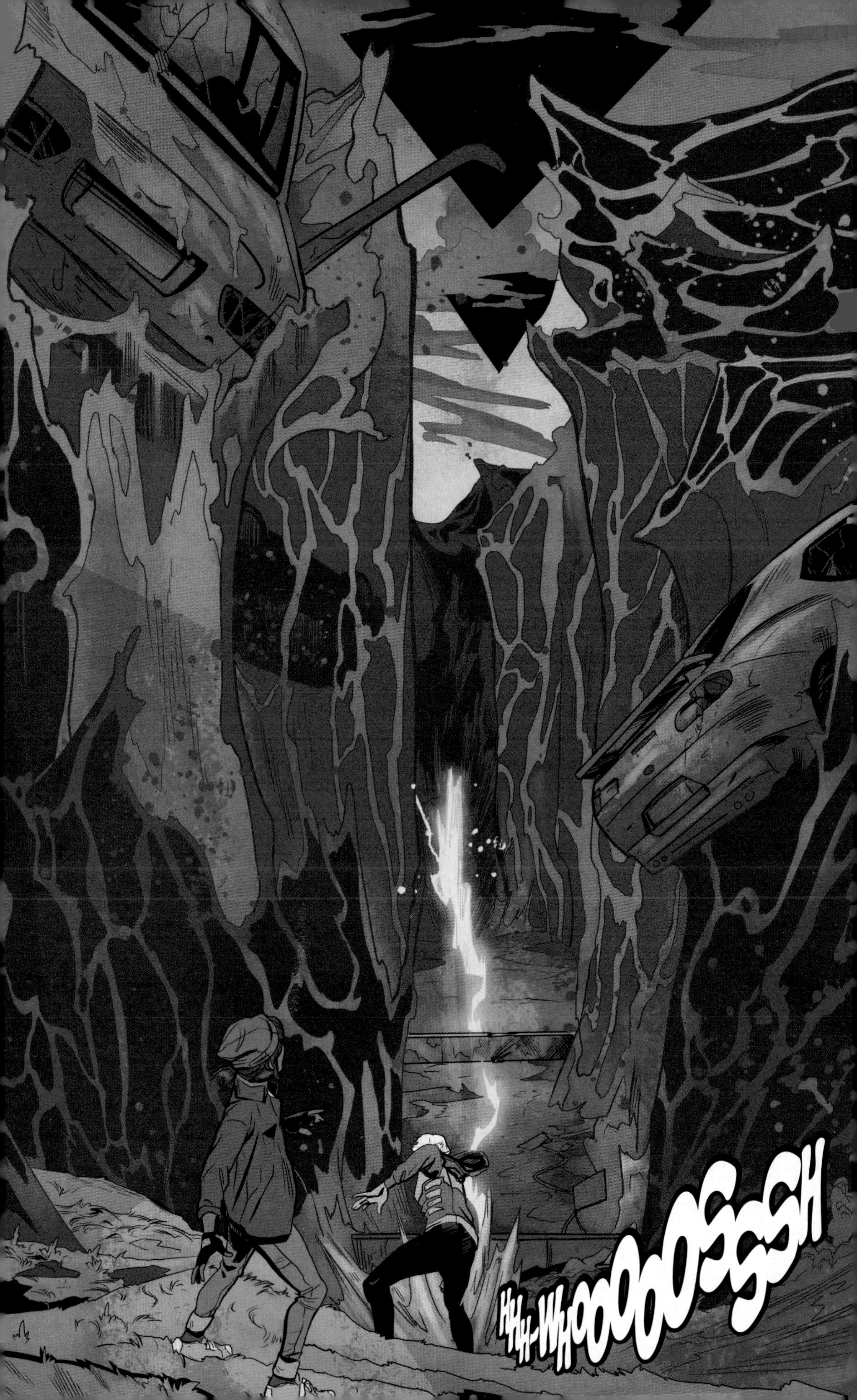
HHH-WHOOOOOOSSSH

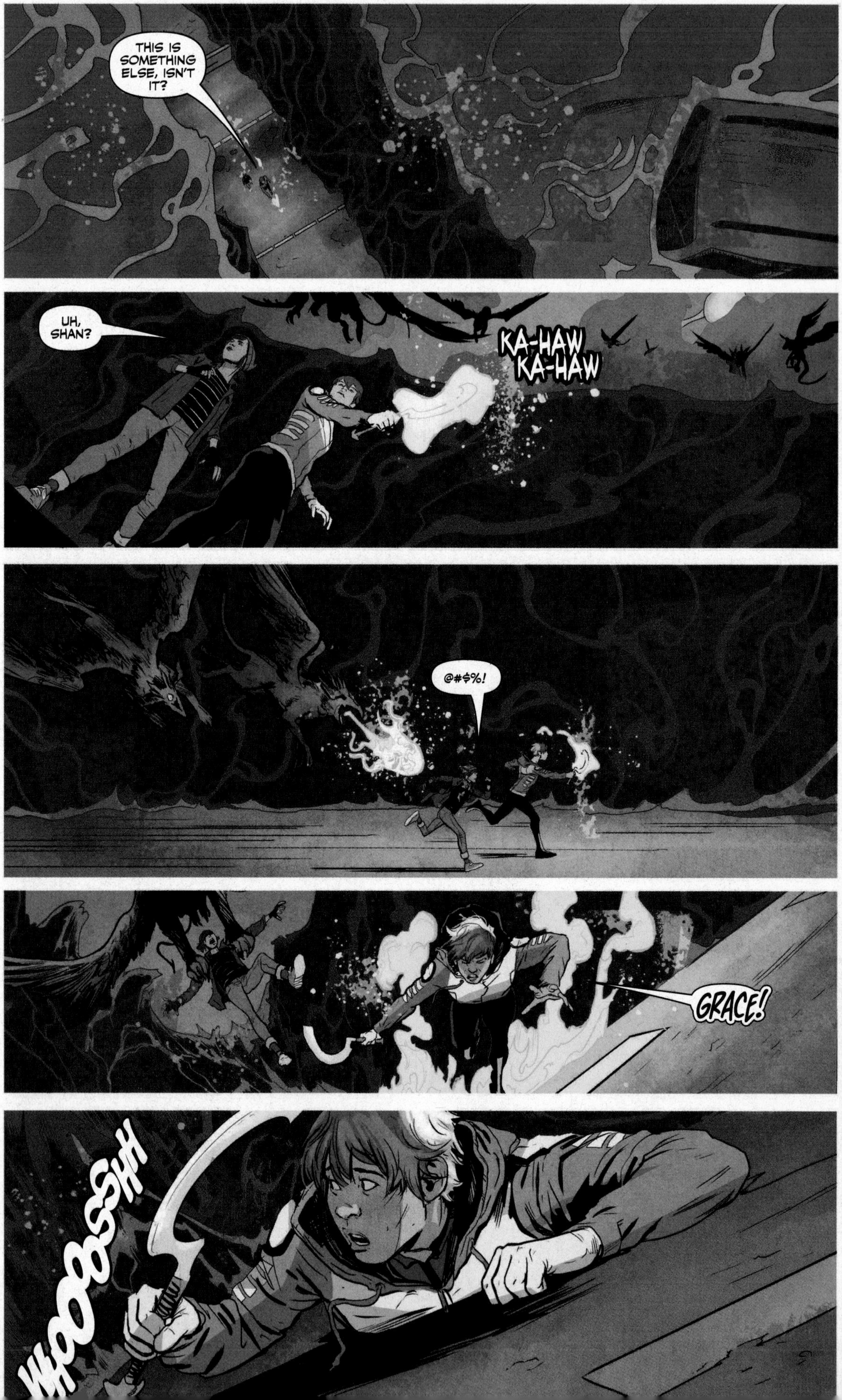
THIS IS SOMETHING ELSE, ISN'T IT?
UH, SHAN?
KA-HAW KA-HAW
@#$%!
GRACE!
WHOOOSSHH

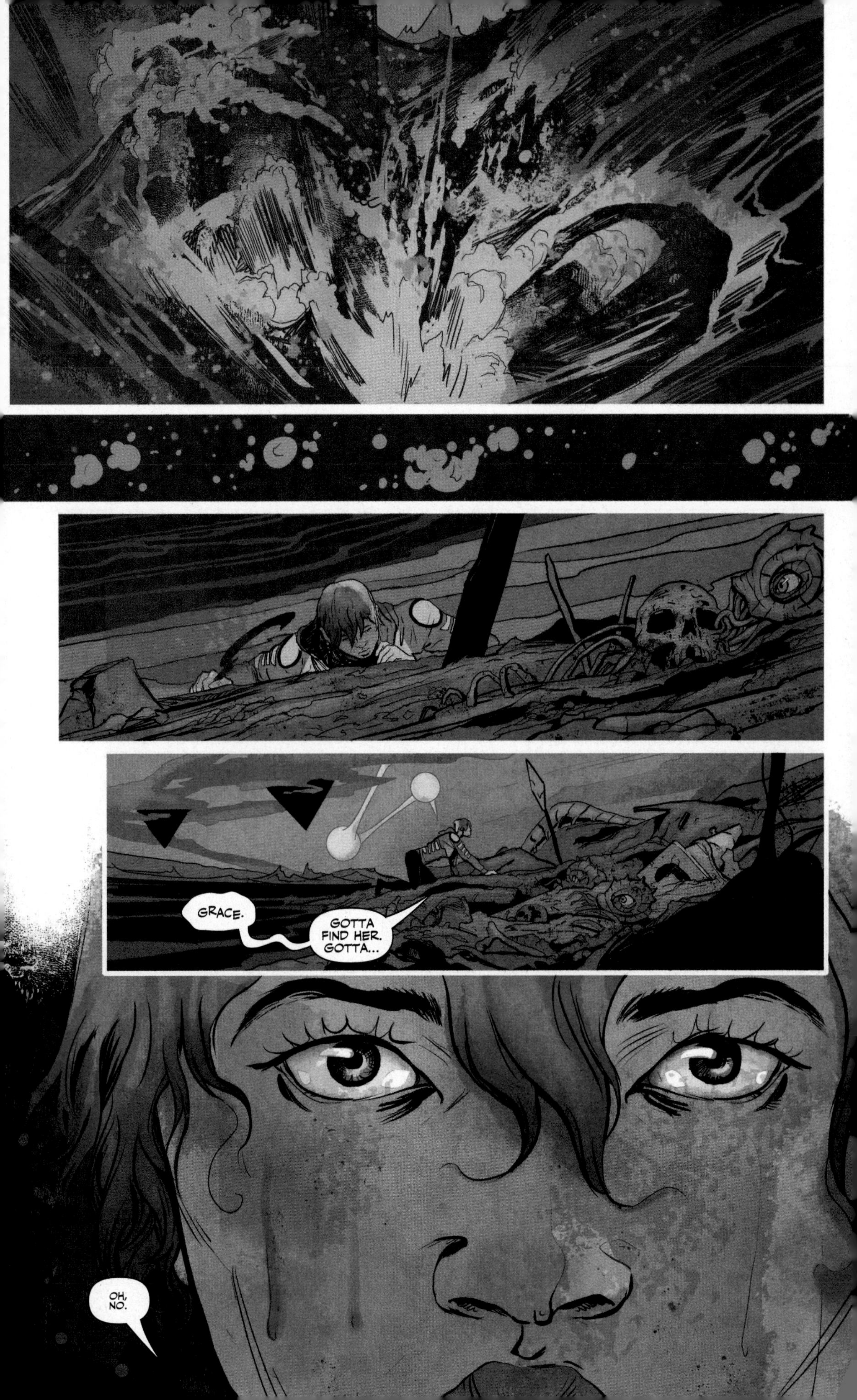
GRACE.
GOTTA FIND HER. GOTTA...
OH, NO.

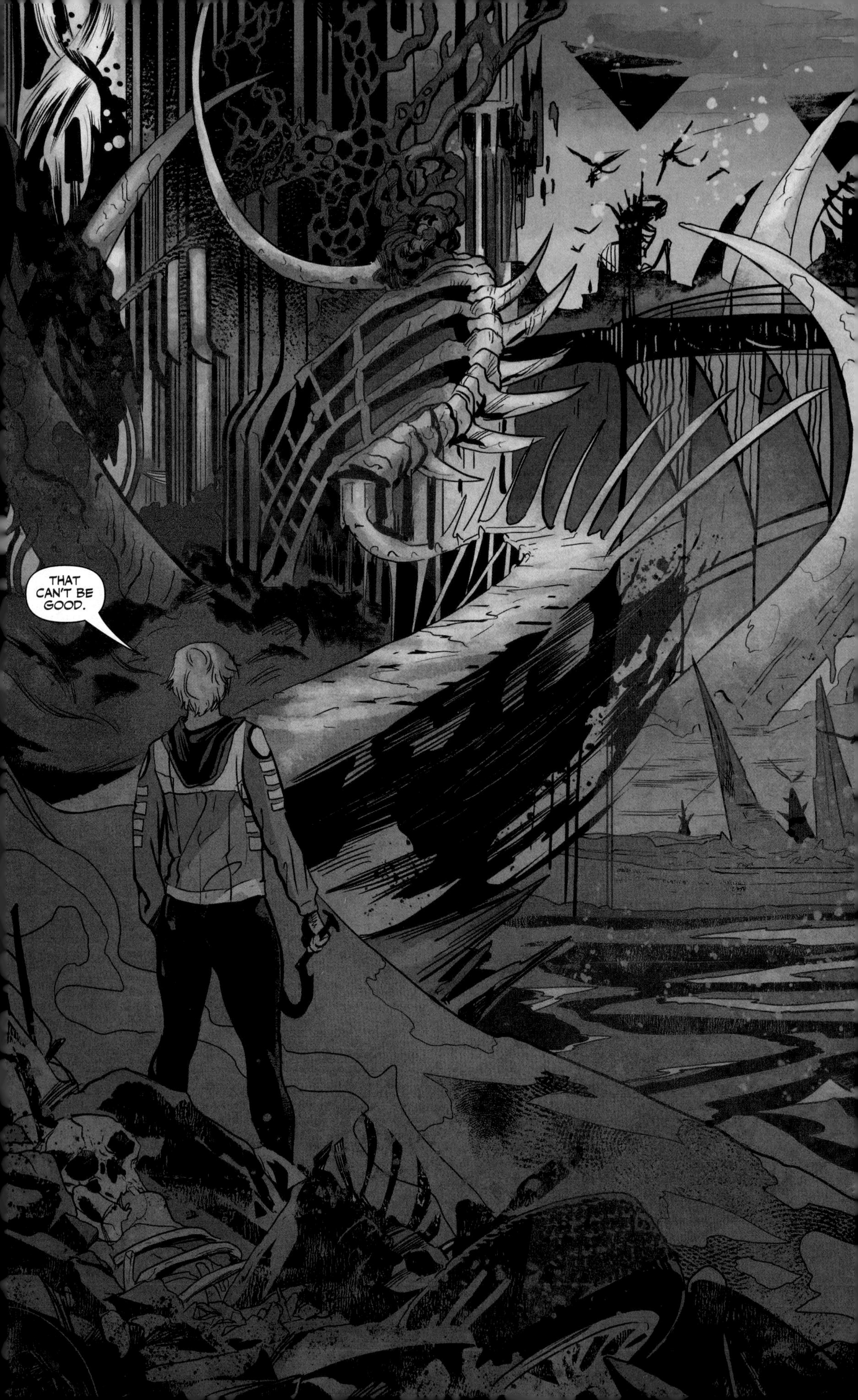
THAT CAN'T BE GOOD.

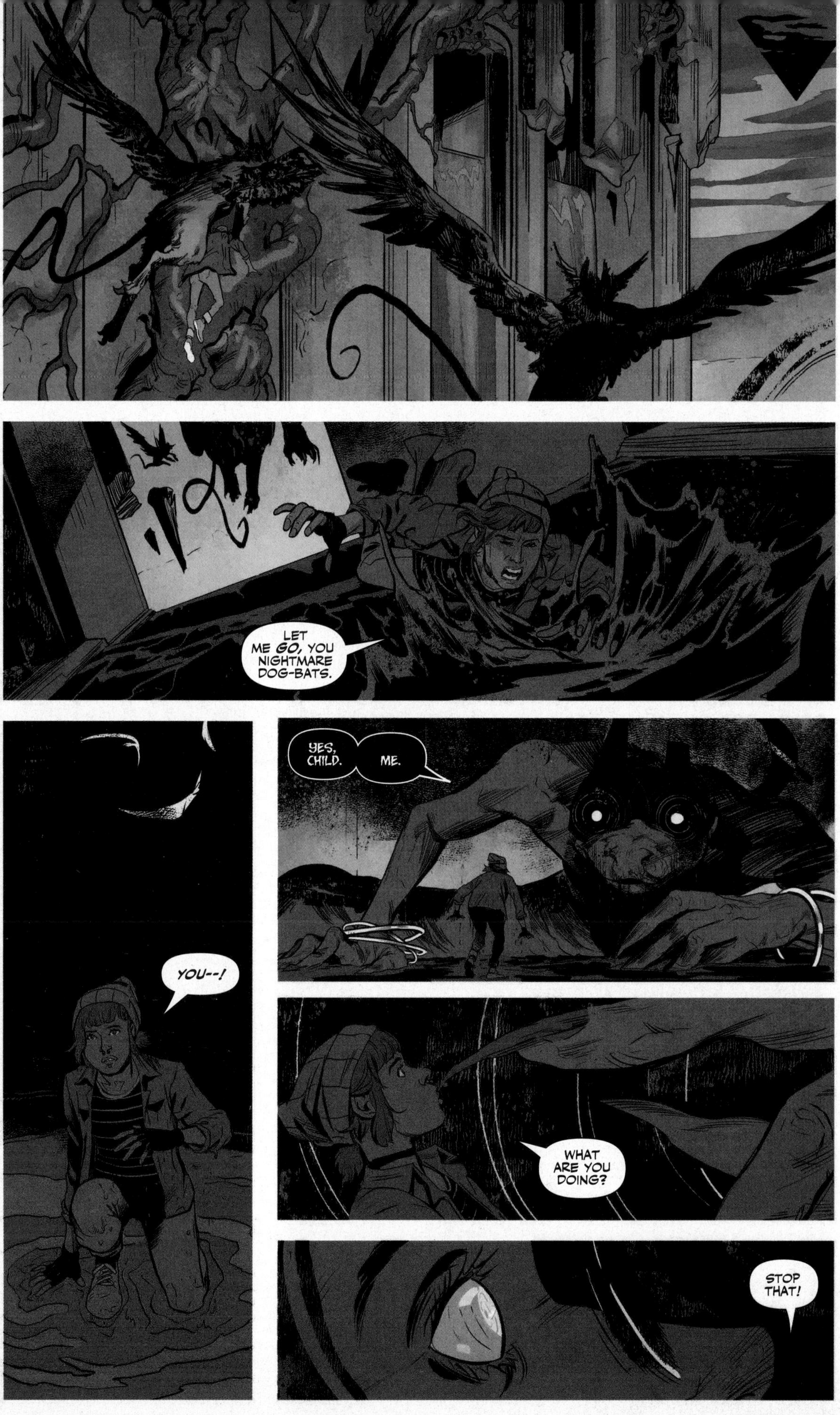
LET ME GO, YOU NIGHTMARE DOG-BATS.
YES, CHILD.
ME.
YOU--!
WHAT ARE YOU DOING?
STOP THAT!

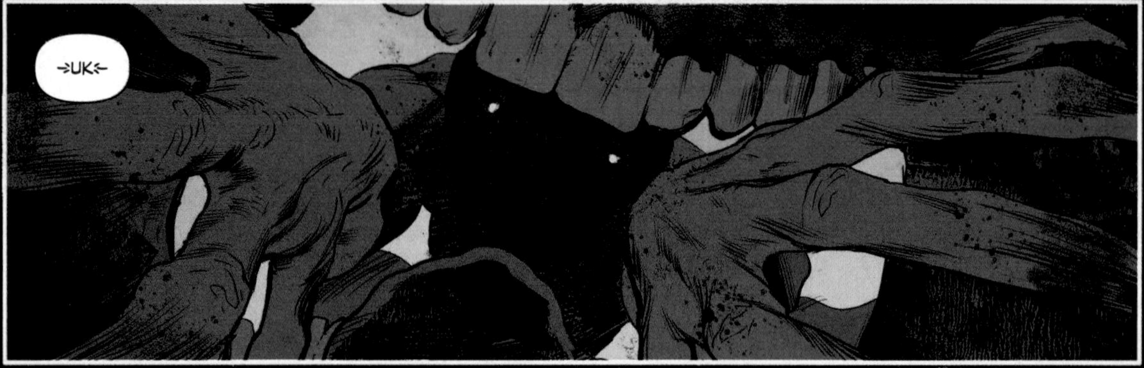

UK

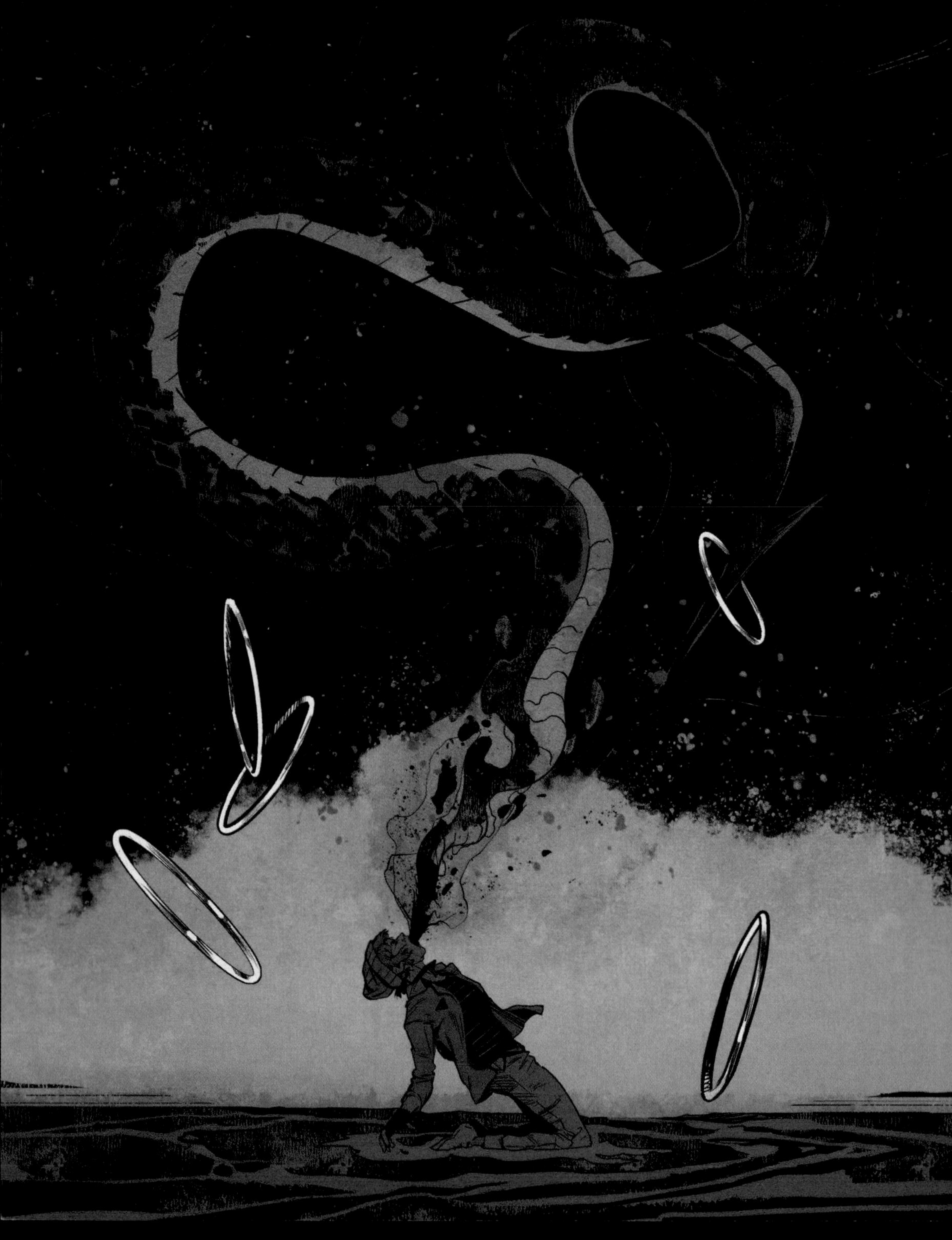

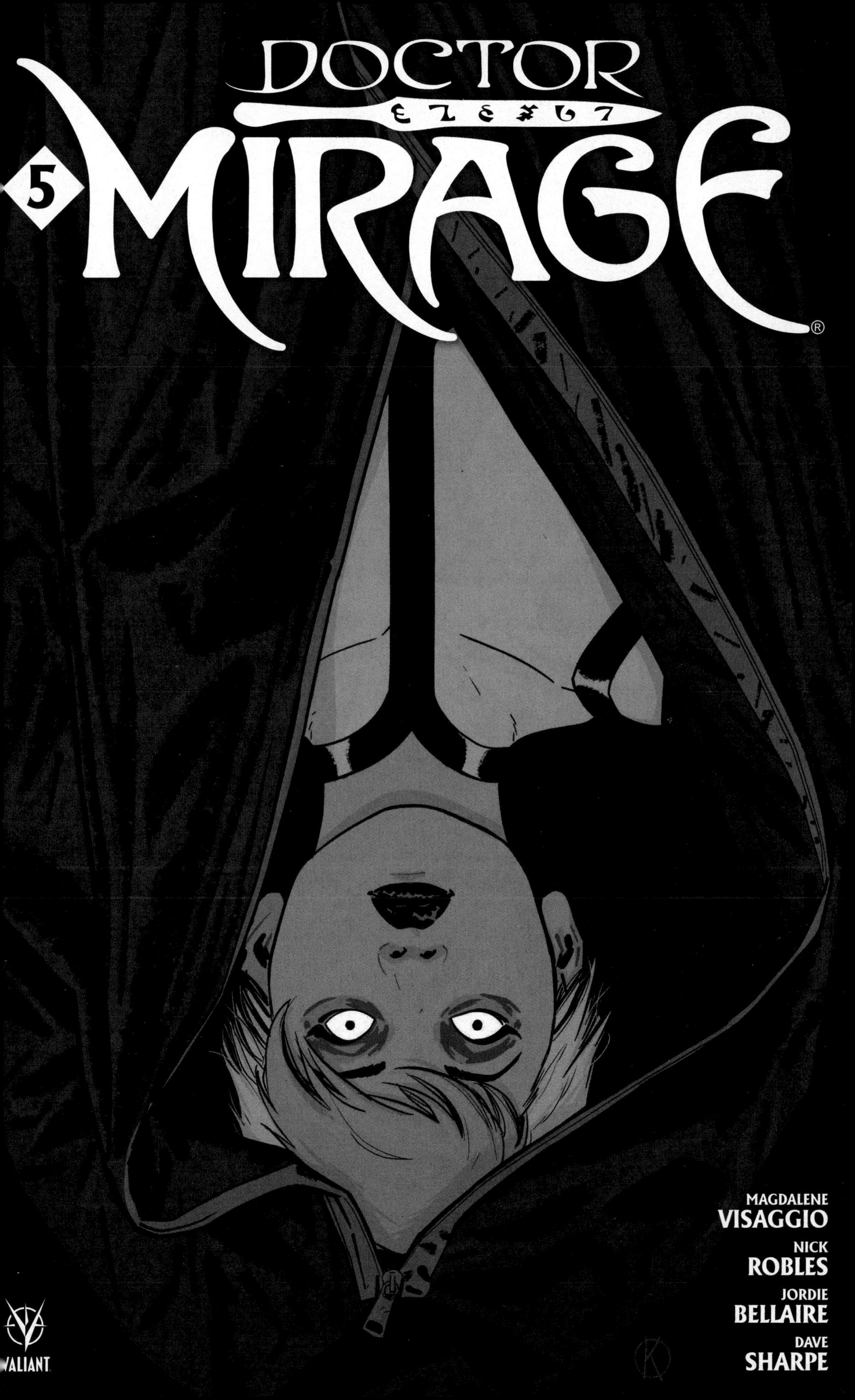
DOCTOR
5
MIRAGE
MAGDALENE
VISAGGIO
NICK
ROBLES
JORDIE
BELLAIRE
DAVE
SHARPE
VALIANT

DOCTOR MIRAGE #5

WRITER: Magdalene Visaggio
ART: Nick Robles
COLORS: Jordie Bellaire
LETTERS: Dave Sharpe
COVER ARTIST: Kano
ASSISTANT EDITOR:
Drew Baumgartner
EDITOR: Lysa Hawkins

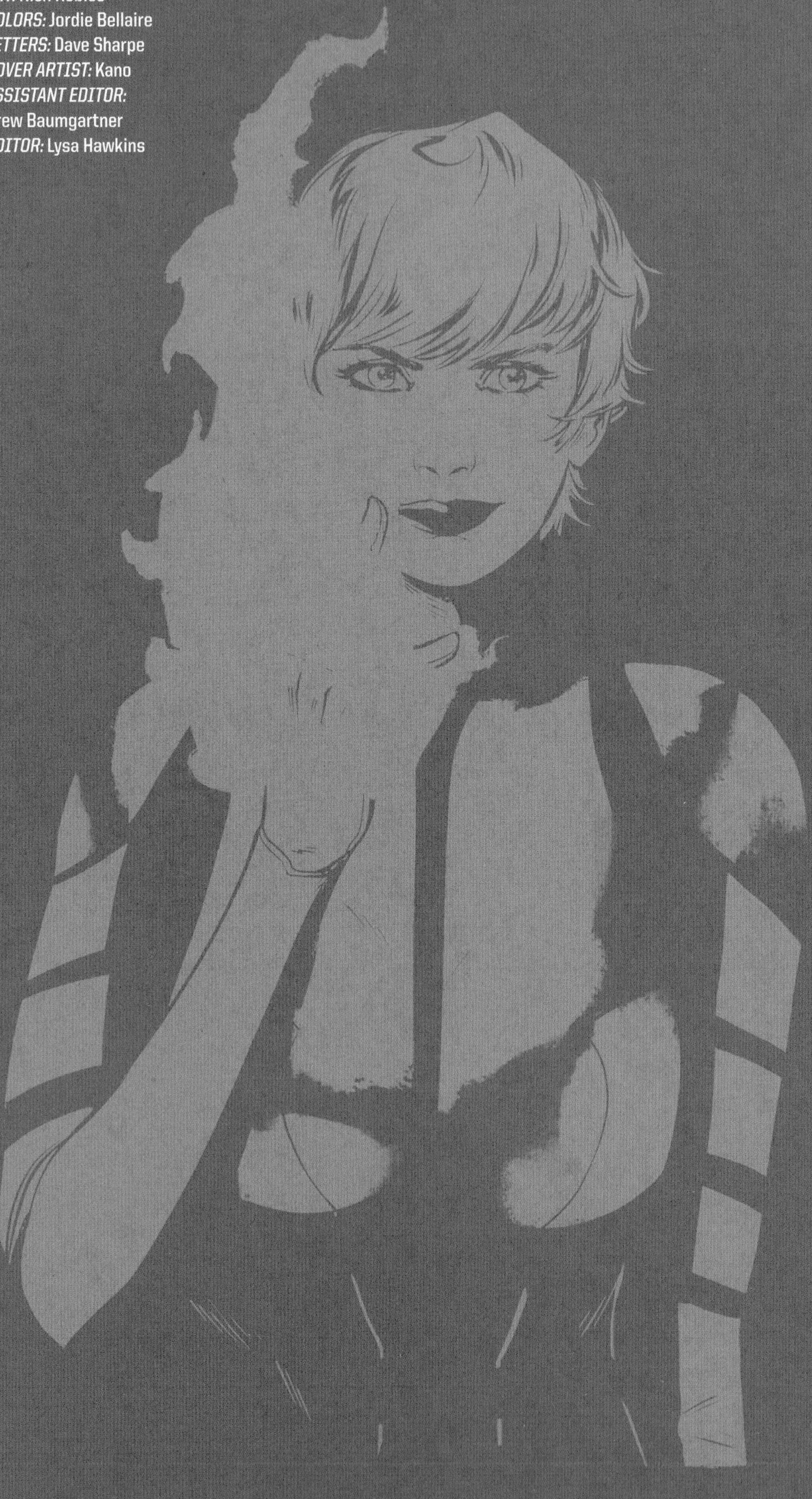

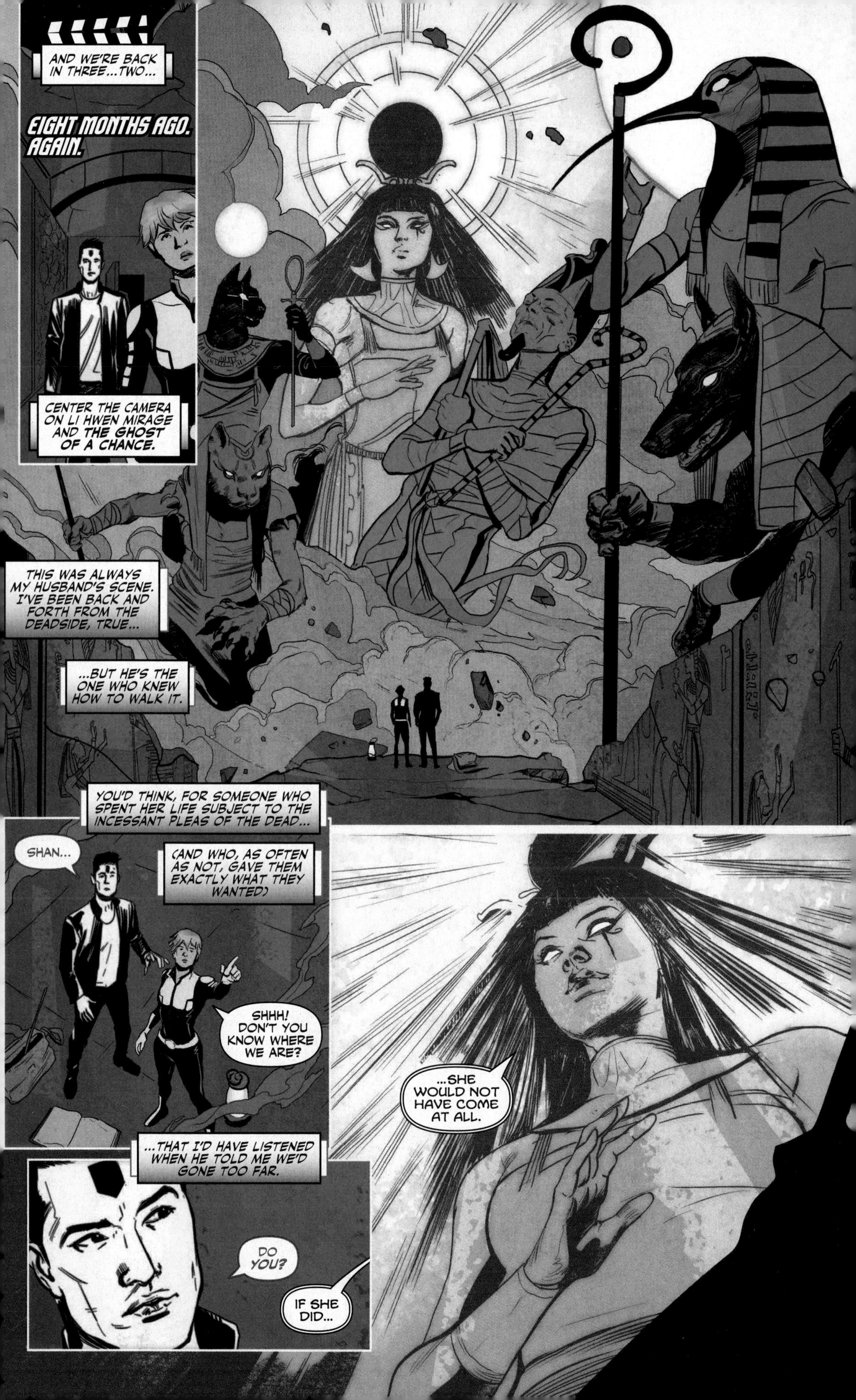
AND WE'RE BACK IN THREE...TWO...
EIGHT MONTHS AGO. AGAIN.
CENTER THE CAMERA ON LI HWEN MIRAGE AND THE GHOST OF A CHANCE.
THIS WAS ALWAYS MY HUSBAND'S SCENE. I'VE BEEN BACK AND FORTH FROM THE DEADSIDE, TRUE...
...BUT HE'S THE ONE WHO KNEW HOW TO WALK IT.
YOU'D THINK, FOR SOMEONE WHO SPENT HER LIFE SUBJECT TO THE INCESSANT PLEAS OF THE DEAD...
SHAN...
(AND WHO, AS OFTEN AS NOT, GAVE THEM EXACTLY WHAT THEY WANTED)
SHHH! DON'T YOU KNOW WHERE WE ARE?
...THAT I'D HAVE LISTENED WHEN HE TOLD ME WE'D GONE TOO FAR.
DO YOU?
IF SHE DID...
...SHE WOULD NOT HAVE COME AT ALL.

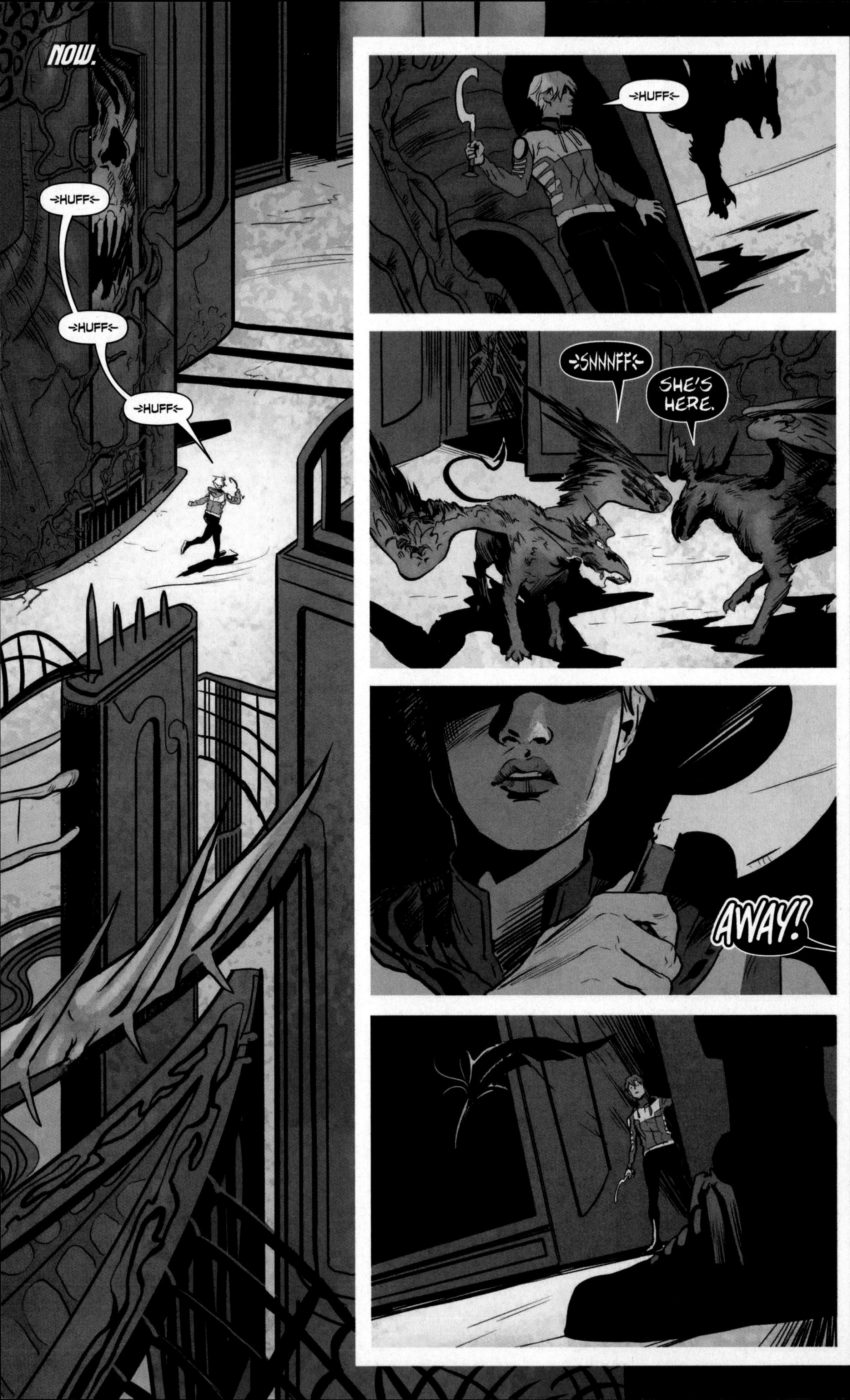
NOW.
HUFF
HUFF
HUFF
HUFF
SNNNFF
SHE'S HERE.
AWAY!

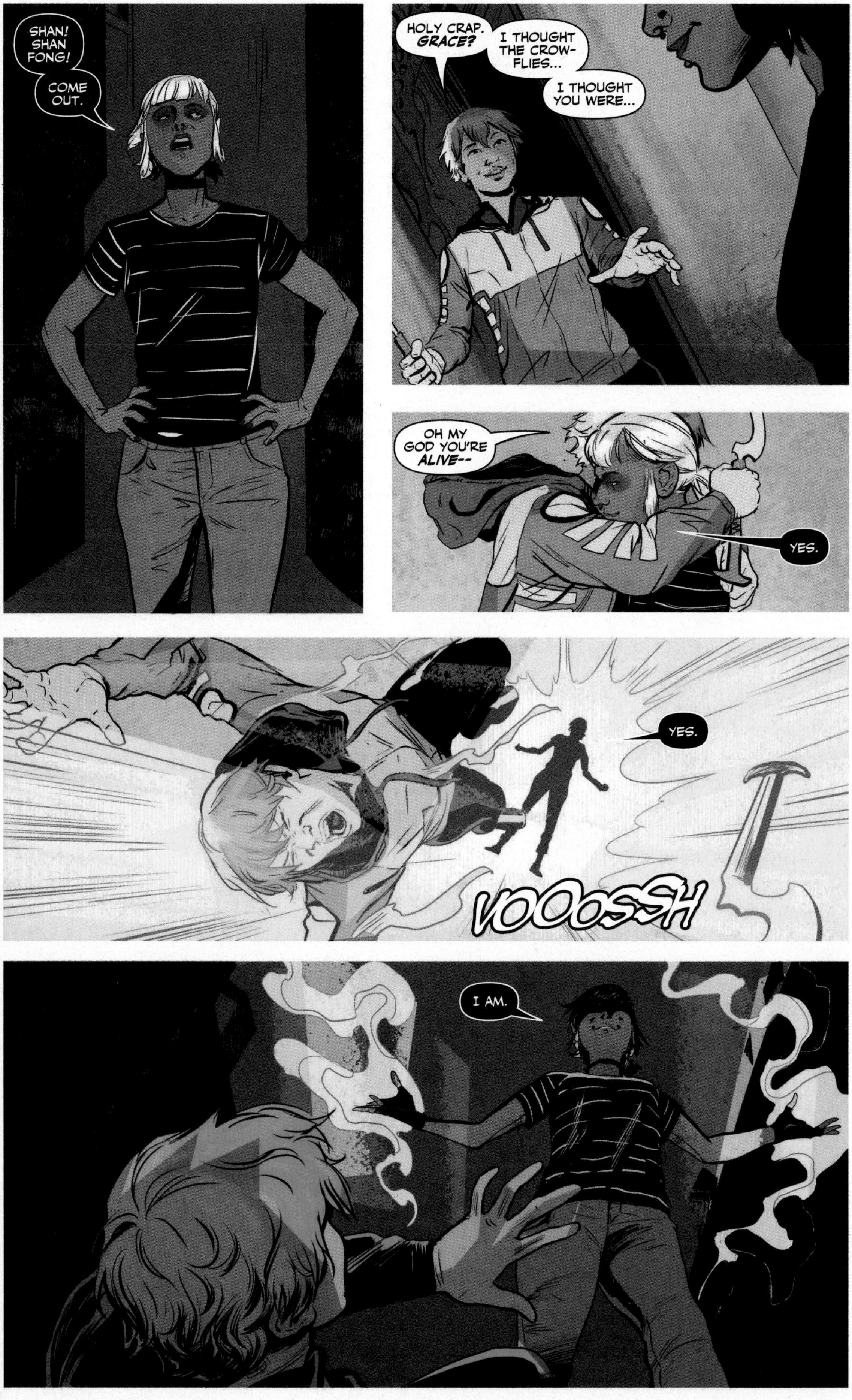
SHAN! SHAN FONG!
COME OUT.
HOLY CRAP. GRACE?
I THOUGHT THE CROW-FLIES...
I THOUGHT YOU WERE...
OH MY GOD YOU'RE ALIVE--
YES.
YES.
VOOOSSH
I AM.

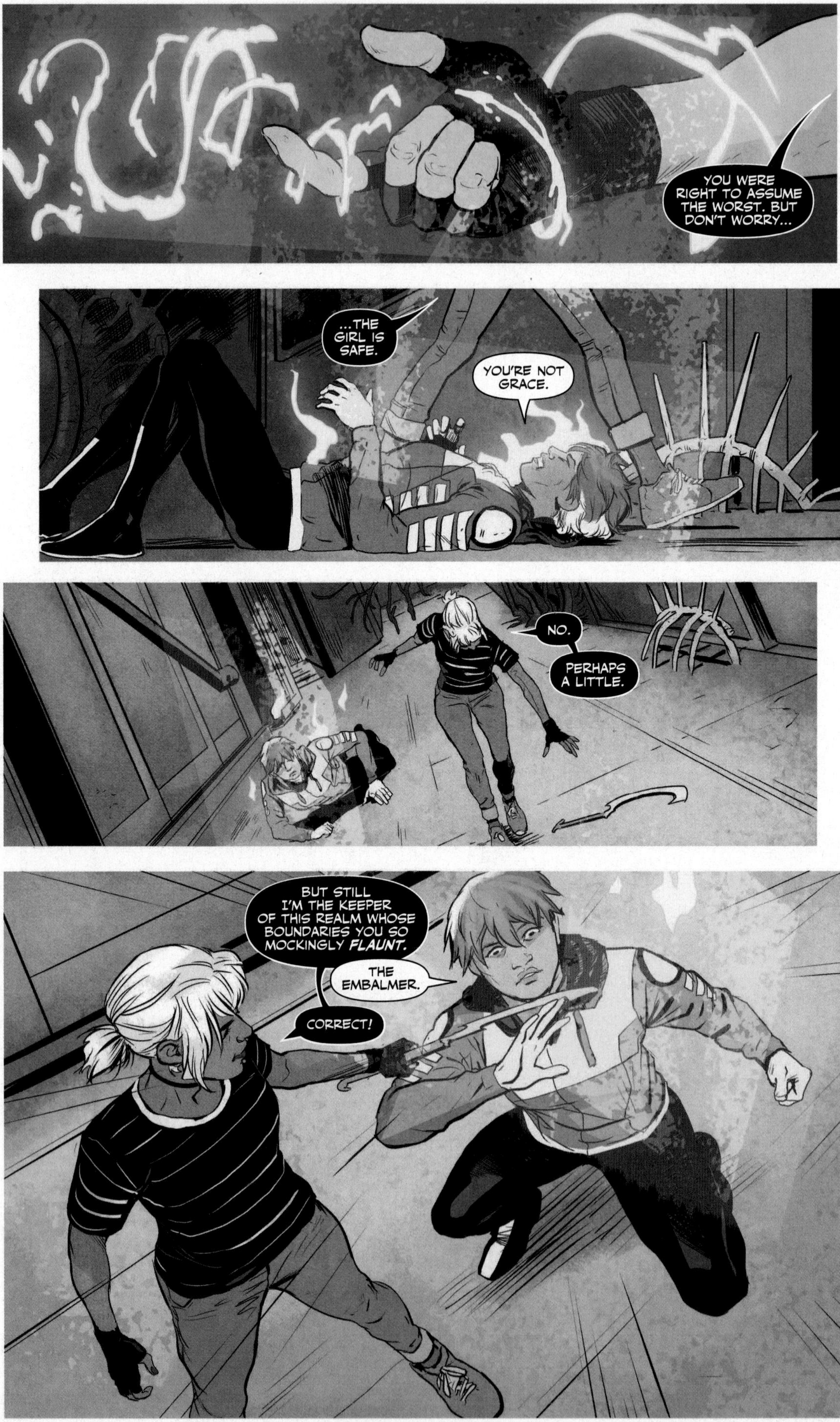
YOU WERE RIGHT TO ASSUME THE WORST. BUT DON'T WORRY...
...THE GIRL IS SAFE.
YOU'RE NOT GRACE.
NO.
PERHAPS A LITTLE.
BUT STILL I'M THE KEEPER OF THIS REALM WHOSE BOUNDARIES YOU SO MOCKINGLY FLAUNT.
THE EMBALMER.
CORRECT!

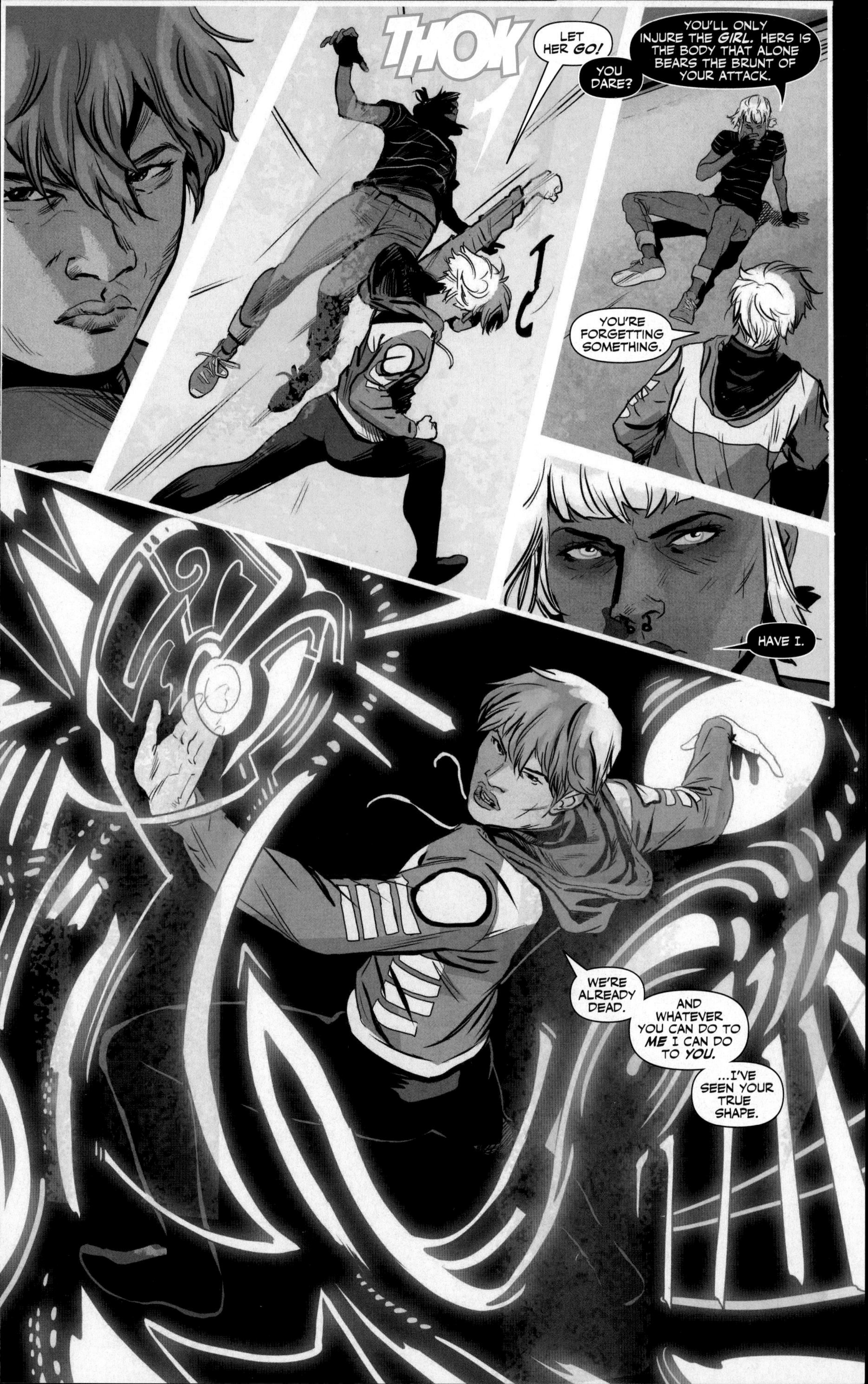
THOK
LET HER GO!
YOU DARE?
YOU'LL ONLY INJURE THE GIRL. HERS IS THE BODY THAT ALONE BEARS THE BRUNT OF YOUR ATTACK.
YOU'RE FORGETTING SOMETHING.
HAVE I.
WE'RE ALREADY DEAD.
AND WHATEVER YOU CAN DO TO ME I CAN DO TO YOU.
...I'VE SEEN YOUR TRUE SHAPE.

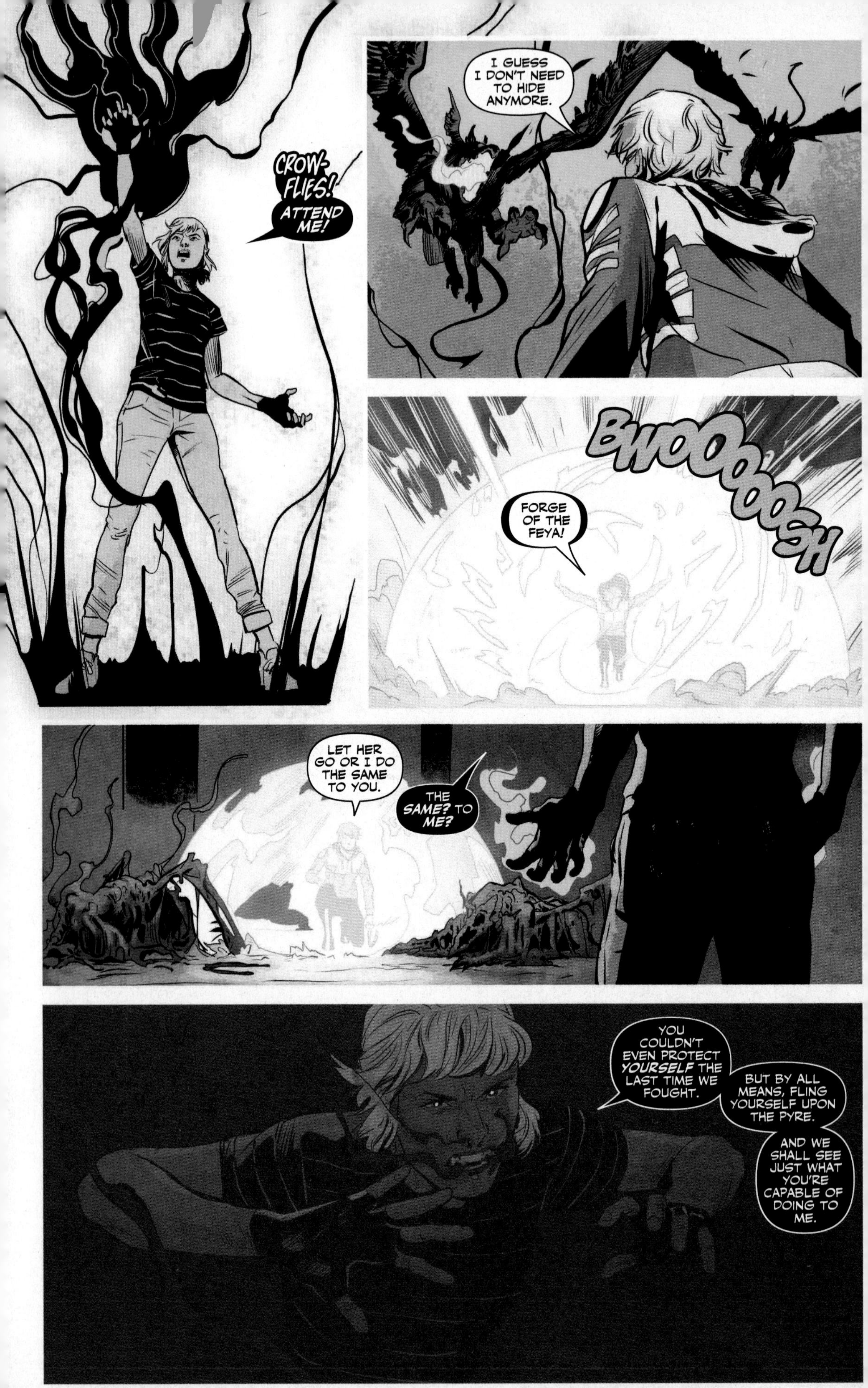
CROW-FLIES! ATTEND ME!
I GUESS I DON'T NEED TO HIDE ANYMORE.
BWOOOOOOSH
FORGE OF THE FEYA!
LET HER GO OR I DO THE SAME TO YOU.
THE SAME? TO ME?
YOU COULDN'T EVEN PROTECT YOURSELF THE LAST TIME WE FOUGHT.
BUT BY ALL MEANS, FLING YOURSELF UPON THE PYRE.
AND WE SHALL SEE JUST WHAT YOU'RE CAPABLE OF DOING TO ME.

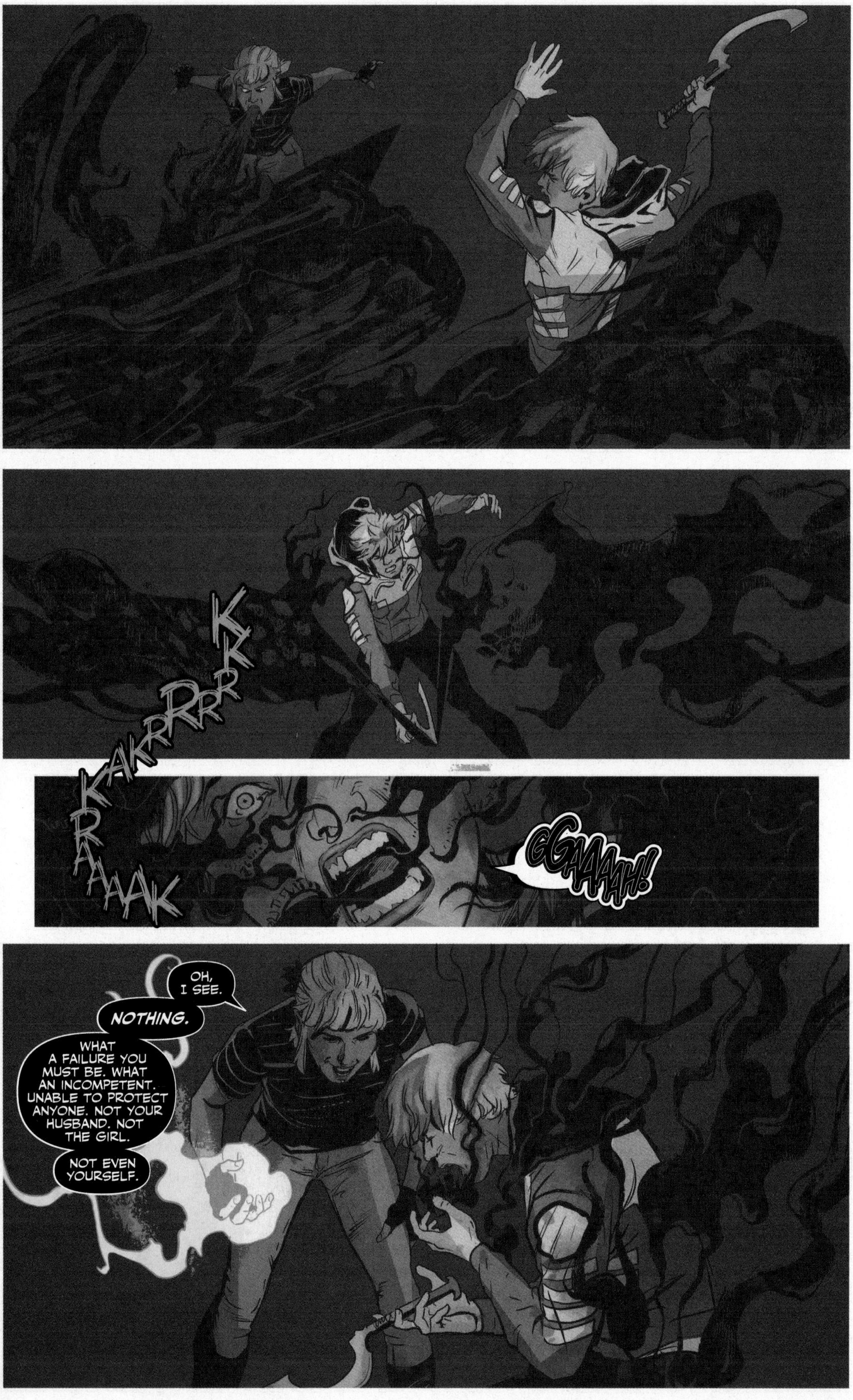
KAKRRRRRKK
KRAAAAK
GGAAAAAH!
OH, I SEE.
NOTHING.
WHAT A FAILURE YOU MUST BE. WHAT AN INCOMPETENT. UNABLE TO PROTECT ANYONE. NOT YOUR HUSBAND. NOT THE GIRL.
NOT EVEN YOURSELF.

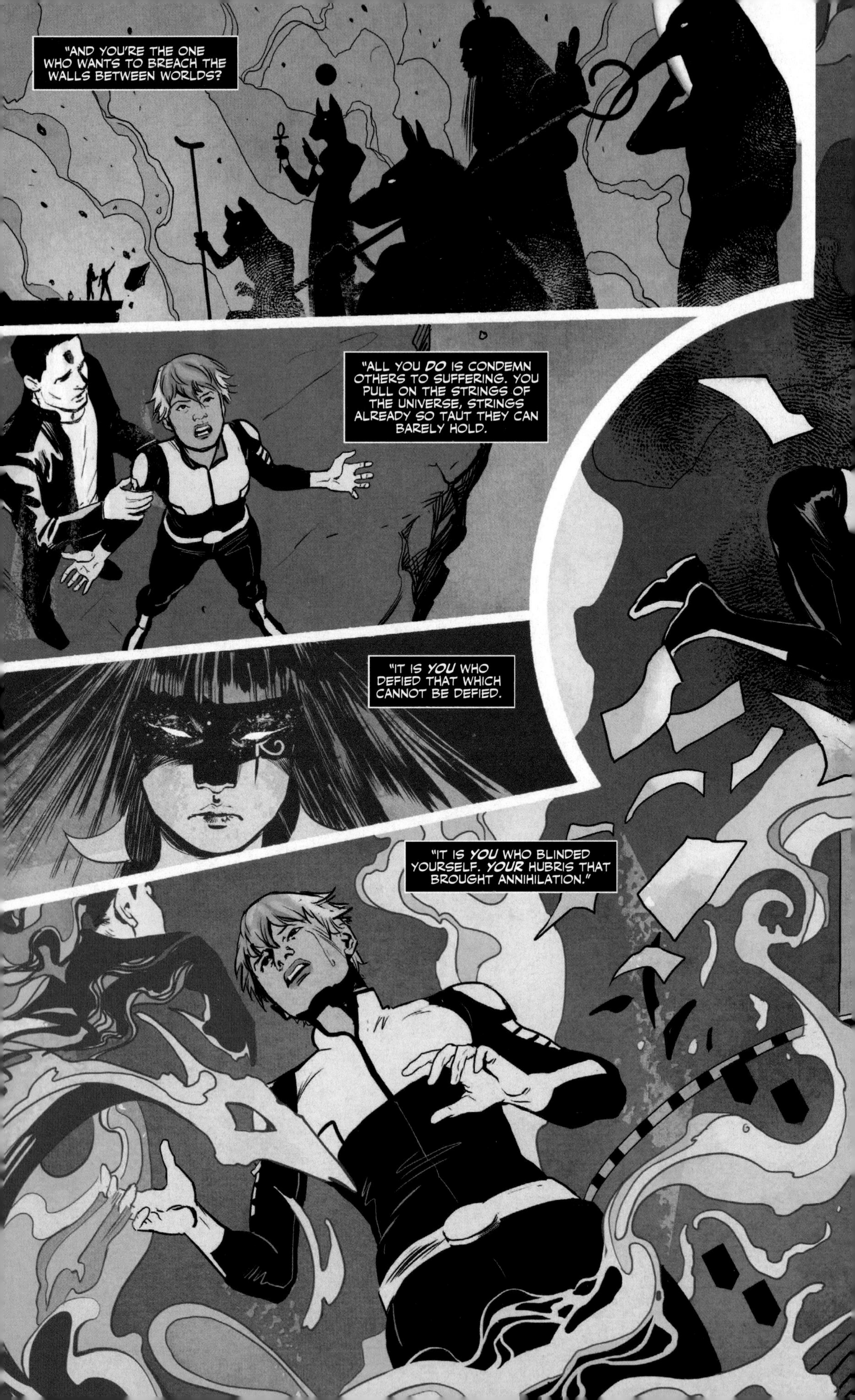
"AND YOU'RE THE ONE WHO WANTS TO BREACH THE WALLS BETWEEN WORLDS?
"ALL YOU DO IS CONDEMN OTHERS TO SUFFERING. YOU PULL ON THE STRINGS OF THE UNIVERSE, STRINGS ALREADY SO TAUT THEY CAN BARELY HOLD.
"IT IS YOU WHO DEFIED THAT WHICH CANNOT BE DEFIED.
"IT IS YOU WHO BLINDED YOURSELF. YOUR HUBRIS THAT BROUGHT ANNIHILATION."

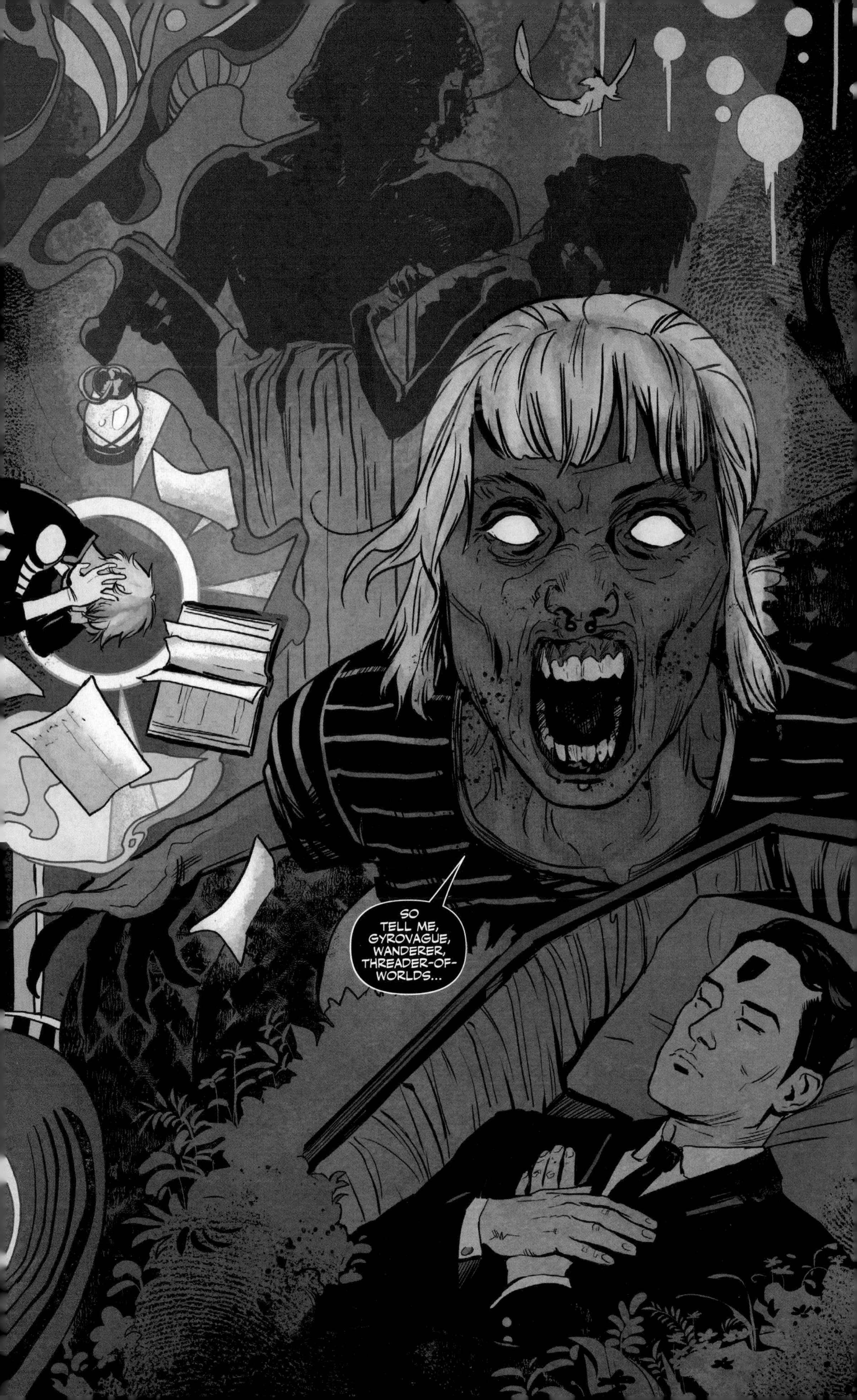
SO TELL ME, GYROVAGUE, WANDERER, THREADER-OF-WORLDS...

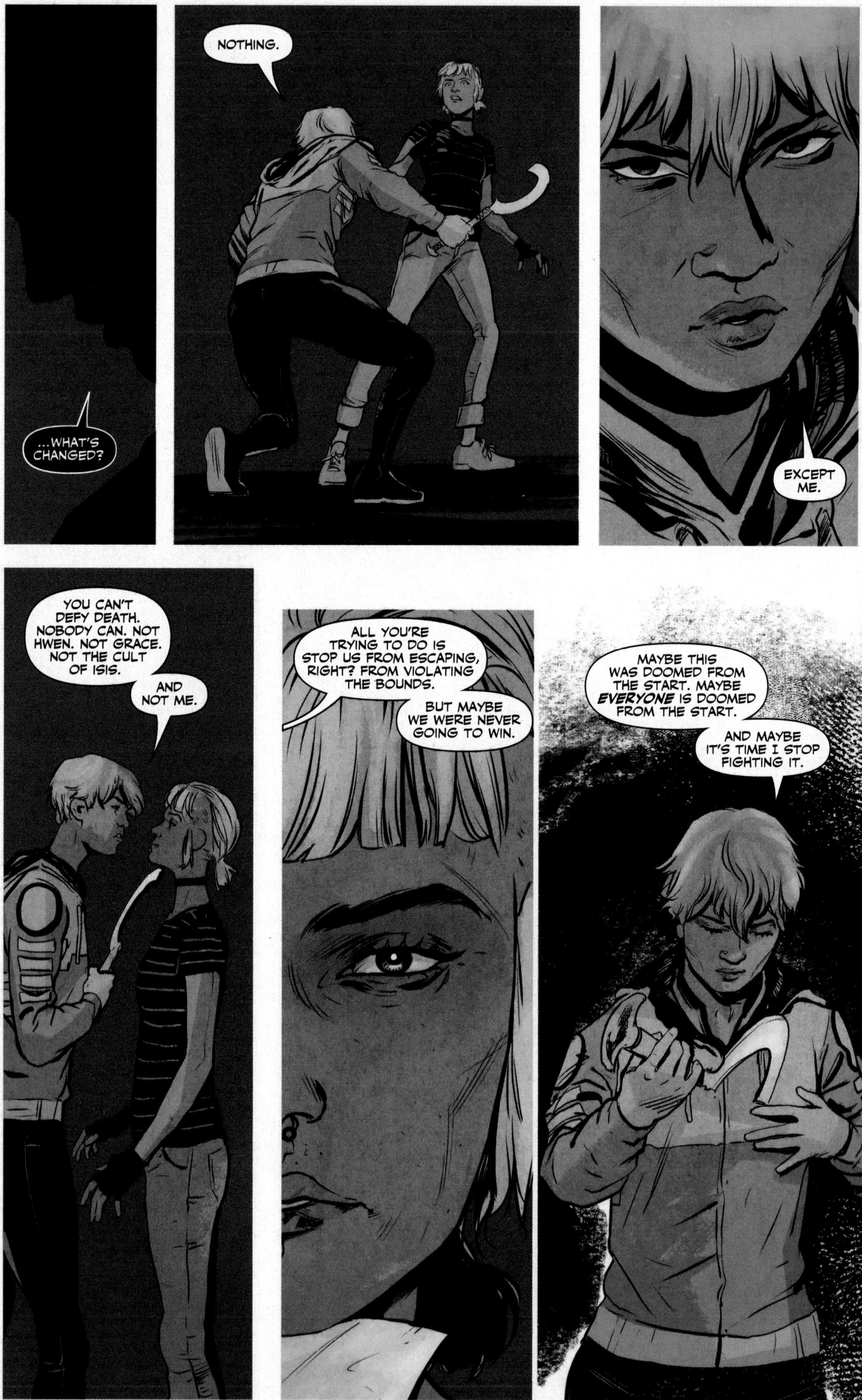
...WHAT'S CHANGED?
NOTHING.
EXCEPT ME.
YOU CAN'T DEFY DEATH. NOBODY CAN. NOT HWEN. NOT GRACE. NOT THE CULT OF ISIS.
AND NOT ME.
ALL YOU'RE TRYING TO DO IS STOP US FROM ESCAPING, RIGHT? FROM VIOLATING THE BOUNDS.
BUT MAYBE WE WERE NEVER GOING TO WIN.
MAYBE THIS WAS DOOMED FROM THE START. MAYBE *EVERYONE* IS DOOMED FROM THE START.
AND MAYBE IT'S TIME I STOP FIGHTING IT.

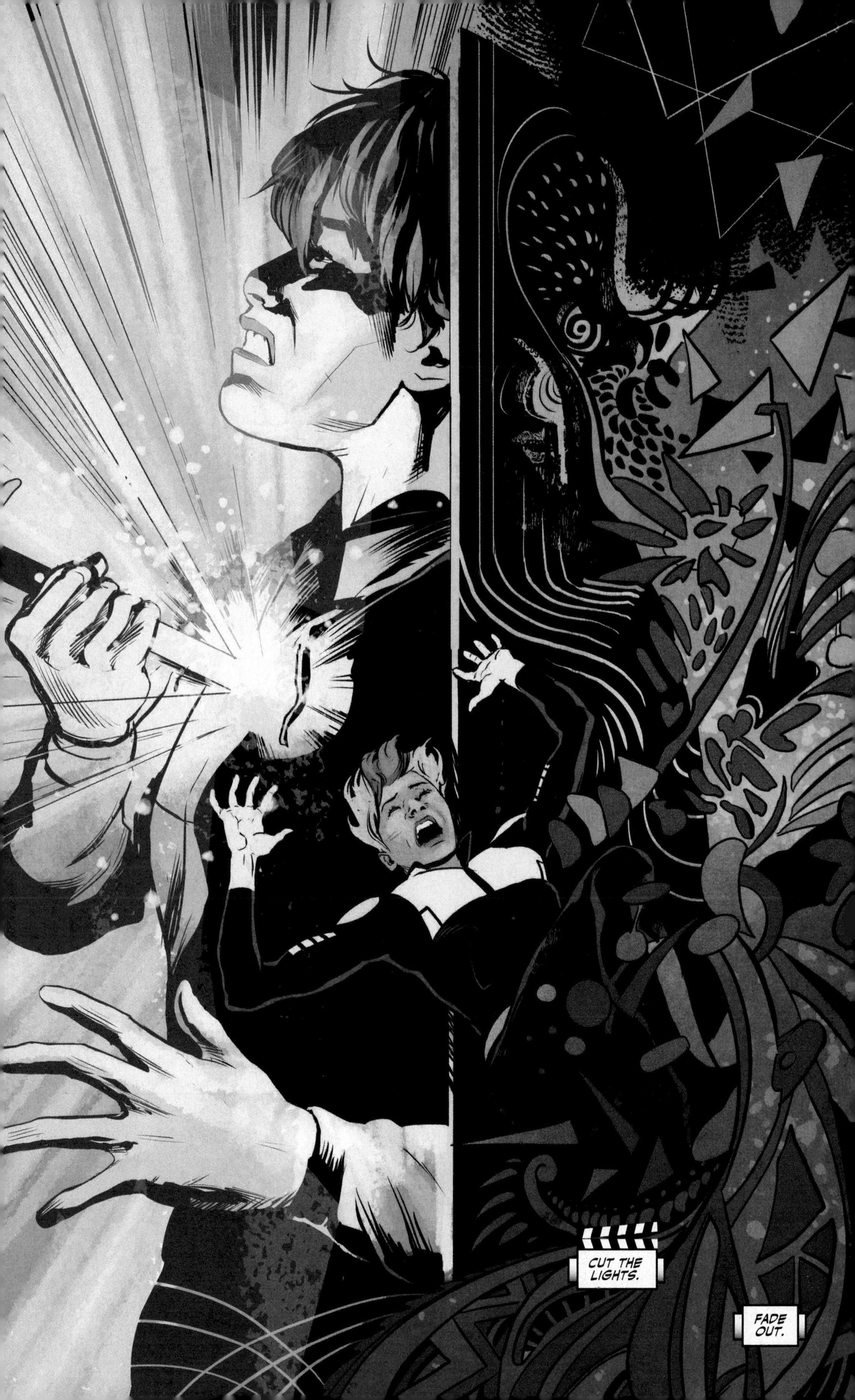
CUT THE LIGHTS.
FADE OUT.

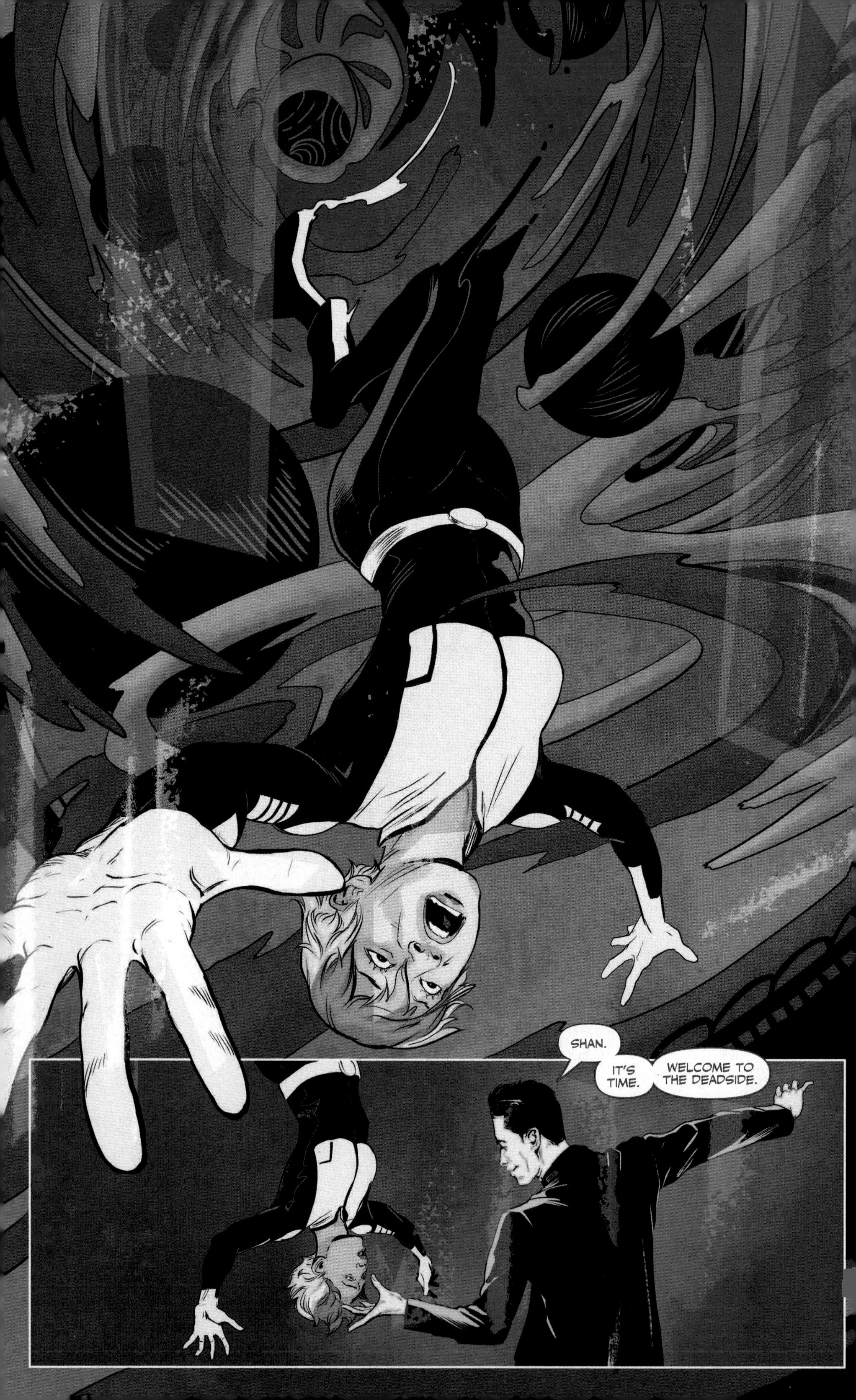
SHAN.
IT'S TIME.
WELCOME TO THE DEADSIDE.

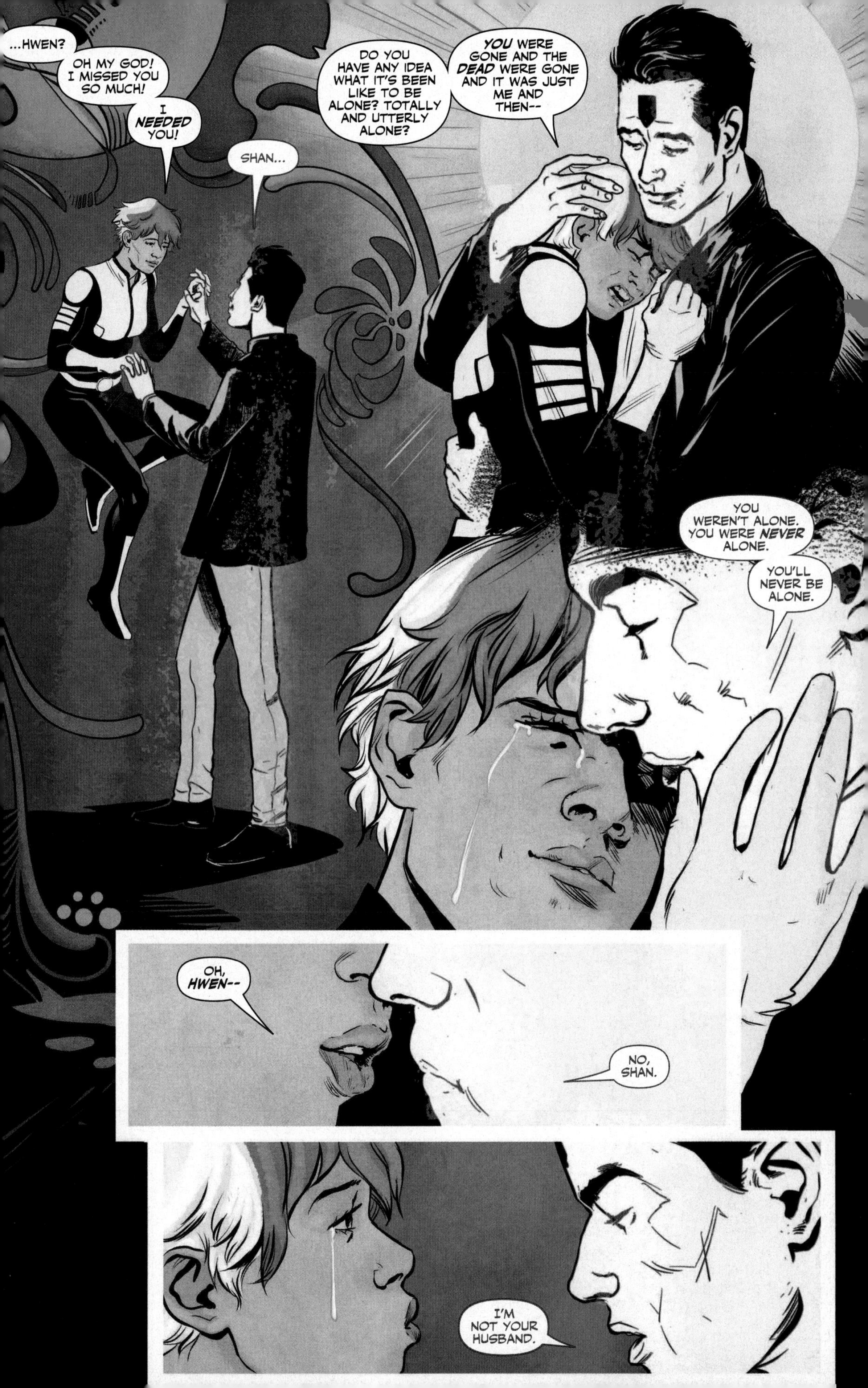
...HWEN?
OH MY GOD! I MISSED YOU SO MUCH!
I *NEEDED* YOU!
SHAN...
DO YOU HAVE ANY IDEA WHAT IT'S BEEN LIKE TO BE ALONE? TOTALLY AND UTTERLY ALONE?
YOU WERE GONE AND THE *DEAD* WERE GONE AND IT WAS JUST ME AND THEN--
YOU WEREN'T ALONE. YOU WERE *NEVER* ALONE.
YOU'LL NEVER BE ALONE.
OH, *HWEN--*
NO, SHAN.
I'M NOT YOUR HUSBAND.

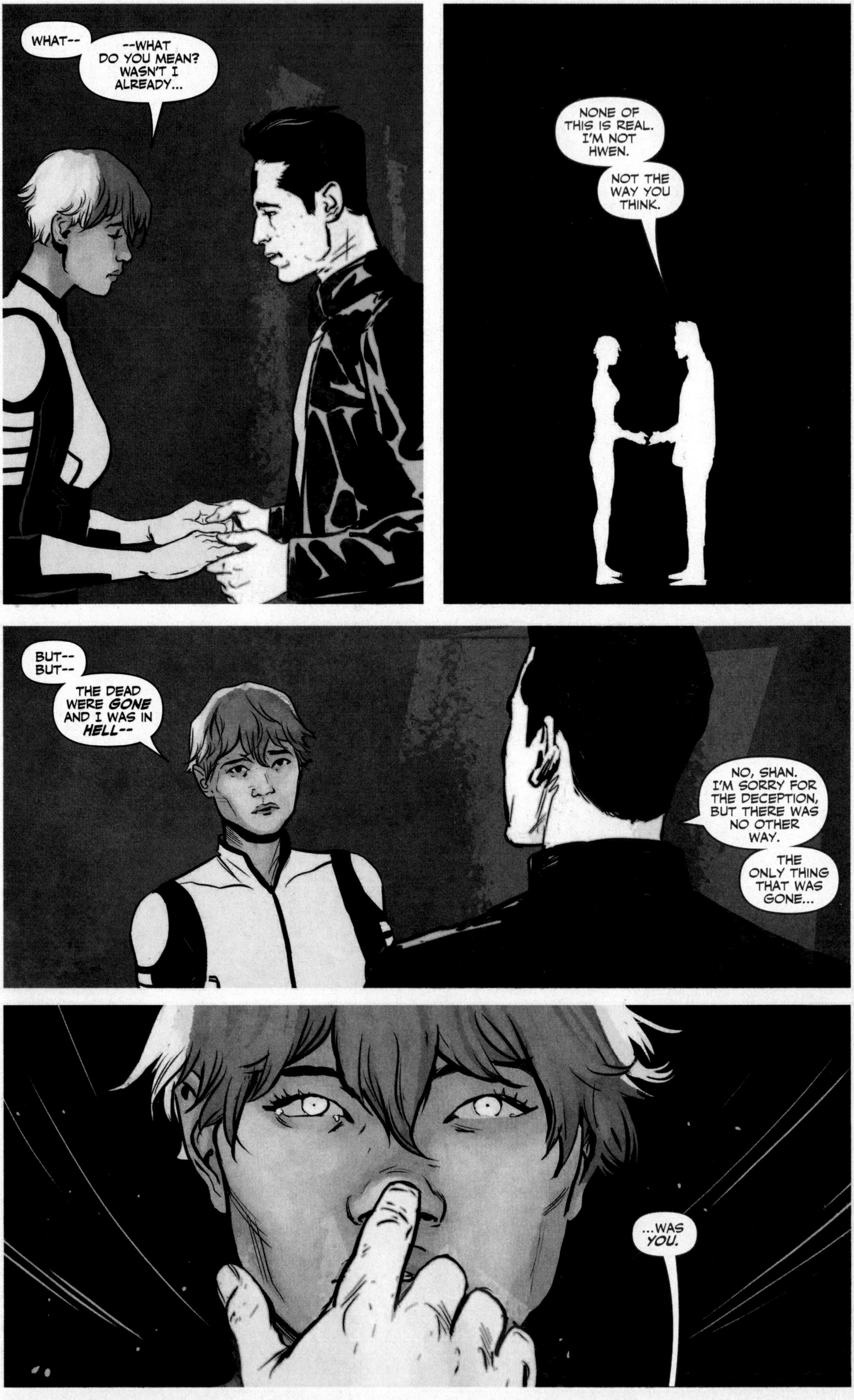
WHAT--
--WHAT DO YOU MEAN? WASN'T I ALREADY...
NONE OF THIS IS REAL. I'M NOT HWEN.
NOT THE WAY YOU THINK.
BUT-- BUT--
THE DEAD WERE GONE AND I WAS IN HELL--
NO, SHAN. I'M SORRY FOR THE DECEPTION, BUT THERE WAS NO OTHER WAY.
THE ONLY THING THAT WAS GONE...
...WAS YOU.

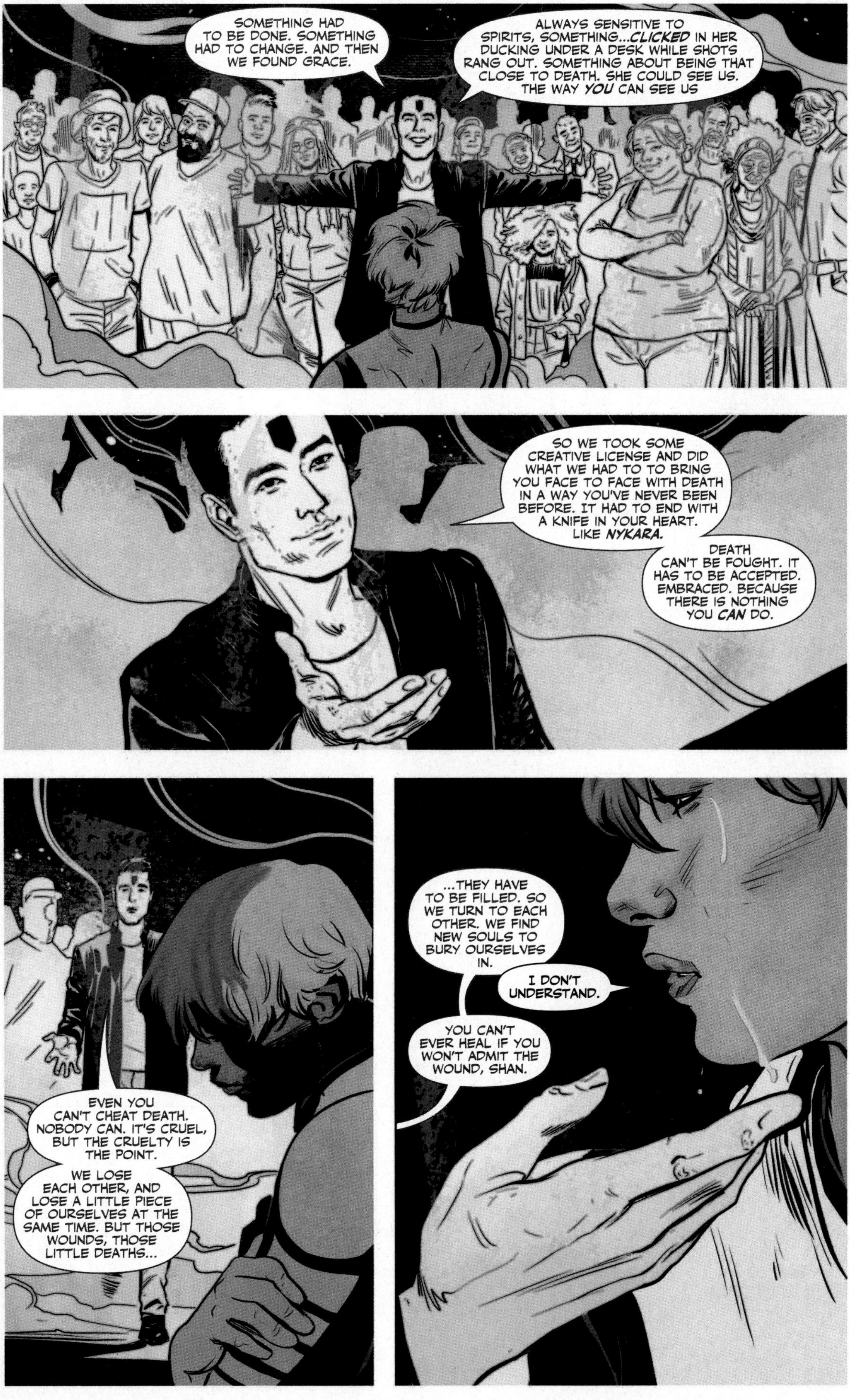
SOMETHING HAD TO BE DONE. SOMETHING HAD TO CHANGE. AND THEN WE FOUND GRACE.
ALWAYS SENSITIVE TO SPIRITS, SOMETHING...CLICKED IN HER DUCKING UNDER A DESK WHILE SHOTS RANG OUT. SOMETHING ABOUT BEING THAT CLOSE TO DEATH. SHE COULD SEE US. THE WAY YOU CAN SEE US
SO WE TOOK SOME CREATIVE LICENSE AND DID WHAT WE HAD TO TO BRING YOU FACE TO FACE WITH DEATH IN A WAY YOU'VE NEVER BEEN BEFORE. IT HAD TO END WITH A KNIFE IN YOUR HEART. LIKE NYKARA.
DEATH CAN'T BE FOUGHT. IT HAS TO BE ACCEPTED. EMBRACED. BECAUSE THERE IS NOTHING YOU CAN DO.
EVEN YOU CAN'T CHEAT DEATH. NOBODY CAN. IT'S CRUEL, BUT THE CRUELTY IS THE POINT.
WE LOSE EACH OTHER, AND LOSE A LITTLE PIECE OF OURSELVES AT THE SAME TIME. BUT THOSE WOUNDS, THOSE LITTLE DEATHS...
...THEY HAVE TO BE FILLED. SO WE TURN TO EACH OTHER. WE FIND NEW SOULS TO BURY OURSELVES IN.
I DON'T UNDERSTAND.
YOU CAN'T EVER HEAL IF YOU WON'T ADMIT THE WOUND, SHAN.

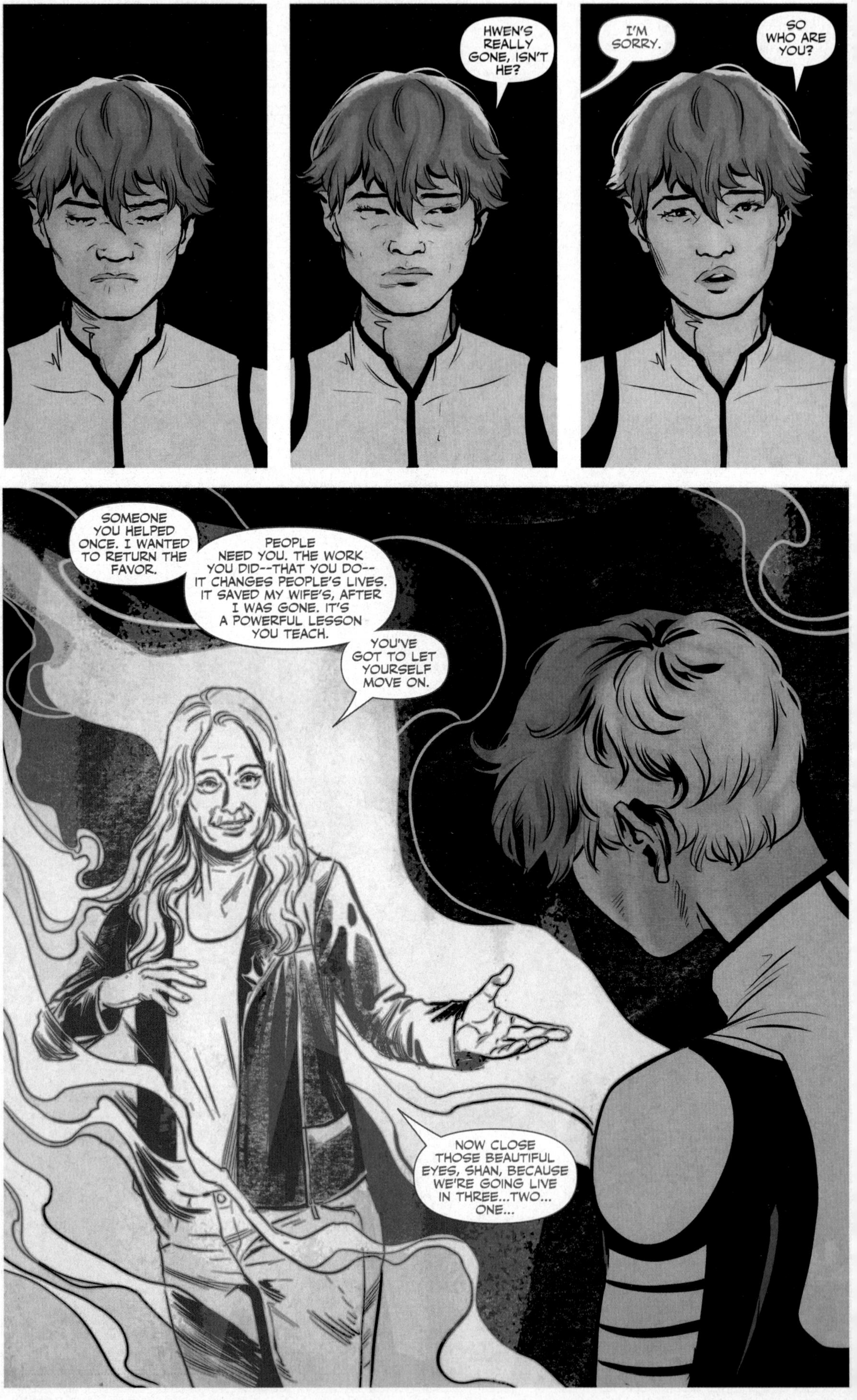
HWEN'S REALLY GONE, ISN'T HE?
I'M SORRY.
SO WHO ARE YOU?
SOMEONE YOU HELPED ONCE. I WANTED TO RETURN THE FAVOR.
PEOPLE NEED YOU. THE WORK YOU DID--THAT YOU DO--IT CHANGES PEOPLE'S LIVES. IT SAVED MY WIFE'S, AFTER I WAS GONE. IT'S A POWERFUL LESSON YOU TEACH.
YOU'VE GOT TO LET YOURSELF MOVE ON.
NOW CLOSE THOSE BEAUTIFUL EYES, SHAN, BECAUSE WE'RE GOING LIVE IN THREE...TWO... ONE...

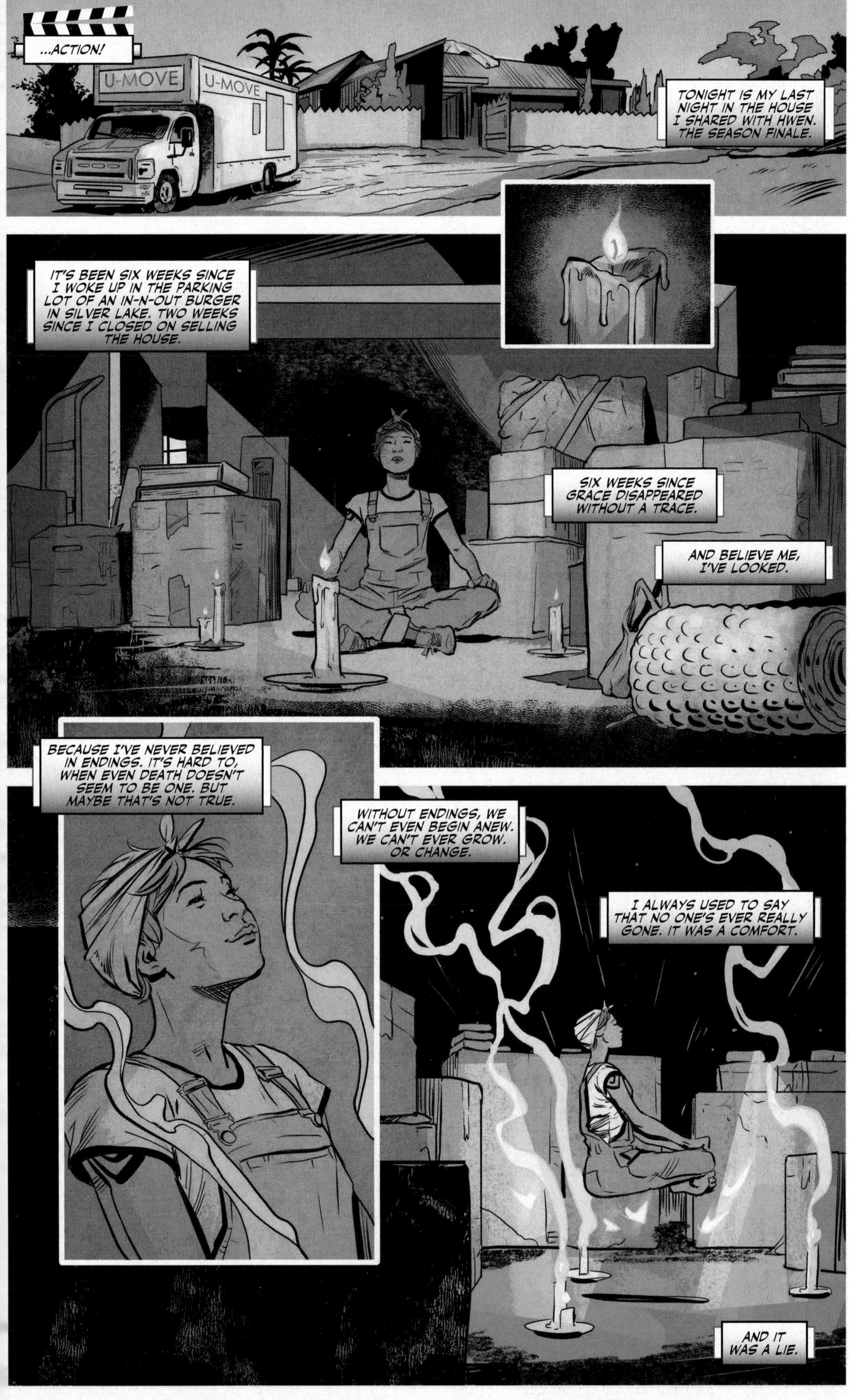
...ACTION!
U-MOVE
U-MOVE
TONIGHT IS MY LAST NIGHT IN THE HOUSE I SHARED WITH HWEN. THE SEASON FINALE.
IT'S BEEN SIX WEEKS SINCE I WOKE UP IN THE PARKING LOT OF AN IN-N-OUT BURGER IN SILVER LAKE. TWO WEEKS SINCE I CLOSED ON SELLING THE HOUSE.
SIX WEEKS SINCE GRACE DISAPPEARED WITHOUT A TRACE.
AND BELIEVE ME, I'VE LOOKED.
BECAUSE I'VE NEVER BELIEVED IN ENDINGS. IT'S HARD TO, WHEN EVEN DEATH DOESN'T SEEM TO BE ONE. BUT MAYBE THAT'S NOT TRUE.
WITHOUT ENDINGS, WE CAN'T EVEN BEGIN ANEW. WE CAN'T EVER GROW. OR CHANGE.
I ALWAYS USED TO SAY THAT NO ONE'S EVER REALLY GONE. IT WAS A COMFORT.
AND IT WAS A LIE.

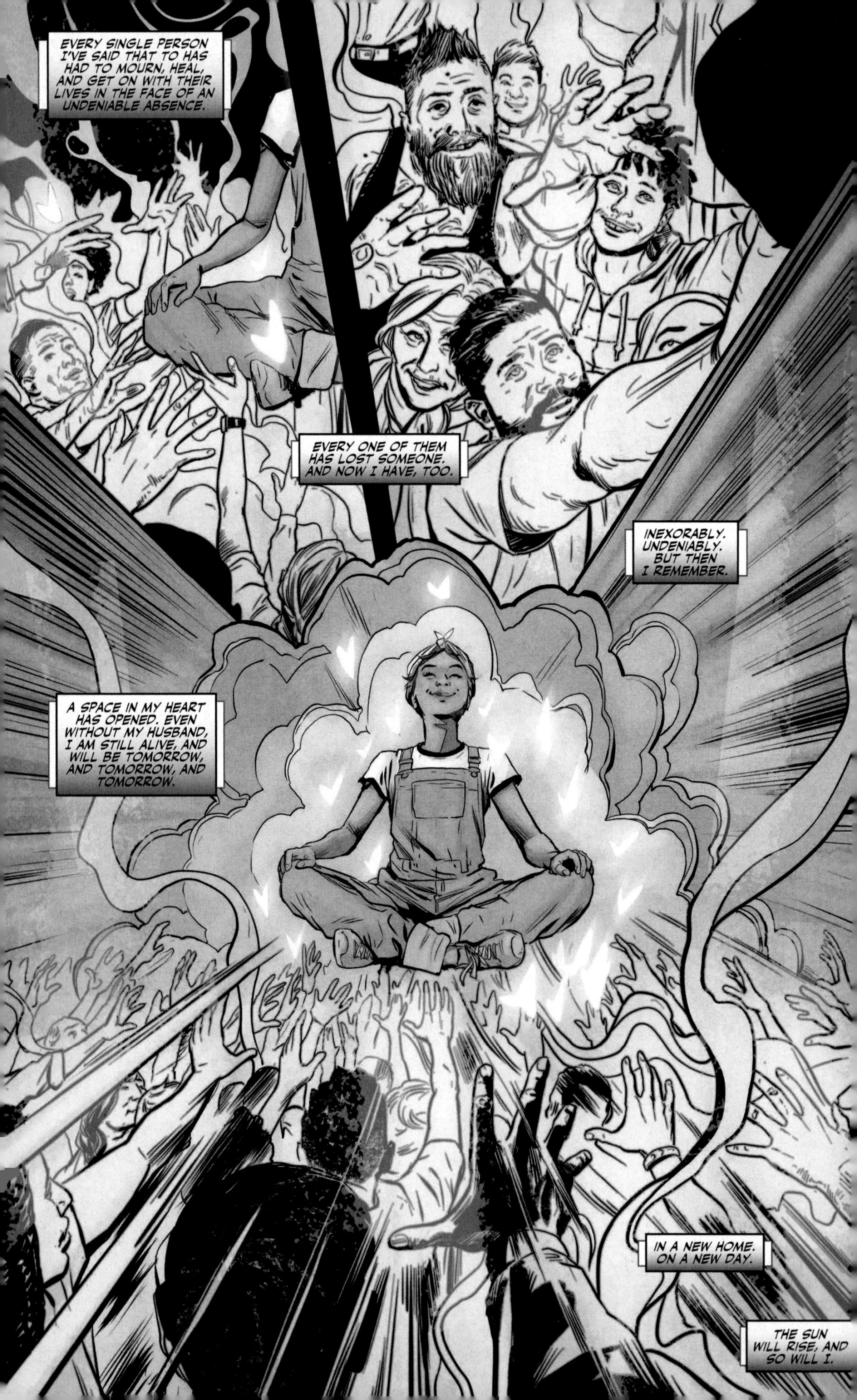
EVERY SINGLE PERSON I'VE SAID THAT TO HAS HAD TO MOURN, HEAL, AND GET ON WITH THEIR LIVES IN THE FACE OF AN UNDENIABLE ABSENCE.
EVERY ONE OF THEM HAS LOST SOMEONE. AND NOW I HAVE, TOO.
INEXORABLY. UNDENIABLY. BUT THEN I REMEMBER.
A SPACE IN MY HEART HAS OPENED. EVEN WITHOUT MY HUSBAND, I AM STILL ALIVE, AND WILL BE TOMORROW, AND TOMORROW, AND TOMORROW.
IN A NEW HOME. ON A NEW DAY.
THE SUN WILL RISE, AND SO WILL I.

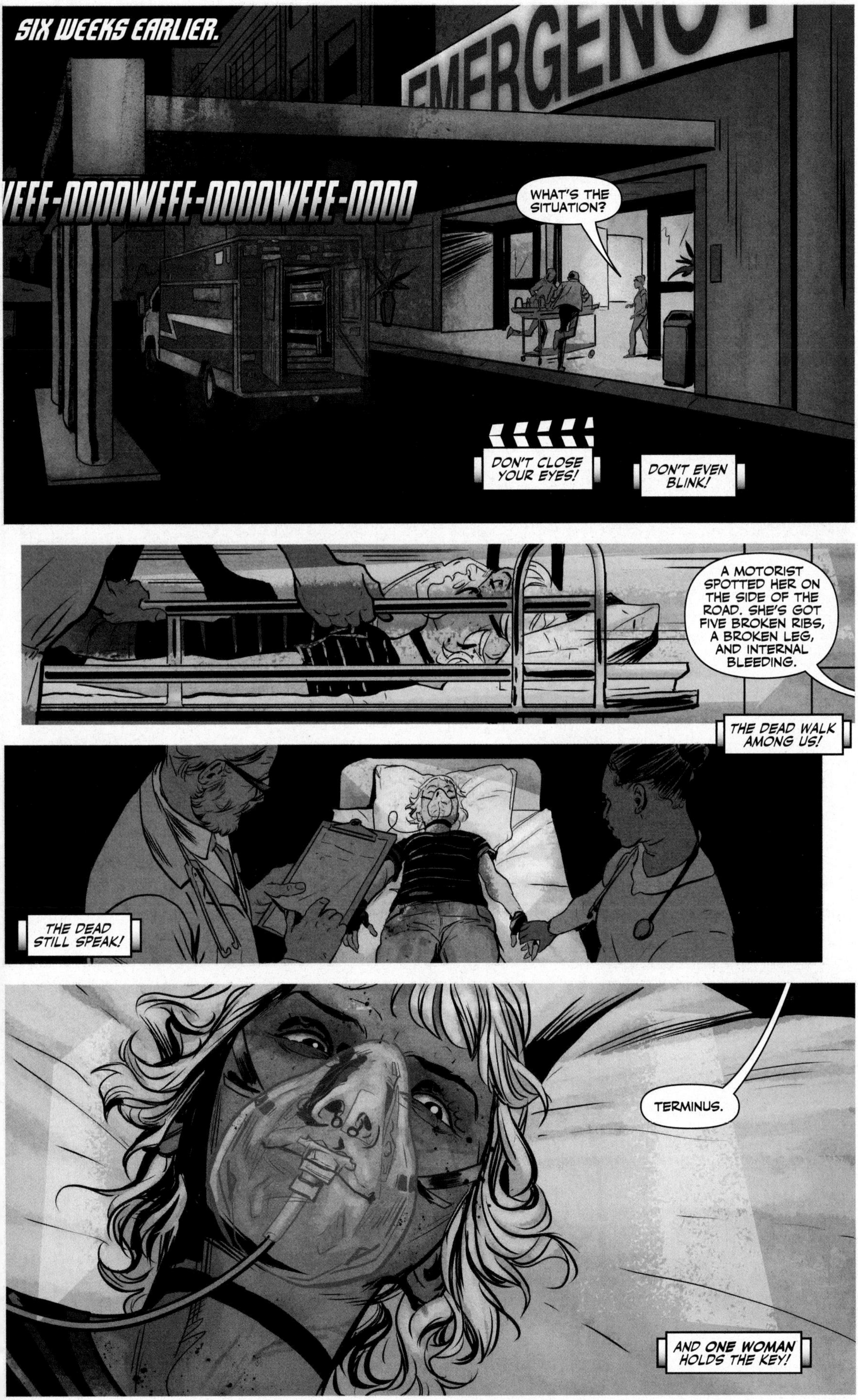
SIX WEEKS EARLIER.
EMERGENC
WEEE-OOOOWEEE-OOOOWEEE-OOOO
WHAT'S THE SITUATION?
DON'T CLOSE YOUR EYES!
DON'T EVEN BLINK!
A MOTORIST SPOTTED HER ON THE SIDE OF THE ROAD. SHE'S GOT FIVE BROKEN RIBS, A BROKEN LEG, AND INTERNAL BLEEDING.
THE DEAD WALK AMONG US!
THE DEAD STILL SPEAK!
TERMINUS.
AND ONE WOMAN HOLDS THE KEY!

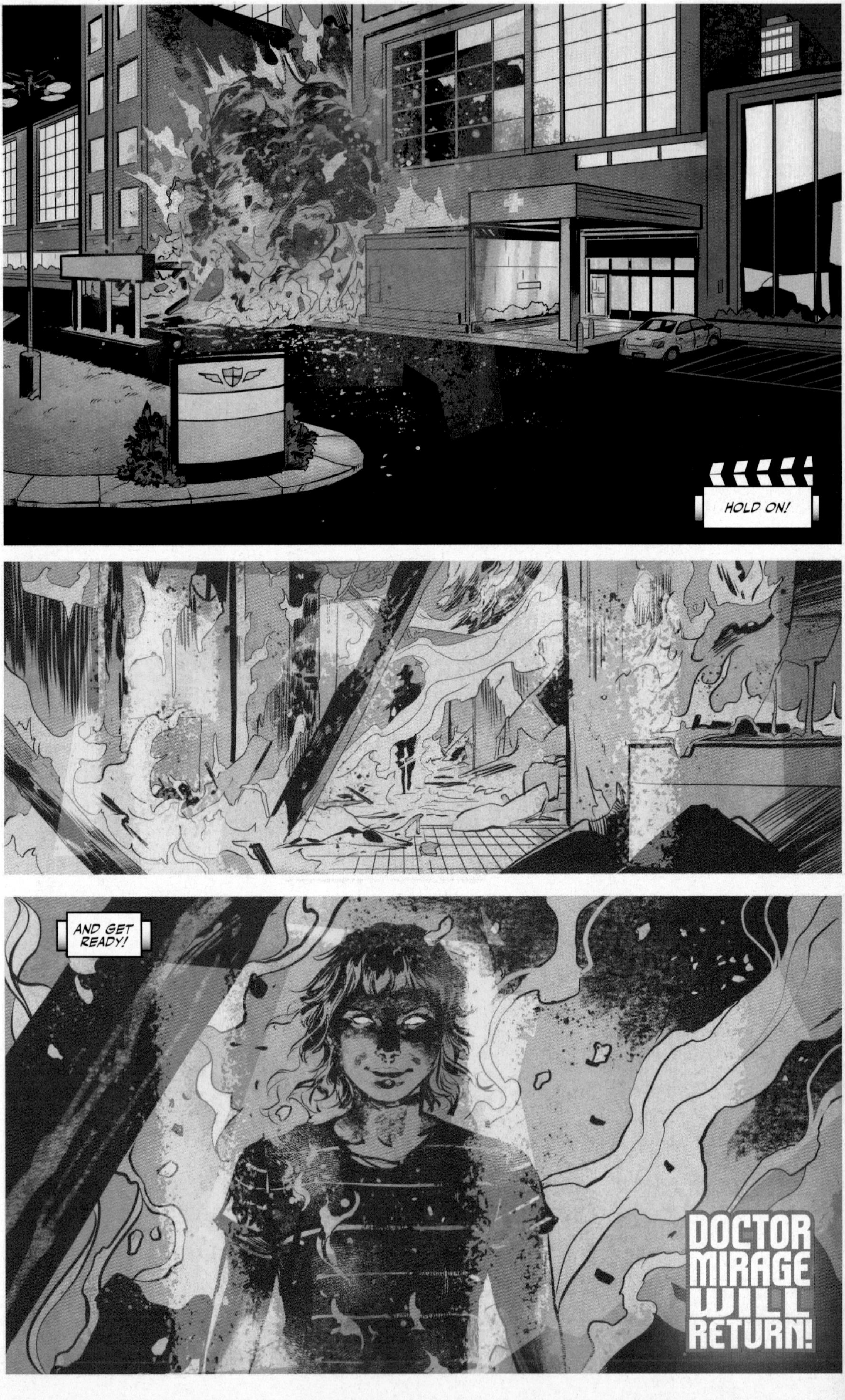
HOLD ON!
AND GET READY!
DOCTOR MIRAGE WILL RETURN!

GALLERY

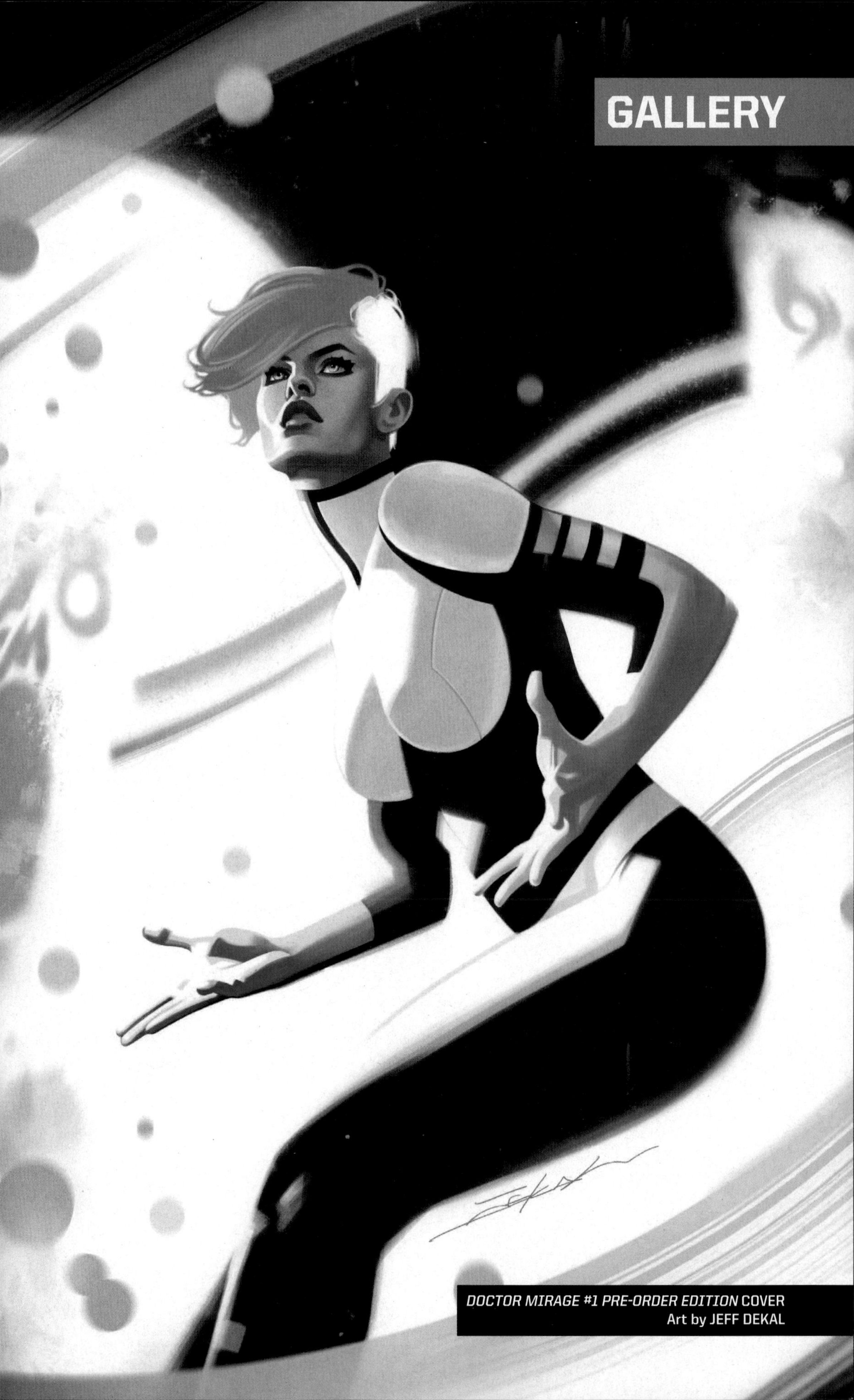

DOCTOR MIRAGE #1 PRE-ORDER EDITION COVER
Art by JEFF DEKAL

DOCTOR MIRAGE #2 COVER B
Art by COLLEEN DORAN

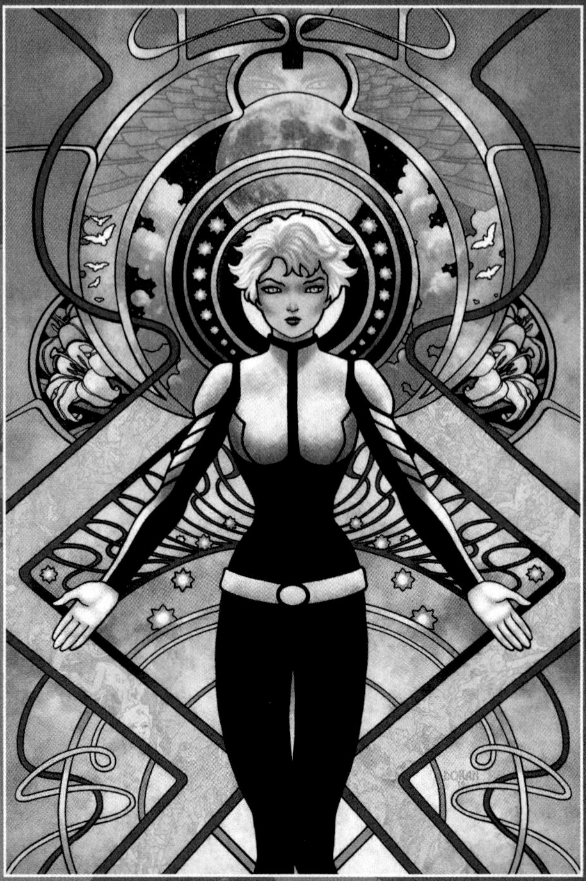
DORAN

DOCTOR MIRAGE #3 PRE-ORDER EDITION COVER
Art by TULA LOTAY

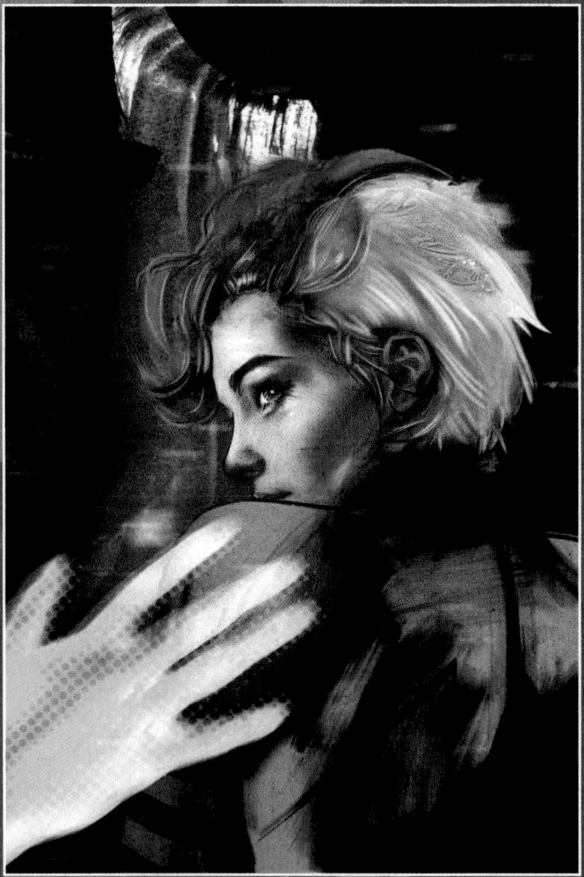

DOCTOR MIRAGE #3 COVER C (facing)
Art by PASQUAL FERRY

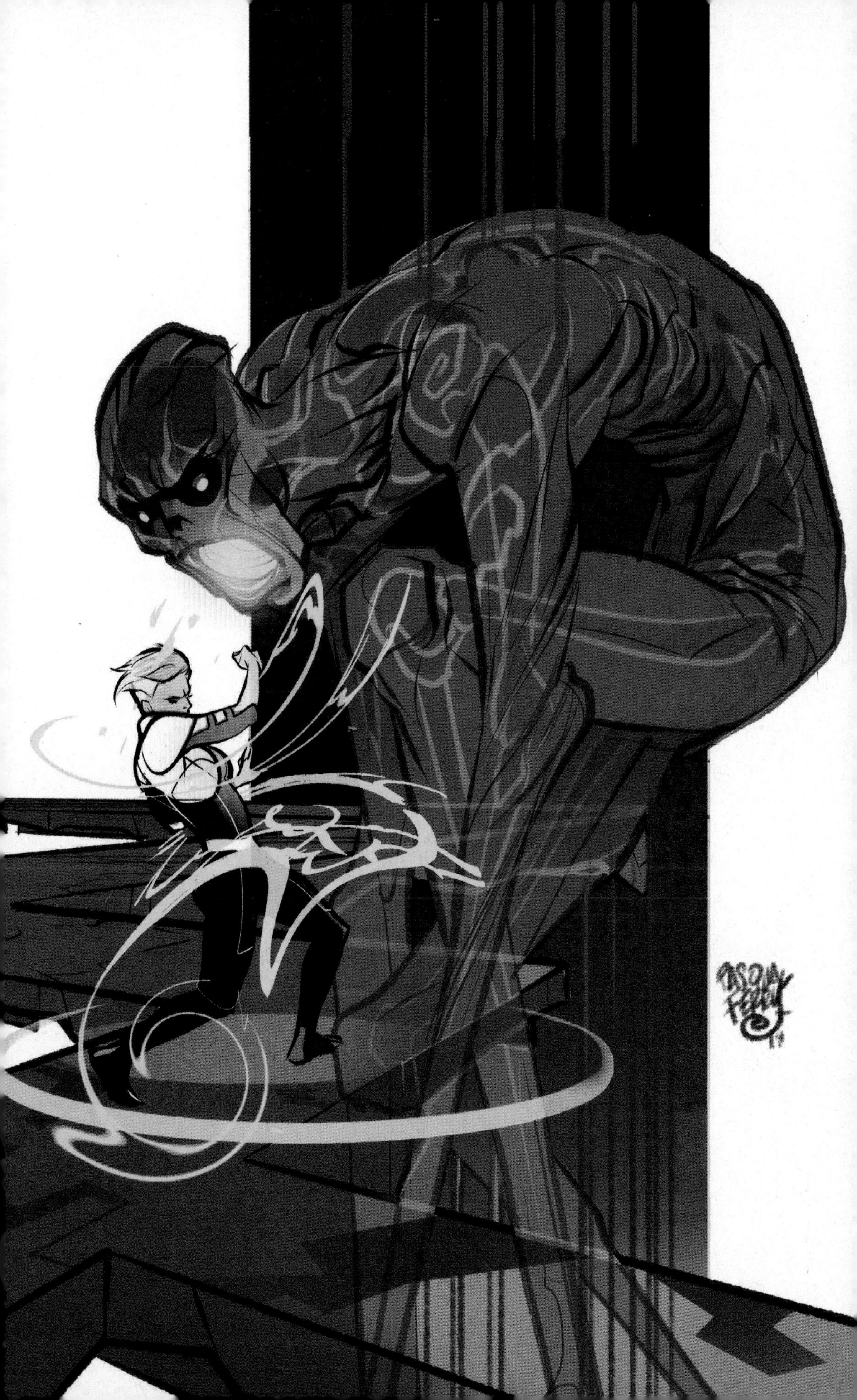

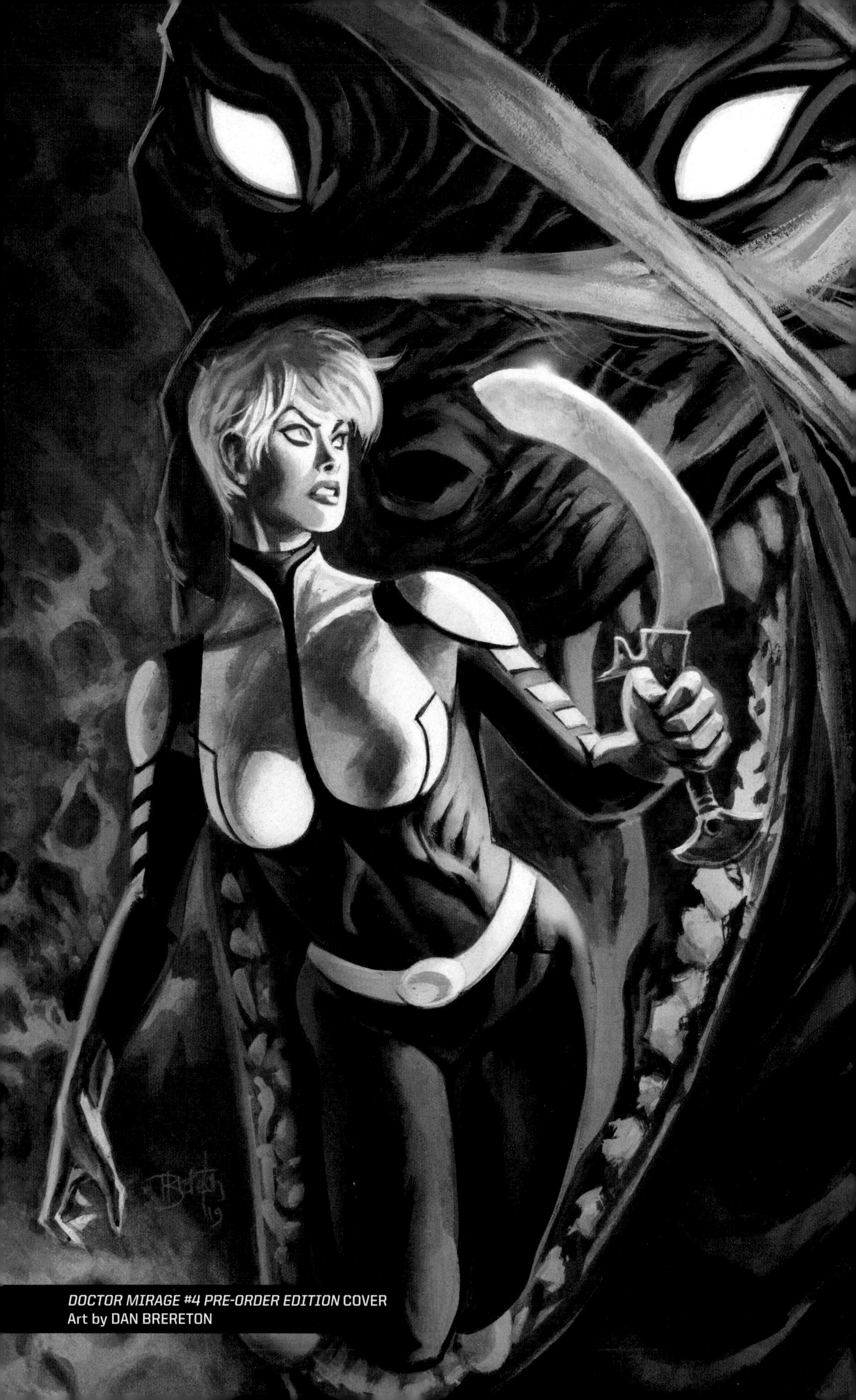

DOCTOR MIRAGE #4 PRE-ORDER EDITION COVER
Art by DAN BRERETON

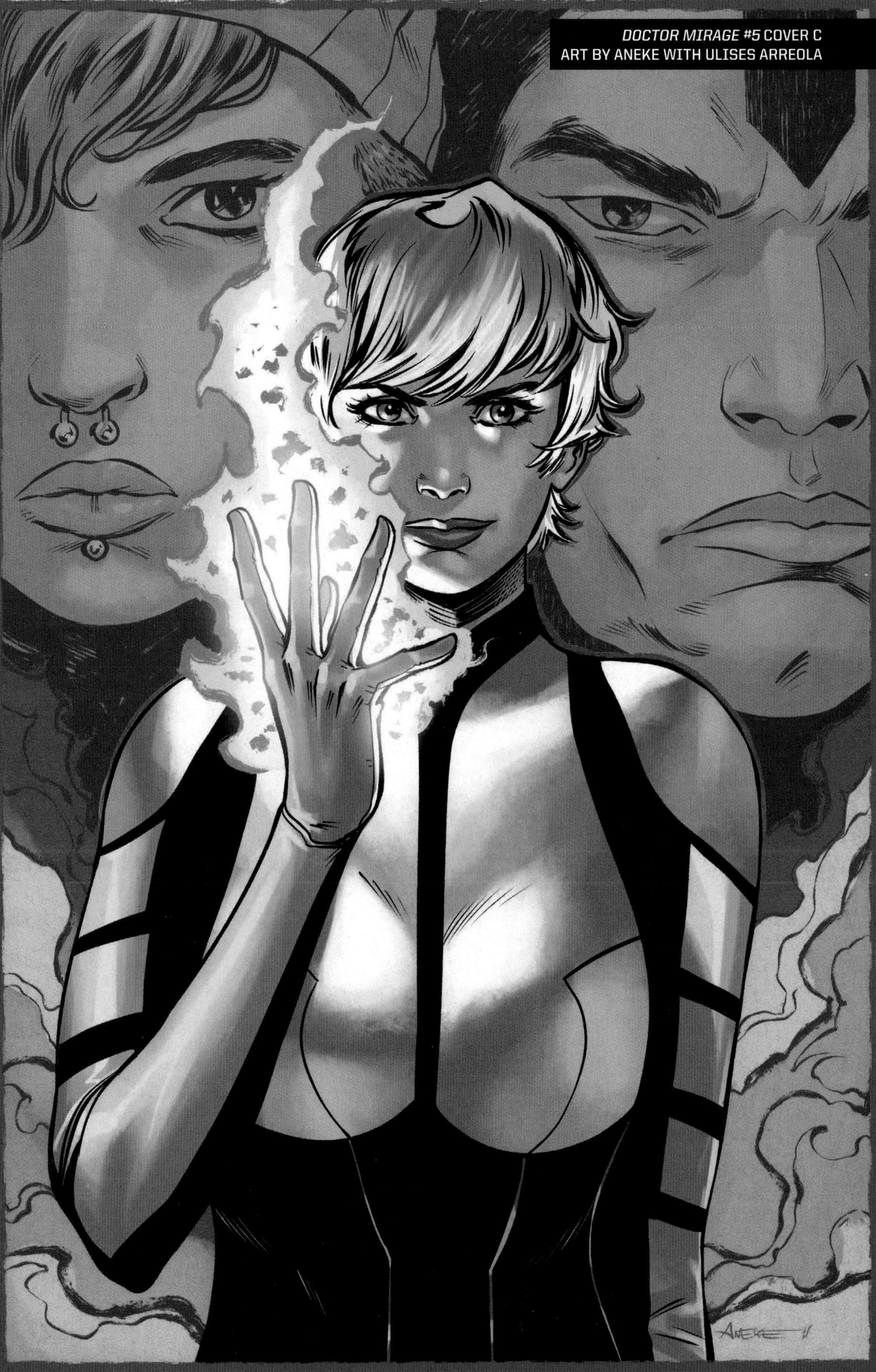
ANEKE

DOCTOR MIRAGE #5 COVER C
ART BY ANEKE WITH ULISES ARREOLA

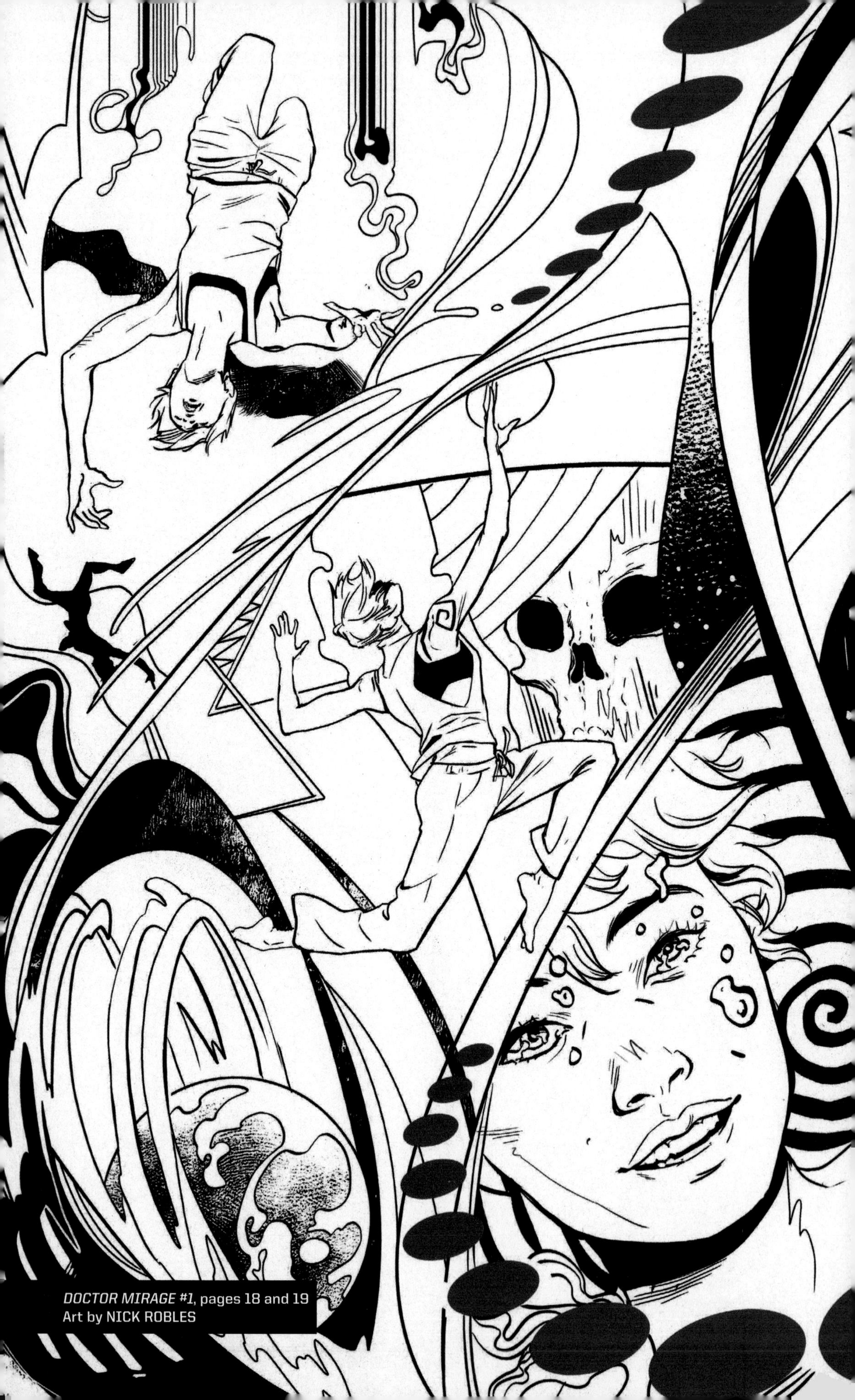

DOCTOR MIRAGE #1, pages 18 and 19
Art by NICK ROBLES

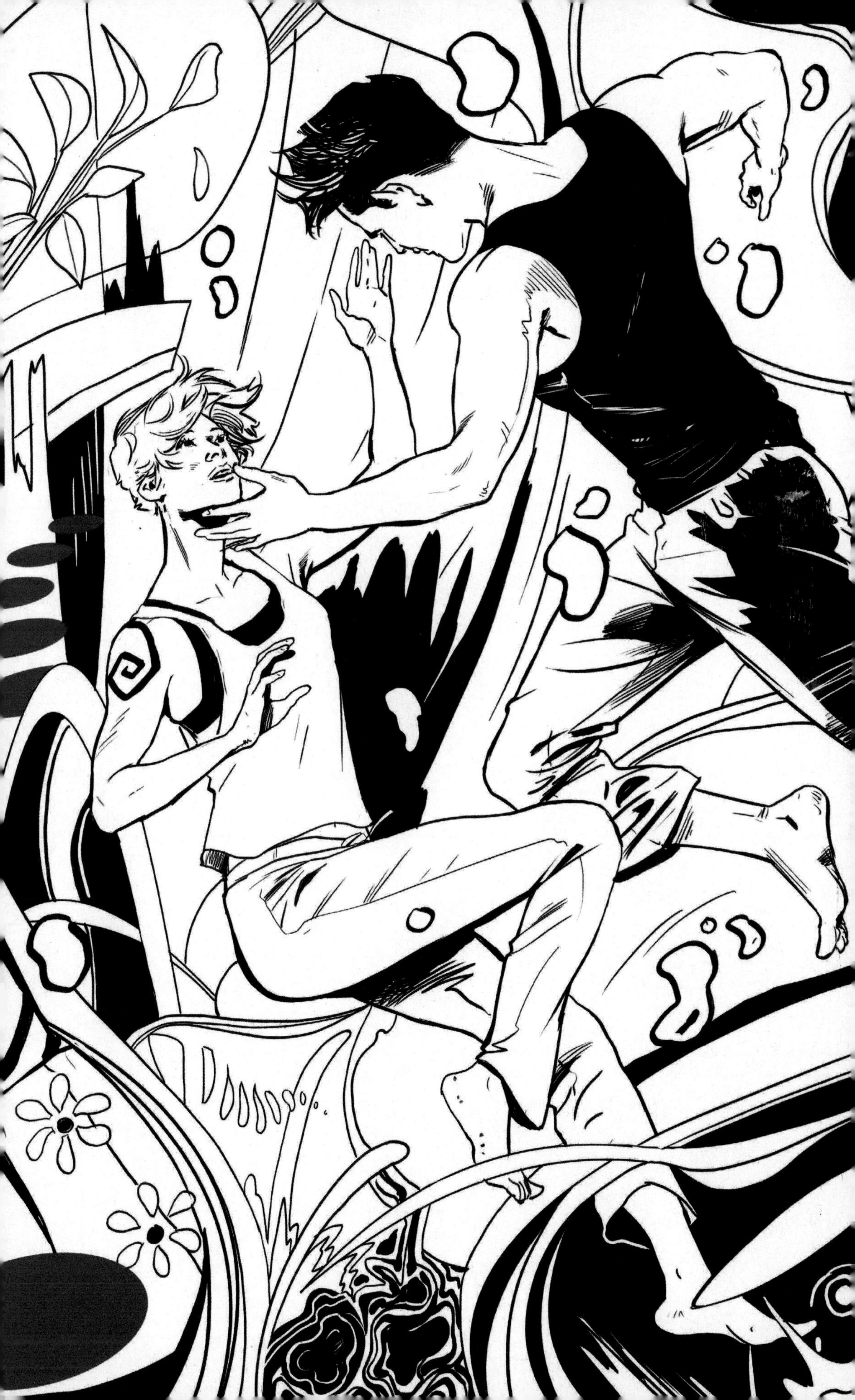

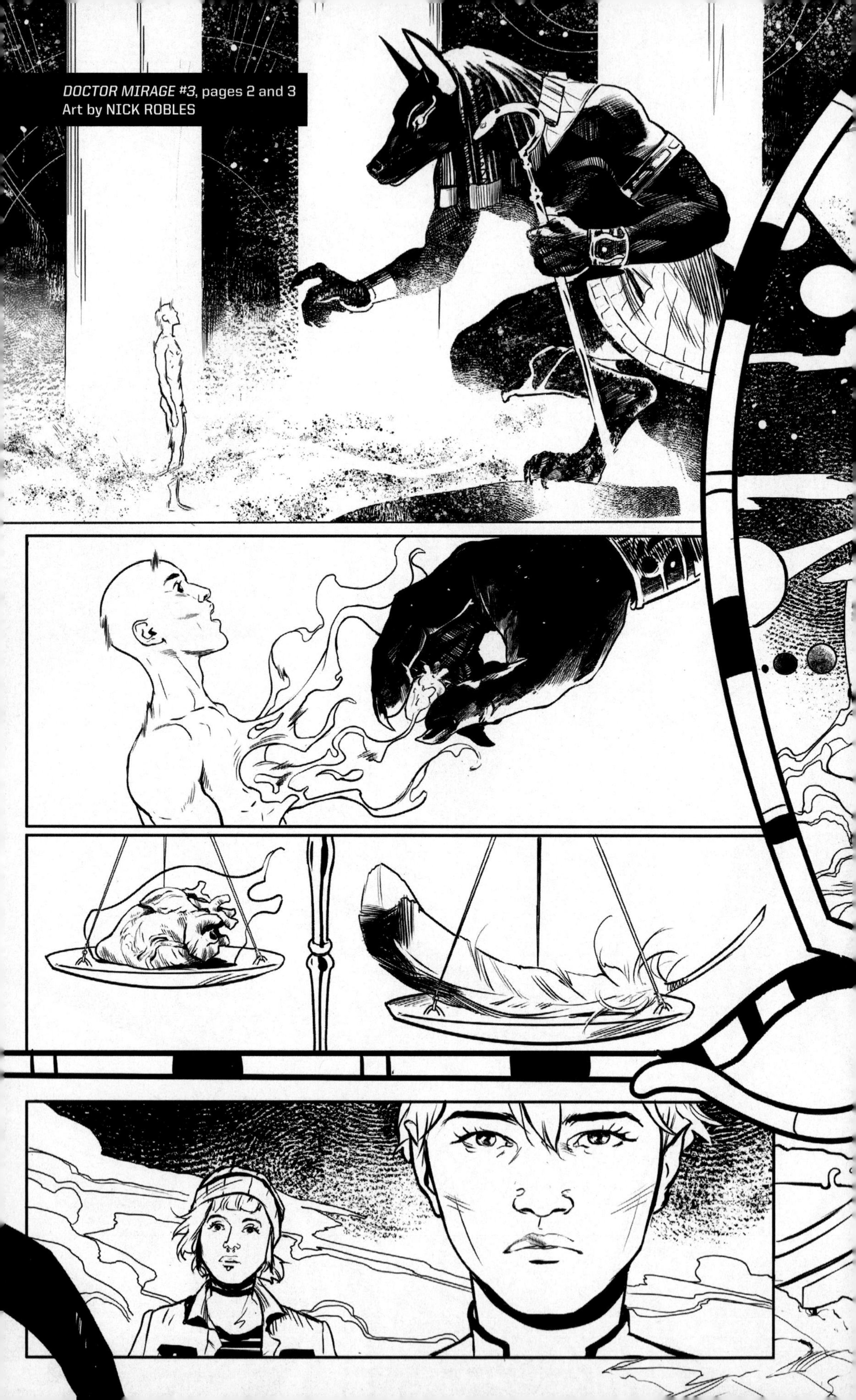

DOCTOR MIRAGE #3, pages 2 and 3
Art by NICK ROBLES

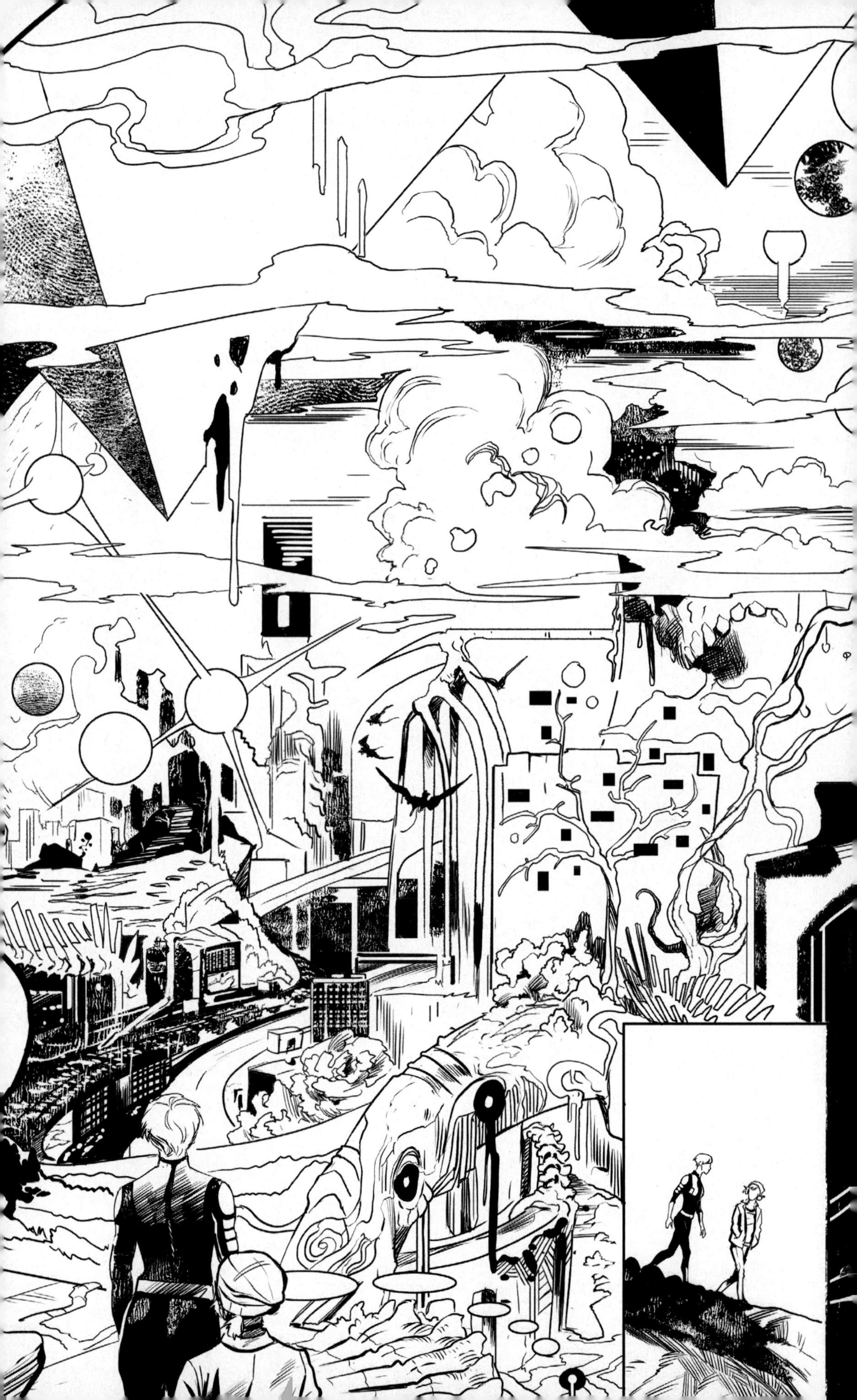

EXPLORE THE VALIANT U

ACTION & ADVENTURE

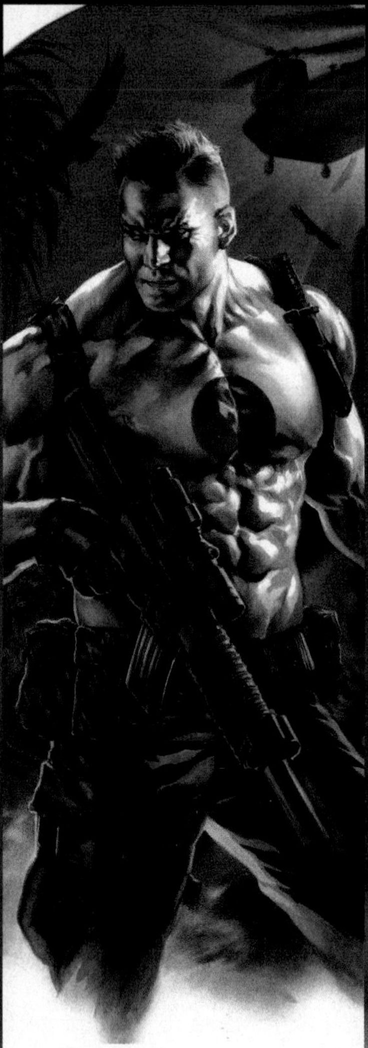

BLOODSHOT BOOK ONE
ISBN: 978-1-68215-342-0
NINJA-K VOL. 1: THE NINJA FILES
ISBN: 978-1-68215-259-1
SAVAGE
ISBN: 978-1-68215-189-1
WRATH OF THE ETERNAL WARRIOR VOL. 1: RISEN
ISBN: 978-1-68215-123-5
X-O MANOWAR (2017) VOL. 1: SOLDIER
ISBN: 978-1-68215-205-8

BLOCKBUSTER ADVENTURE

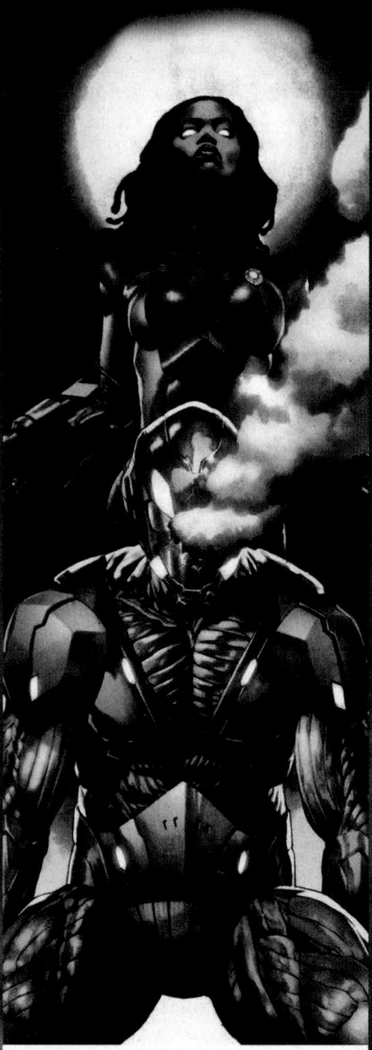

4001 A.D.
ISBN: 978-1-68215-143-3
ARMOR HUNTERS
ISBN: 978-1-939346-45-2
BOOK OF DEATH
ISBN: 978-1-939346-97-1
FALLEN WORLD
ISBN: 978-1-68215-331-4
HARBINGER WARS
ISBN: 978-1-939346-09-4
HARBINGER WARS 2
ISBN: 978-1-68215-289-8
INCURSION
ISBN: 978-1-68215-303-1
THE VALIANT
ISBN: 978-1-939346-60-5

COMEDY

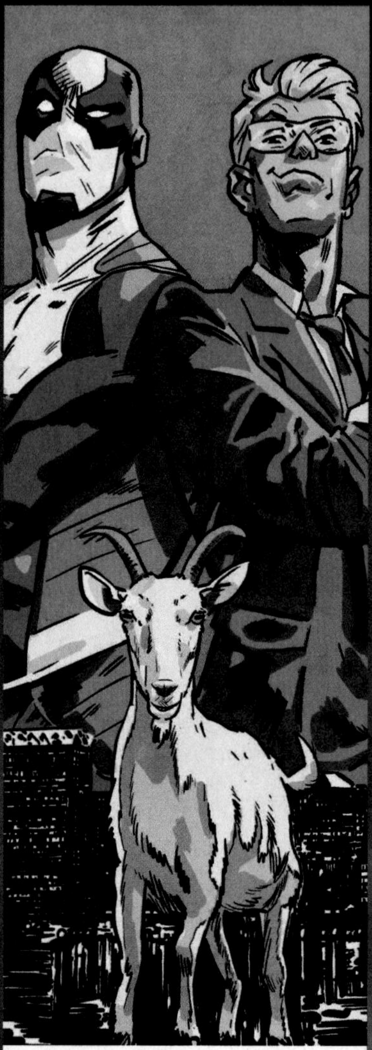

A&A: THE ADVENTURES OF ARCHER & ARMSTRONG VOL. 1: IN THE BAG
ISBN: 978-1-68215-149-5
THE DELINQUENTS
ISBN: 978-1-939346-51-3
QUANTUM AND WOODY! (2017) VOL. 1: KISS KISS, KLANG KLANG
ISBN: 978-1-68215-269-0

IVERSE STARTING AT $9.99

HORROR & MYSTERY

SCIENCE FICTION & FANTASY

TEEN ADVENTURE

BRITANNIA
ISBN: 978-1-68215-185-3
THE DEATH-DEFYING DOCTOR MIRAGE
ISBN: 978-1-939346-49-0
PUNK MAMBO
ISBN: 978-1-68215-330-7
RAPTURE
ISBN: 978-1-68215-225-6
SHADOWMAN (2018) VOL. 1:
FEAR OF THE DARK
ISBN: 978-1-68215-239-3

DIVINITY
ISBN: 978-1-939346-76-6
THE FORGOTTEN QUEEN
ISBN: 978-1-68215-324-6
IMPERIUM VOL. 1: COLLECTING MONSTERS
ISBN: 978-1-939346-75-9
IVAR, TIMEWALKER VOL. 1: MAKING
HISTORY
ISBN: 978-1-939346-63-6
RAI VOL. 1: WELCOME TO NEW JAPAN
ISBN: 978-1-939346-41-4
WAR MOTHER
ISBN: 978-1-68215-237-9

FAITH VOL. 1: HOLLYWOOD AND VINE
ISBN: 978-1-68215-121-1
GENERATION ZERO VOL. 1:
WE ARE THE FUTURE
ISBN: 978-1-68215-175-4
HARBINGER RENEGADE VOL. 1:
THE JUDGMENT OF SOLOMON
ISBN: 978-1-68215-169-3
LIVEWIRE VOL. 1: FUGITIVE
ISBN: 978-1-68215-301-7
SECRET WEAPONS
ISBN: 978-1-68215-229-4

Discover the entire Valiant Universe of titles at VALIANTENTERTAINMENT.COM/ALL-SERIES/